Garfield gets cookin'

BY JIM DAVIS

Ballantine Books • New York

A Ballantine Book
Published by The Ballantine Publishing Group

Copyright © 2001 by PAWS, Incorporated. All rights reserved.

"GARFIELD" and the GARFIELD characters are registered and unregistered trademarks of PAWS, Inc.

All rights reserved under International and Pan-American Copyright Conventions. Published in the United States by The Ballantine Publishing Group, a division of Random House, Inc., New York, and simultaneously in Canada by Random House of Canada Limited, Toronto.

Ballantine is a registered trademark and the Ballantine colophon is a trademark of Random House, Inc.

www.randomhouse.com/BB/

A Library of Congress card number is available from the publisher upon request.

ISBN 0-345-44582-1

Manufactured in the United States of America

First Edition: October 2001

10 9 8 7 6 5 4 3 2 1

Top Ten Dating Dodges Women Use On Jon

10. "Sorry, I Don't Date Outside My Species."

9. "I'll Be Washing My hair All That Week. Each One. Individually."

8. "I'm Getting a Sex-change Operation."

7. "I Came Down With a Severe Case of Toe Jam."

6. "Darn, I have to Pick Up My Wombat From the Taxidermist that Night."

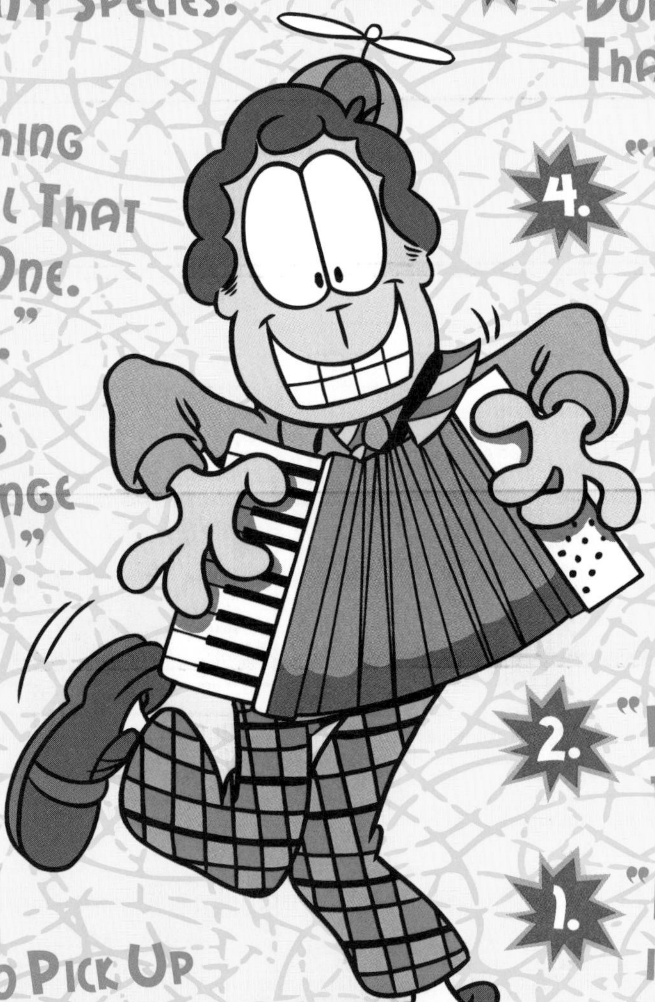

5. "No Can Do. I'm Donating My Kidney That Weekend."

4. "That's the Night I Wax My Grandmother's Mustache."

3. "I have to Stay home and Floss My Otter."

2. "I'm Allergic to Geeks."

1. "I'd Rather Swim in Piranha-infested Waters Dressed as a Meat Loaf."

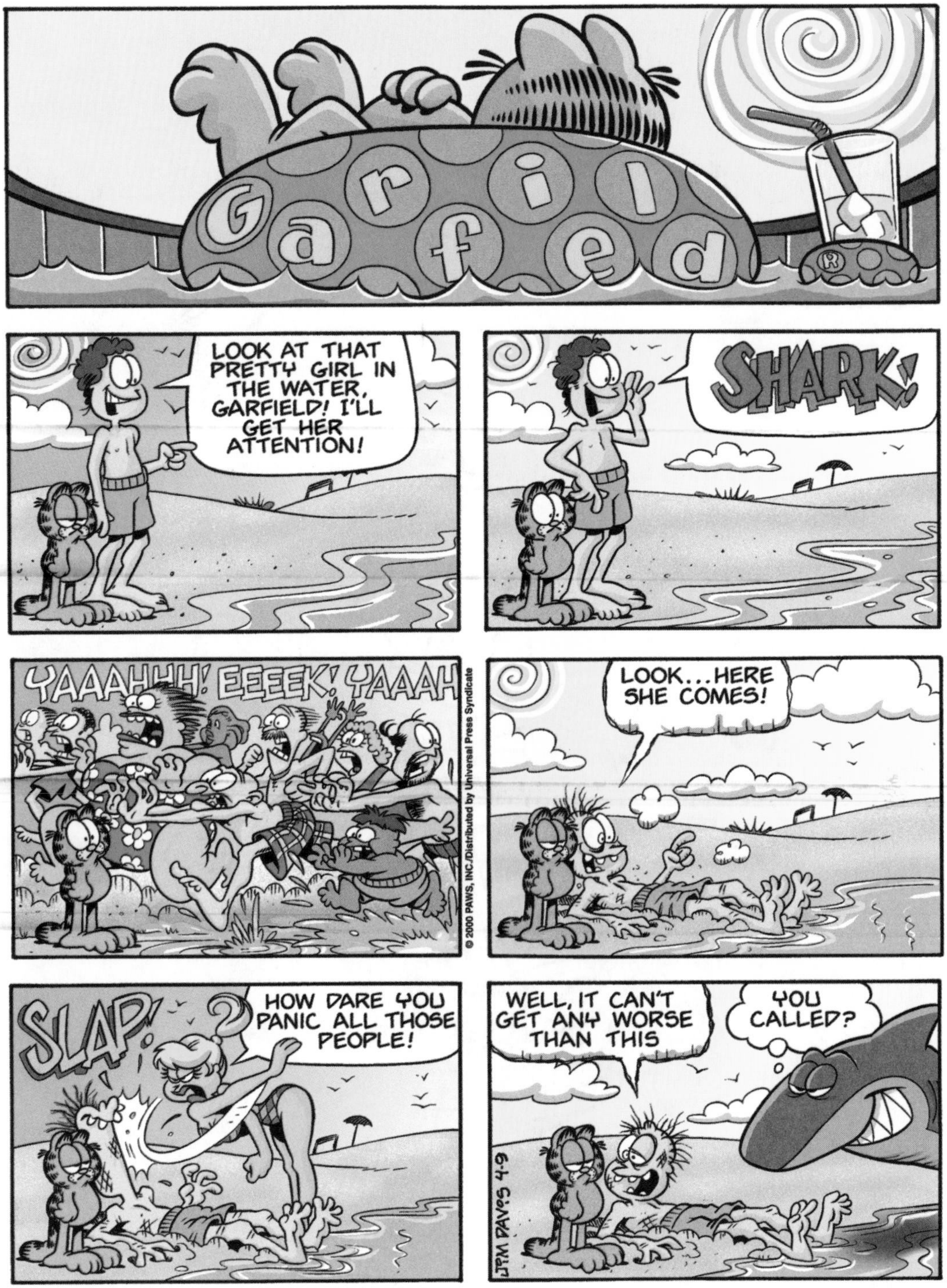
Garfield
LOOK AT THAT PRETTY GIRL IN THE WATER, GARFIELD! I'LL GET HER ATTENTION!
SHARK!
YAAAHHH! EEEEK! YAAAH
© 2000 PAWS, INC./Distributed by Universal Press Syndicate
LOOK...HERE SHE COMES!
SLAP
HOW DARE YOU PANIC ALL THOSE PEOPLE!
JPM DAVIS 4-9
WELL, IT CAN'T GET ANY WORSE THAN THIS
YOU CALLED?

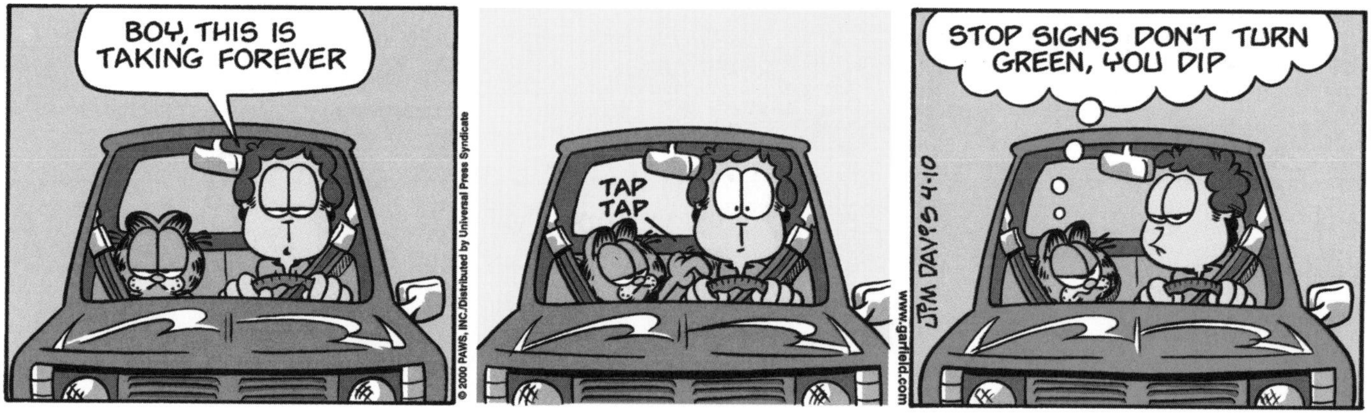
BOY, THIS IS TAKING FOREVER
TAP TAP
STOP SIGNS DON'T TURN GREEN, YOU DIP
© 2000 PAWS, INC./Distributed by Universal Press Syndicate
www.garfield.com
JIM DAVIS 4-10

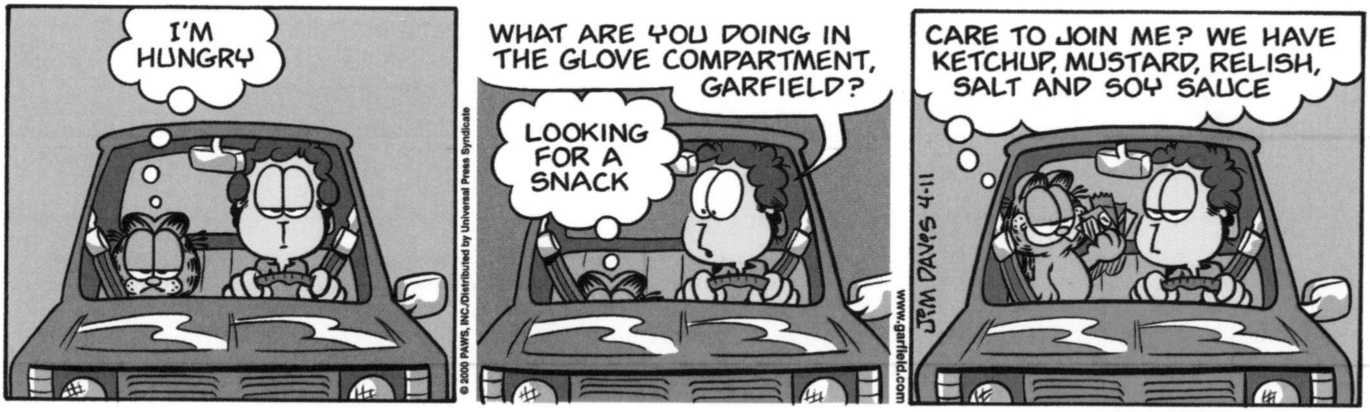
I'M HUNGRY
WHAT ARE YOU DOING IN THE GLOVE COMPARTMENT, GARFIELD?
LOOKING FOR A SNACK
CARE TO JOIN ME? WE HAVE KETCHUP, MUSTARD, RELISH, SALT AND SOY SAUCE
© 2000 PAWS, INC./Distributed by Universal Press Syndicate
www.garfield.com
JIM DAVIS 4-11

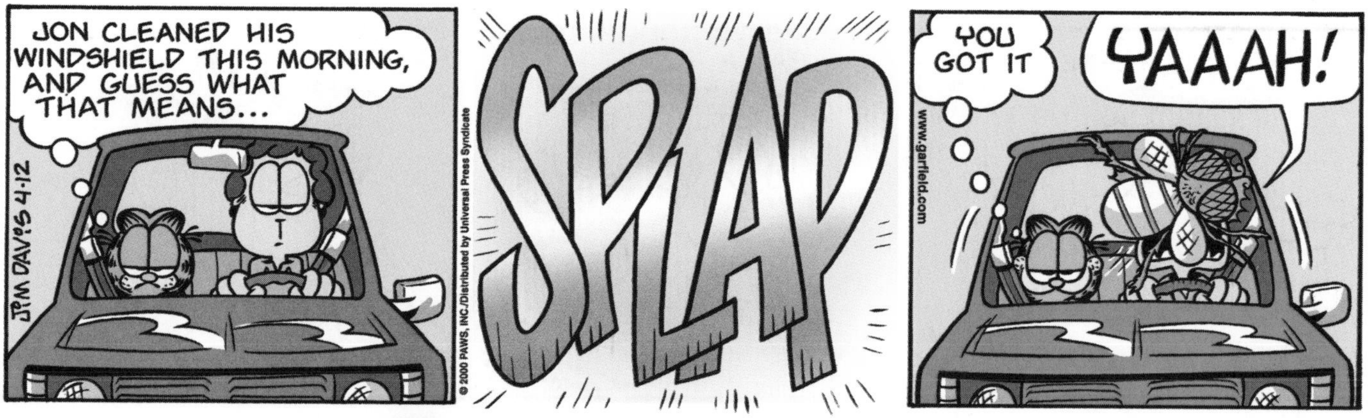
JON CLEANED HIS WINDSHIELD THIS MORNING, AND GUESS WHAT THAT MEANS...
SPLAP
YOU GOT IT
YAAAH!
JIM DAVIS 4-12
© 2000 PAWS, INC./Distributed by Universal Press Syndicate
www.garfield.com

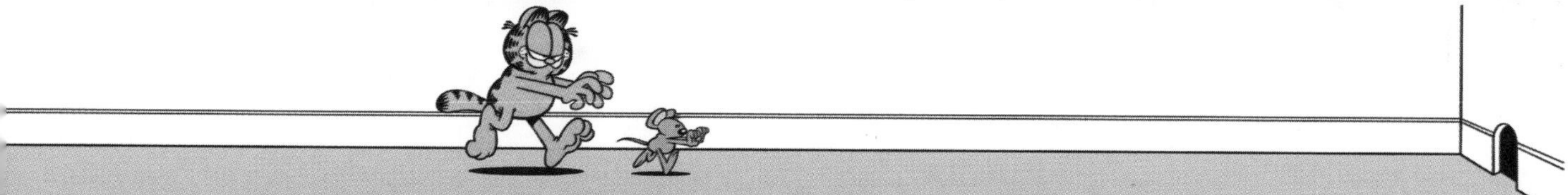

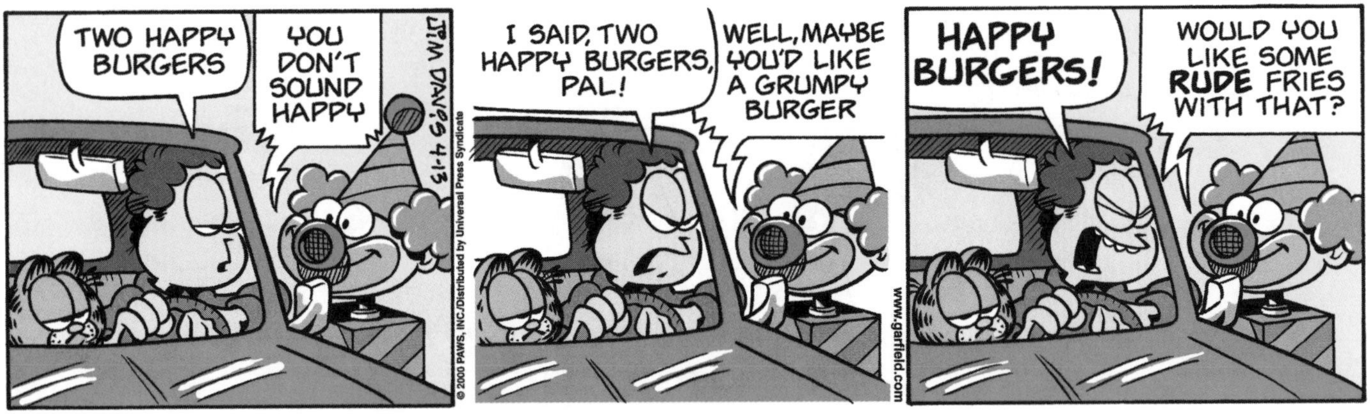
JIM DAVIS 4-13
© 2000 PAWS, INC./Distributed by Universal Press Syndicate
TWO HAPPY BURGERS
YOU DON'T SOUND HAPPY
I SAID, TWO HAPPY BURGERS, PAL!
WELL, MAYBE YOU'D LIKE A GRUMPY BURGER
www.garfield.com
HAPPY BURGERS!
WOULD YOU LIKE SOME RUDE FRIES WITH THAT?

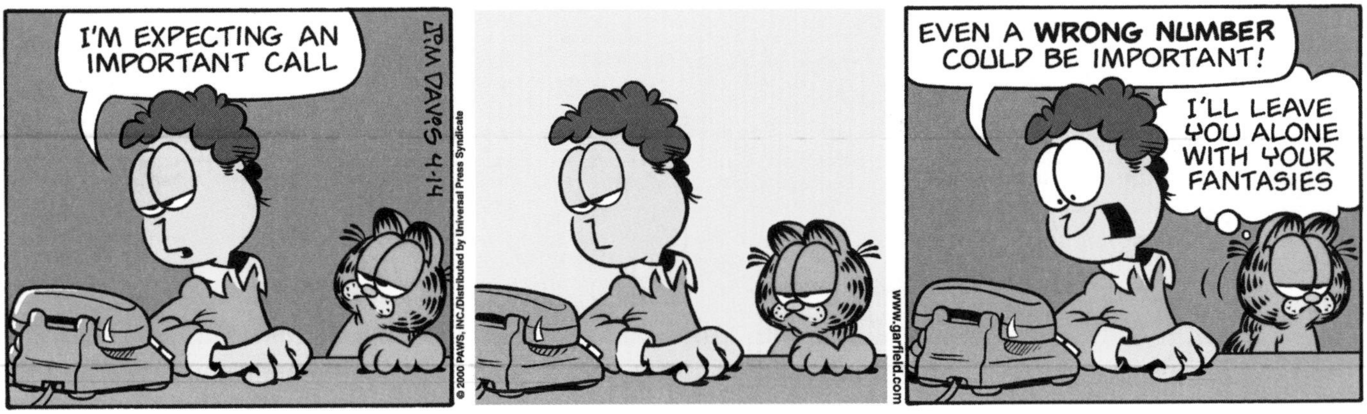
JIM DAVIS 4-14
© 2000 PAWS, INC./Distributed by Universal Press Syndicate
I'M EXPECTING AN IMPORTANT CALL
www.garfield.com
EVEN A WRONG NUMBER COULD BE IMPORTANT!
I'LL LEAVE YOU ALONE WITH YOUR FANTASIES

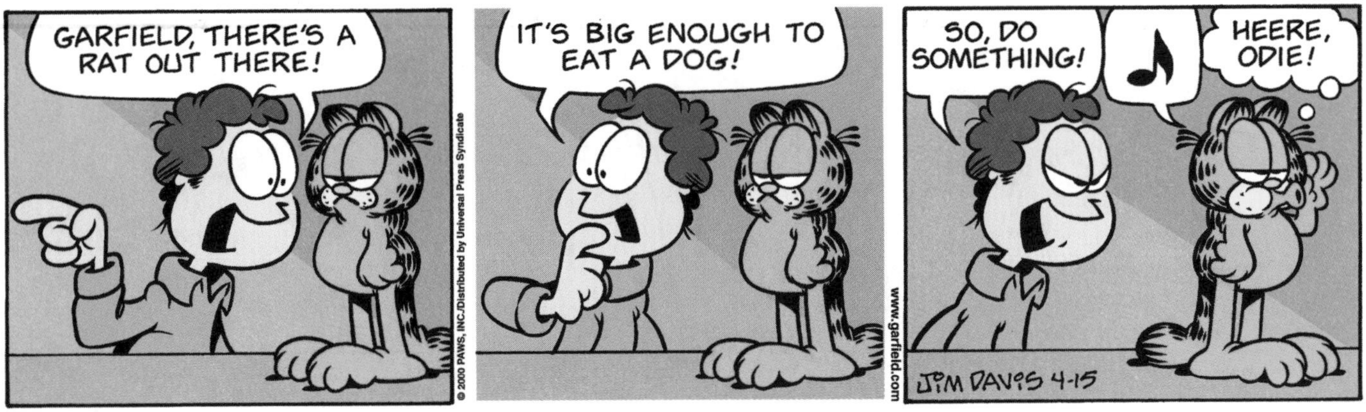
GARFIELD, THERE'S A RAT OUT THERE!
© 2000 PAWS, INC./Distributed by Universal Press Syndicate
IT'S BIG ENOUGH TO EAT A DOG!
www.garfield.com
SO, DO SOMETHING!
♪
HEERE, ODIE!
JIM DAVIS 4-15

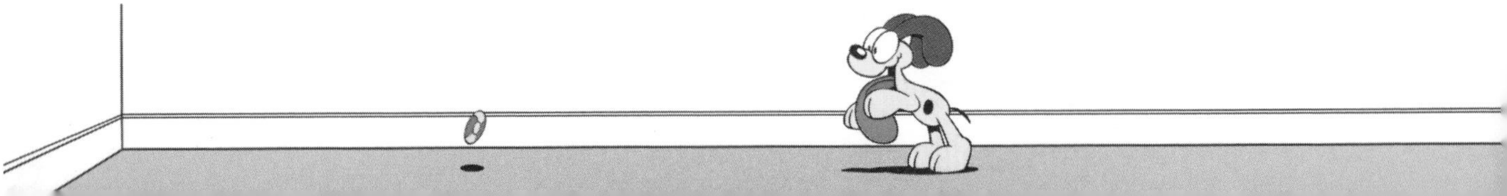

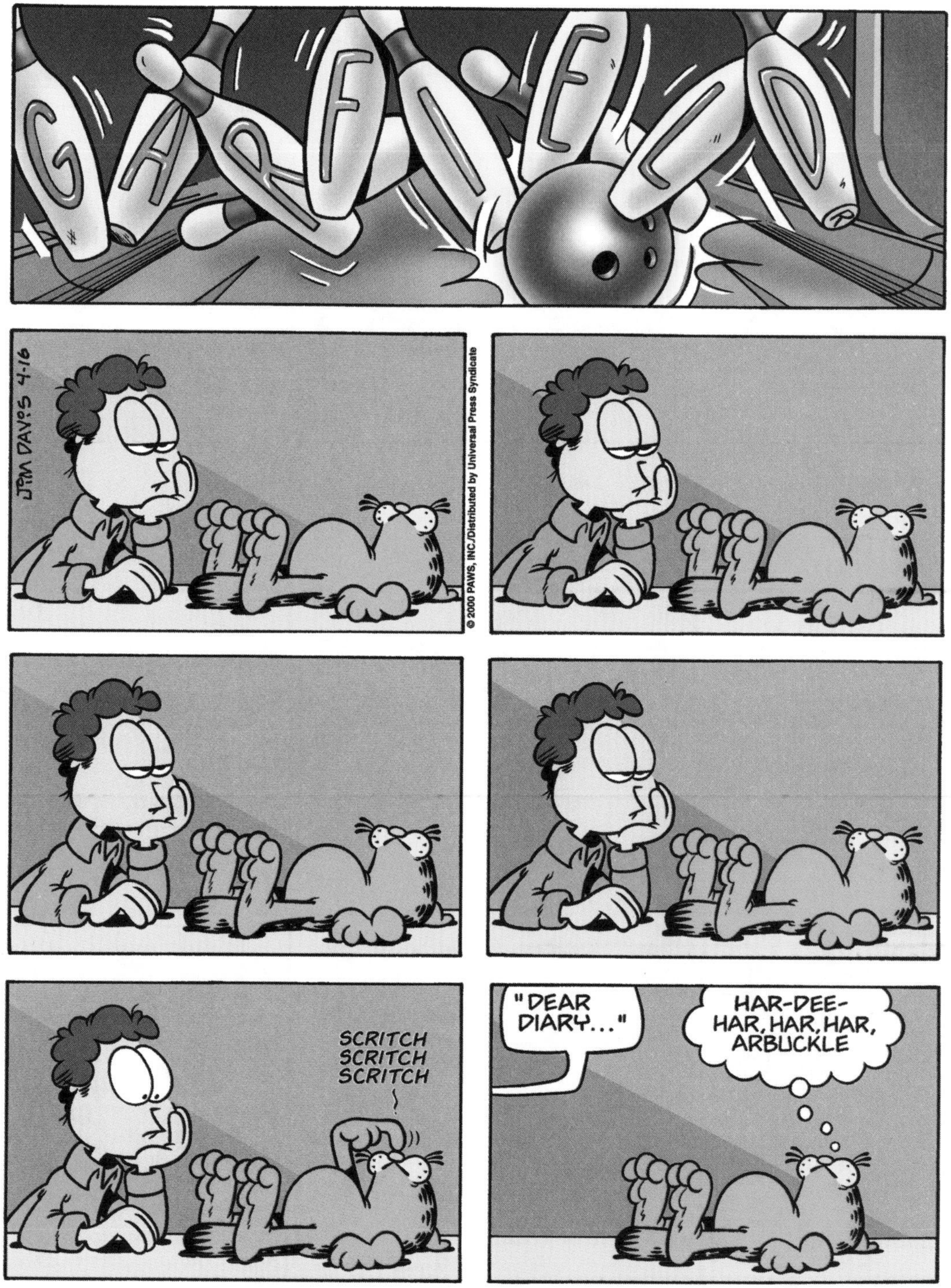
GARFIELD
JIM DAVIS 4-16
© 2000 PAWS, INC./Distributed by Universal Press Syndicate
SCRITCH SCRITCH SCRITCH
"DEAR DIARY..."
HAR-DEE-HAR, HAR, HAR, ARBUCKLE

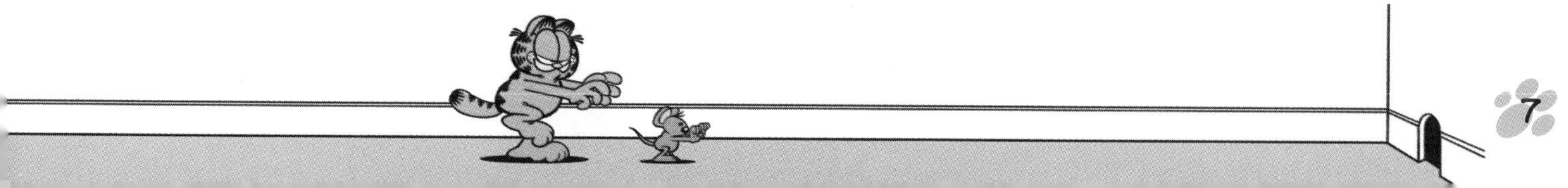

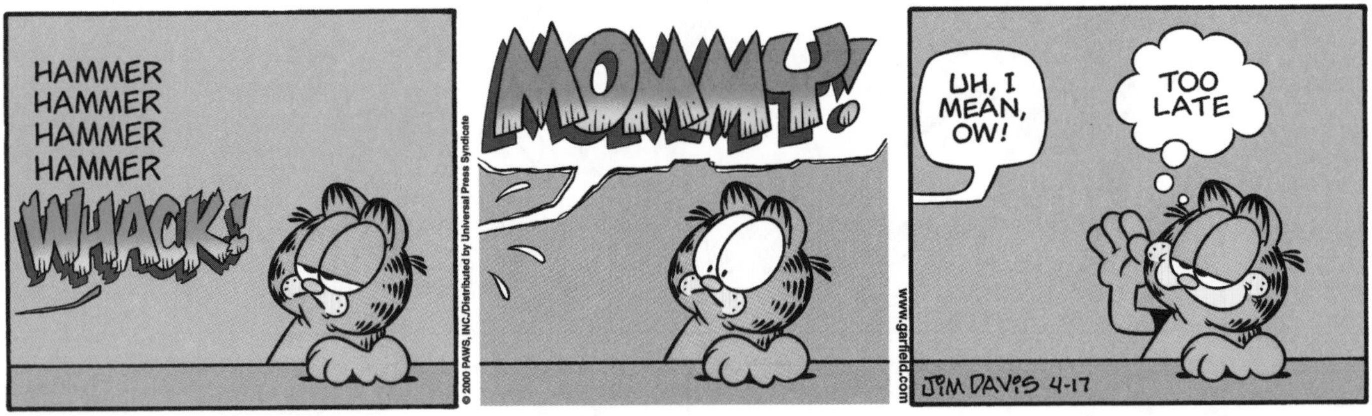
HAMMER
HAMMER
HAMMER
HAMMER
WHACK!
MOMMY!
© 2000 PAWS, INC./Distributed by Universal Press Syndicate
UH, I MEAN, OW!
TOO LATE
www.garfield.com
JIM DAVIS 4-17

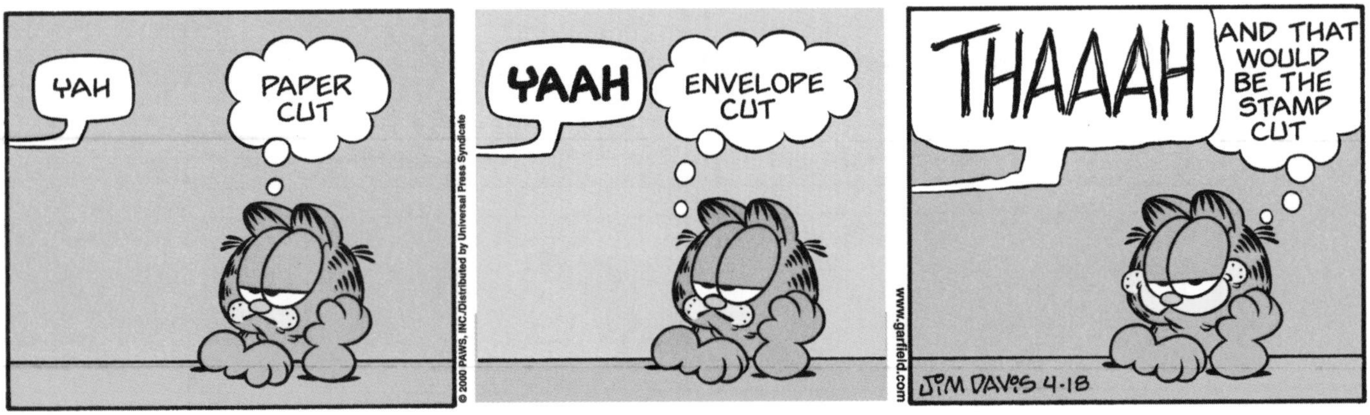
YAH
PAPER CUT
YAAH
ENVELOPE CUT
© 2000 PAWS, INC./Distributed by Universal Press Syndicate
THAAAH
AND THAT WOULD BE THE STAMP CUT
www.garfield.com
JIM DAVIS 4-18

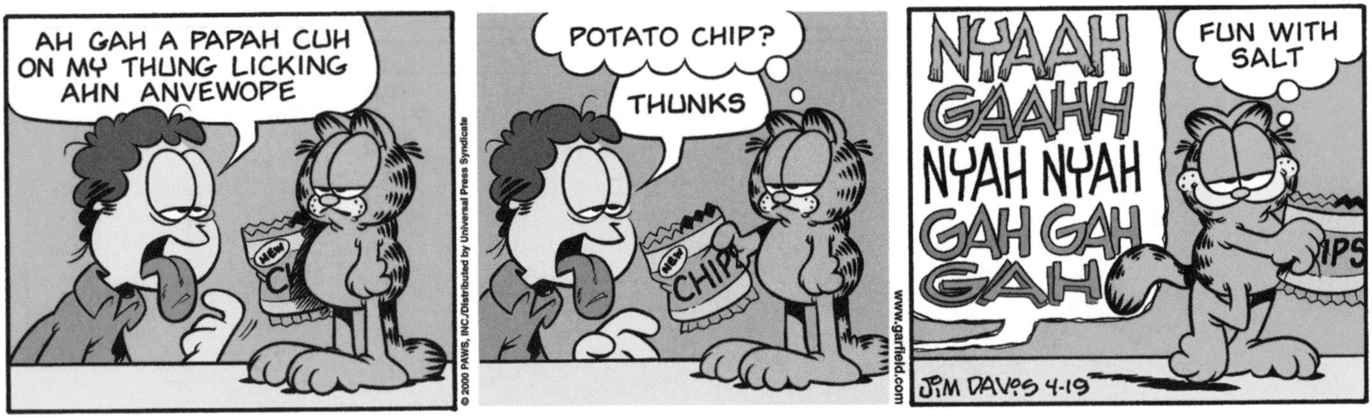
AH GAH A PAPAH CUH ON MY THUNG LICKING AHN ANVEWOPE
POTATO CHIP?
THUNKS
CHIP
© 2000 PAWS, INC./Distributed by Universal Press Syndicate
NYAAH
GAAHH
NYAH NYAH
GAH GAH
GAH
FUN WITH SALT
www.garfield.com
JIM DAVIS 4-19

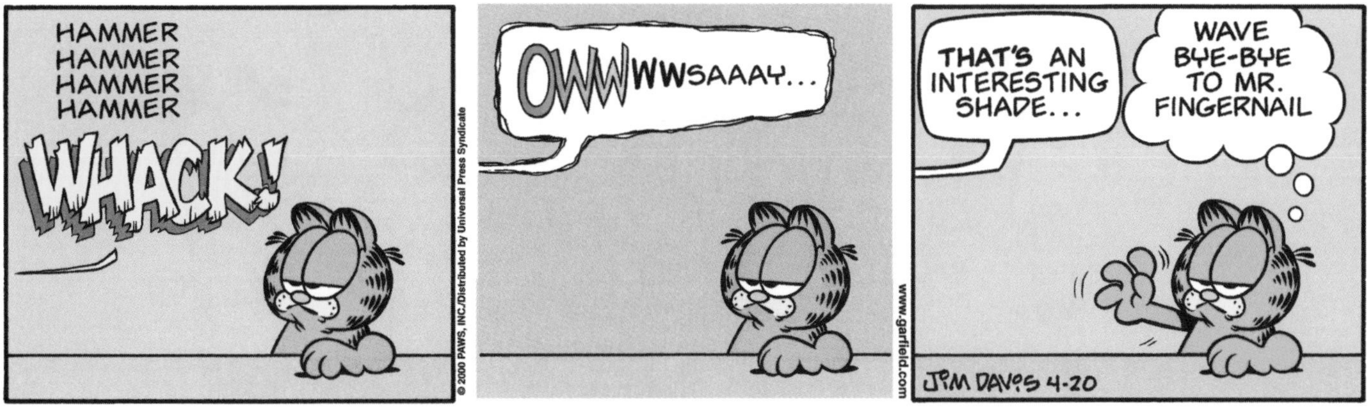
HAMMER
HAMMER
HAMMER
HAMMER
WHACK!
OWWWWSAAAY...
THAT'S AN INTERESTING SHADE...
WAVE BYE-BYE TO MR. FINGERNAIL
© 2000 PAWS, INC./Distributed by Universal Press Syndicate
www.garfield.com
JIM DAVIS 4-20

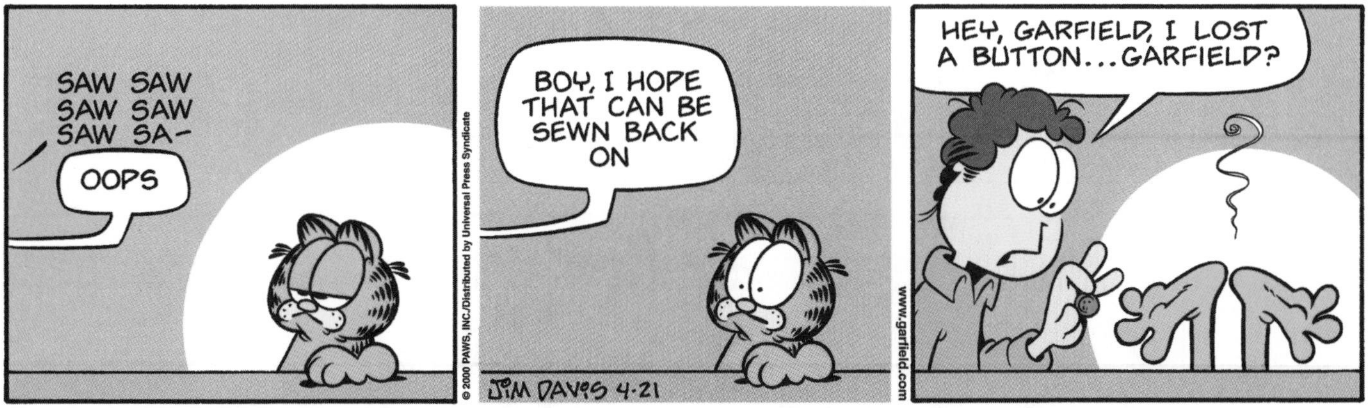
SAW SAW
SAW SAW
SAW SA-
OOPS
BOY, I HOPE THAT CAN BE SEWN BACK ON
HEY, GARFIELD, I LOST A BUTTON...GARFIELD?
© 2000 PAWS, INC./Distributed by Universal Press Syndicate
www.garfield.com
JIM DAVIS 4-21

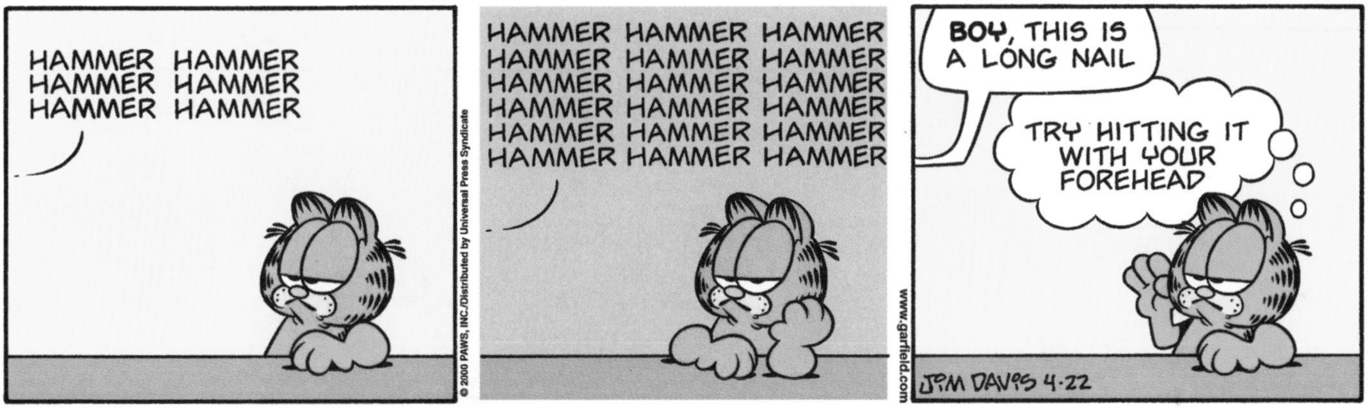
HAMMER HAMMER
HAMMER HAMMER
HAMMER HAMMER
HAMMER HAMMER HAMMER
HAMMER HAMMER HAMMER
HAMMER HAMMER HAMMER
HAMMER HAMMER HAMMER
HAMMER HAMMER HAMMER
HAMMER HAMMER HAMMER
BOY, THIS IS A LONG NAIL
TRY HITTING IT WITH YOUR FOREHEAD
© 2000 PAWS, INC./Distributed by Universal Press Syndicate
www.garfield.com
JIM DAVIS 4-22

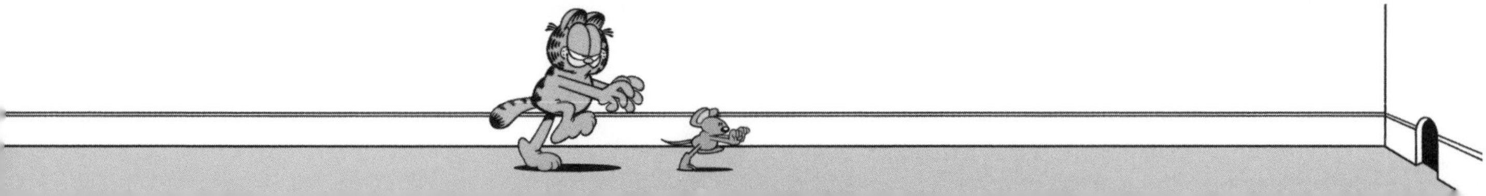

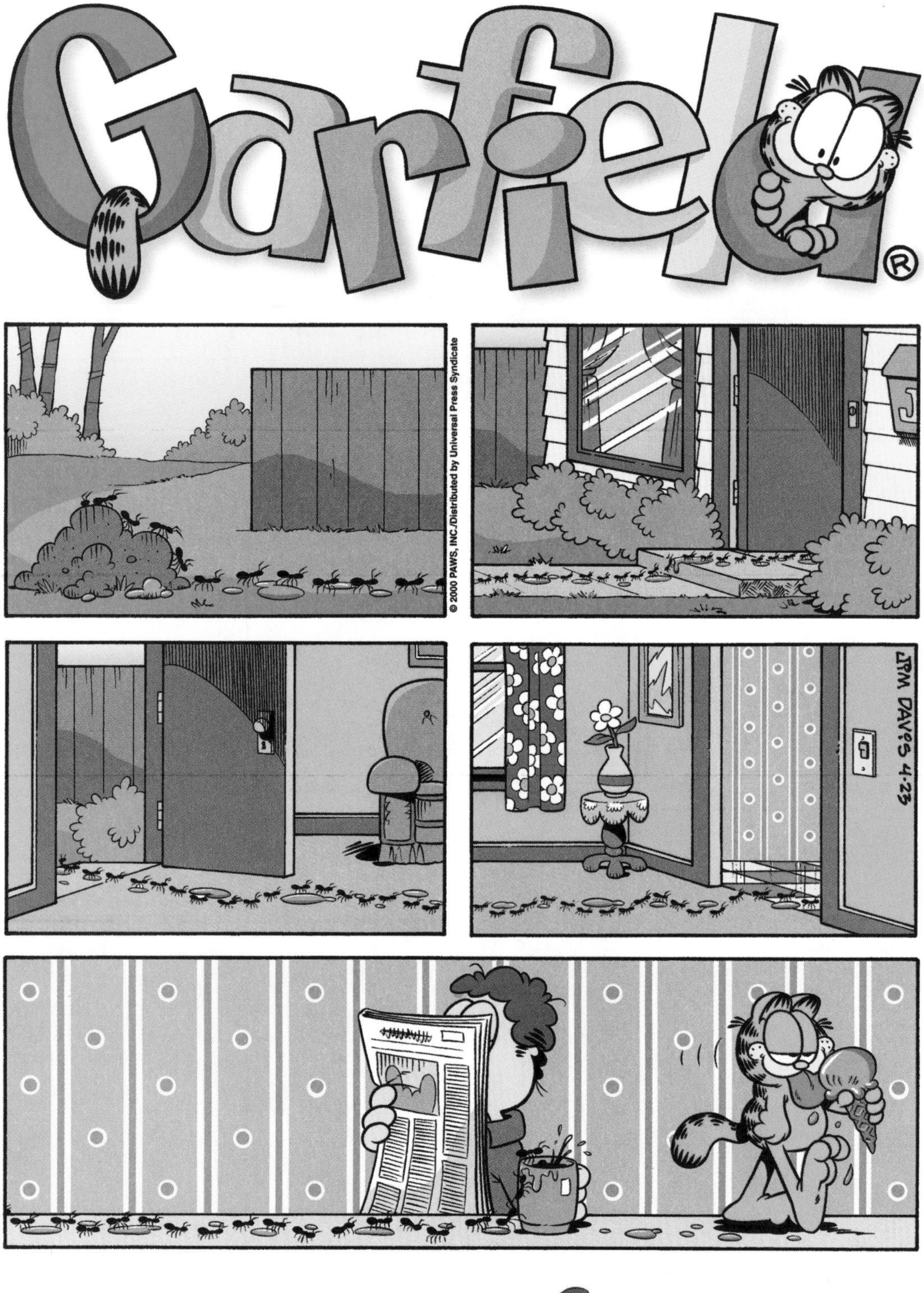
Garfield®
© 2000 PAWS, INC./Distributed by Universal Press Syndicate
JIM DAVIS 4·23

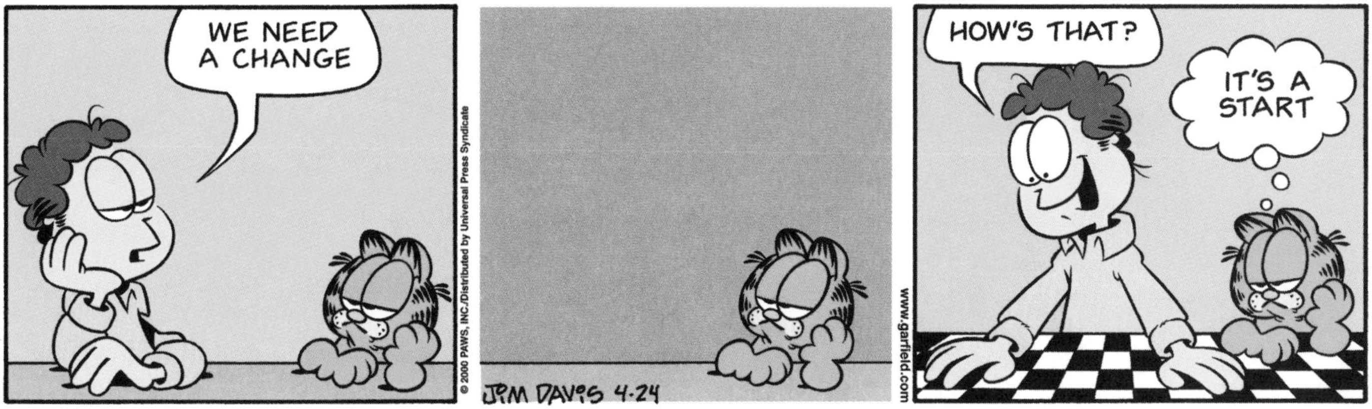
WE NEED A CHANGE
© 2000 PAWS, INC./Distributed by Universal Press Syndicate
JIM DAVIS 4-24
www.garfield.com
HOW'S THAT?
IT'S A START

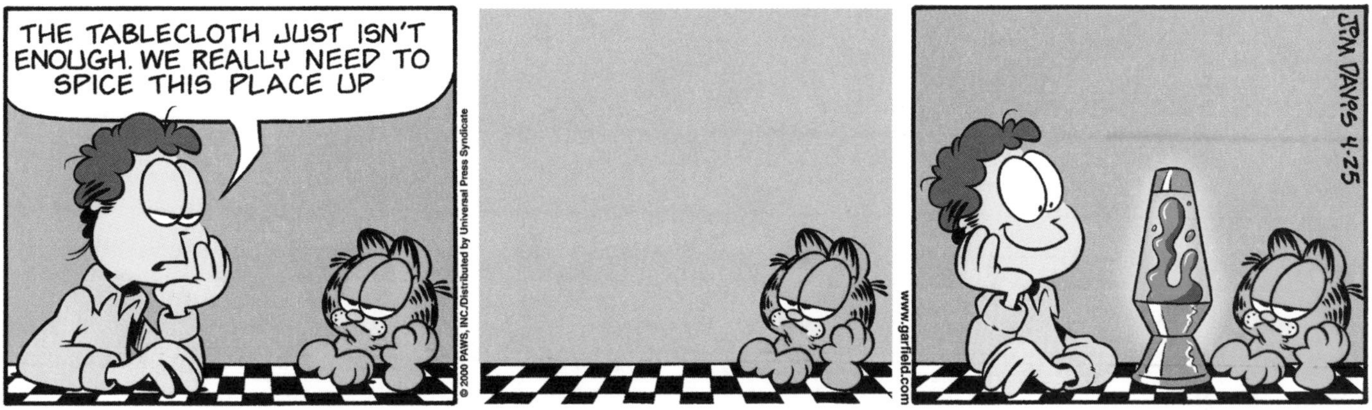
THE TABLECLOTH JUST ISN'T ENOUGH. WE REALLY NEED TO SPICE THIS PLACE UP
© 2000 PAWS, INC./Distributed by Universal Press Syndicate
www.garfield.com
JIM DAVIS 4-25

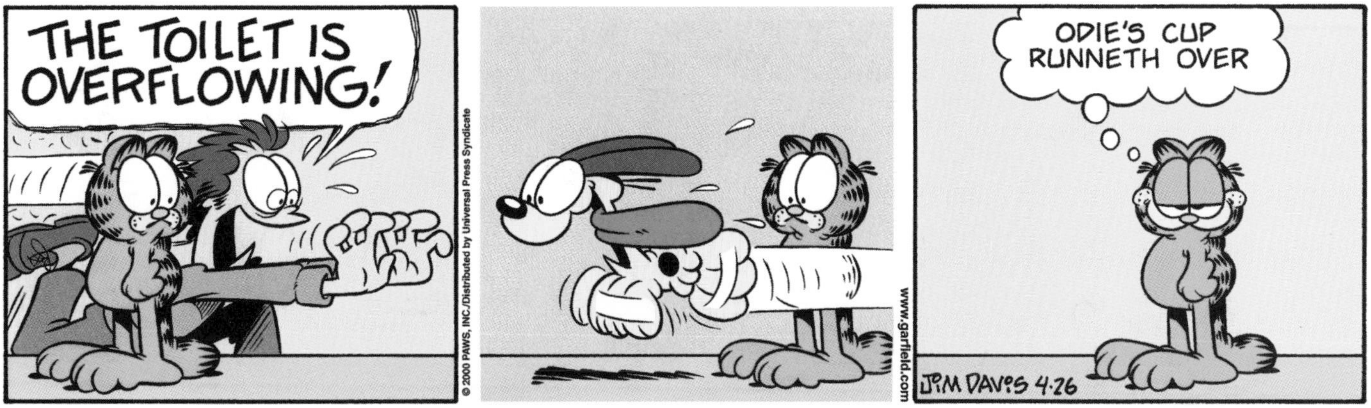
THE TOILET IS OVERFLOWING!
© 2000 PAWS, INC./Distributed by Universal Press Syndicate
www.garfield.com
JIM DAVIS 4-26
ODIE'S CUP RUNNETH OVER

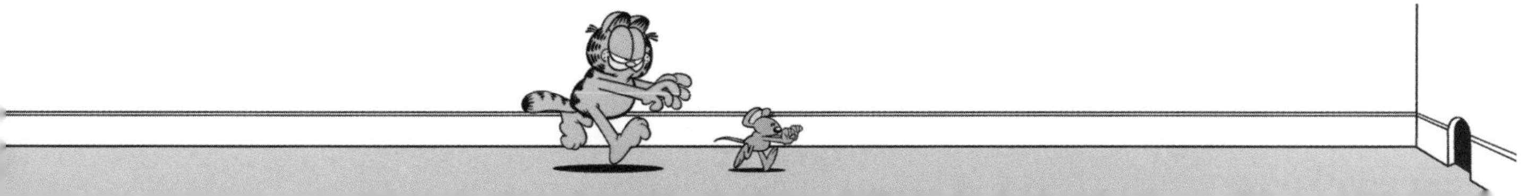

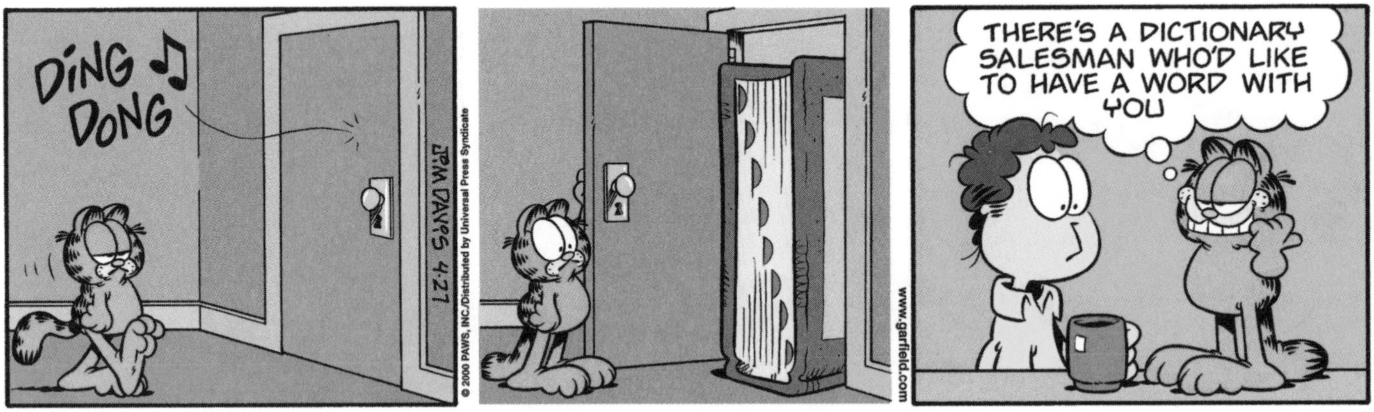
DING ♫ DONG
JIM DAVIS 4·27
© 2000 PAWS, INC./Distributed by Universal Press Syndicate
THERE'S A DICTIONARY SALESMAN WHO'D LIKE TO HAVE A WORD WITH YOU
www.garfield.com

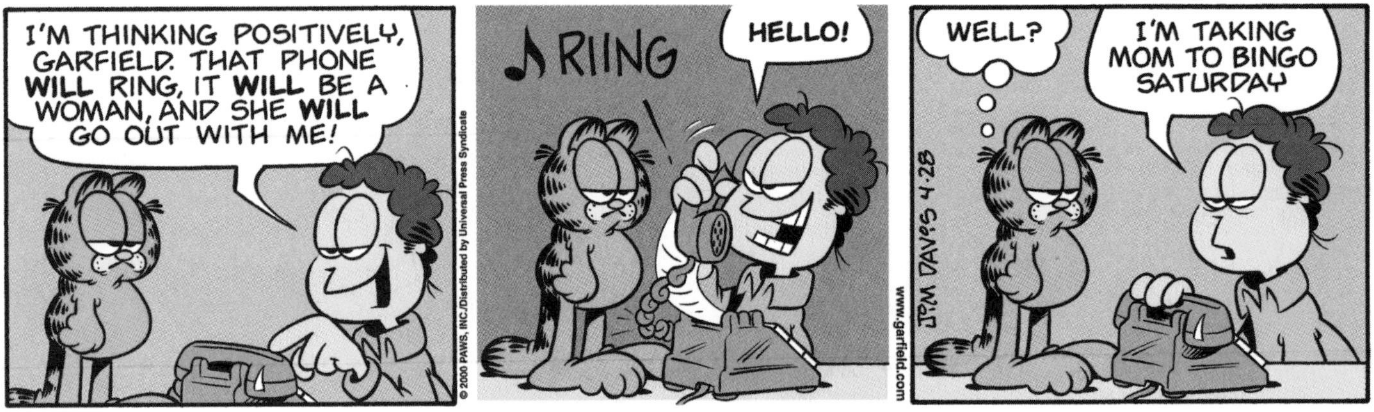
I'M THINKING POSITIVELY, GARFIELD. THAT PHONE **WILL** RING, IT **WILL** BE A WOMAN, AND SHE **WILL** GO OUT WITH ME!
© 2000 PAWS, INC./Distributed by Universal Press Syndicate
♪ RIING
HELLO!
WELL?
I'M TAKING MOM TO BINGO SATURDAY
JIM DAVIS 4·28
www.garfield.com

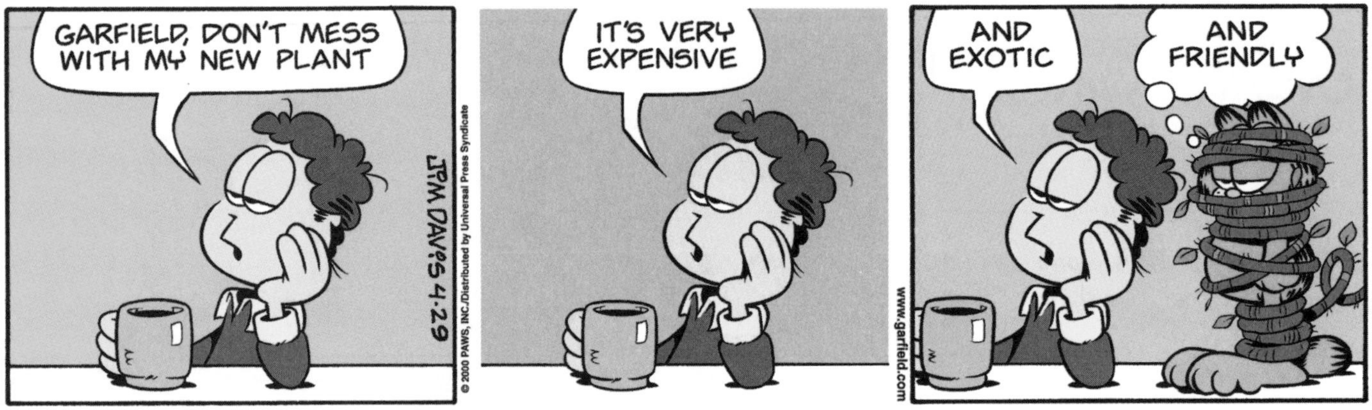
GARFIELD, DON'T MESS WITH MY NEW PLANT
JIM DAVIS 4·29
© 2000 PAWS, INC./Distributed by Universal Press Syndicate
IT'S VERY EXPENSIVE
AND EXOTIC
AND FRIENDLY
www.garfield.com

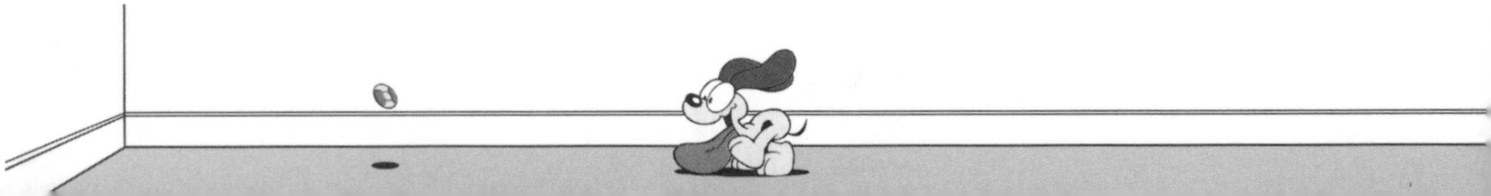

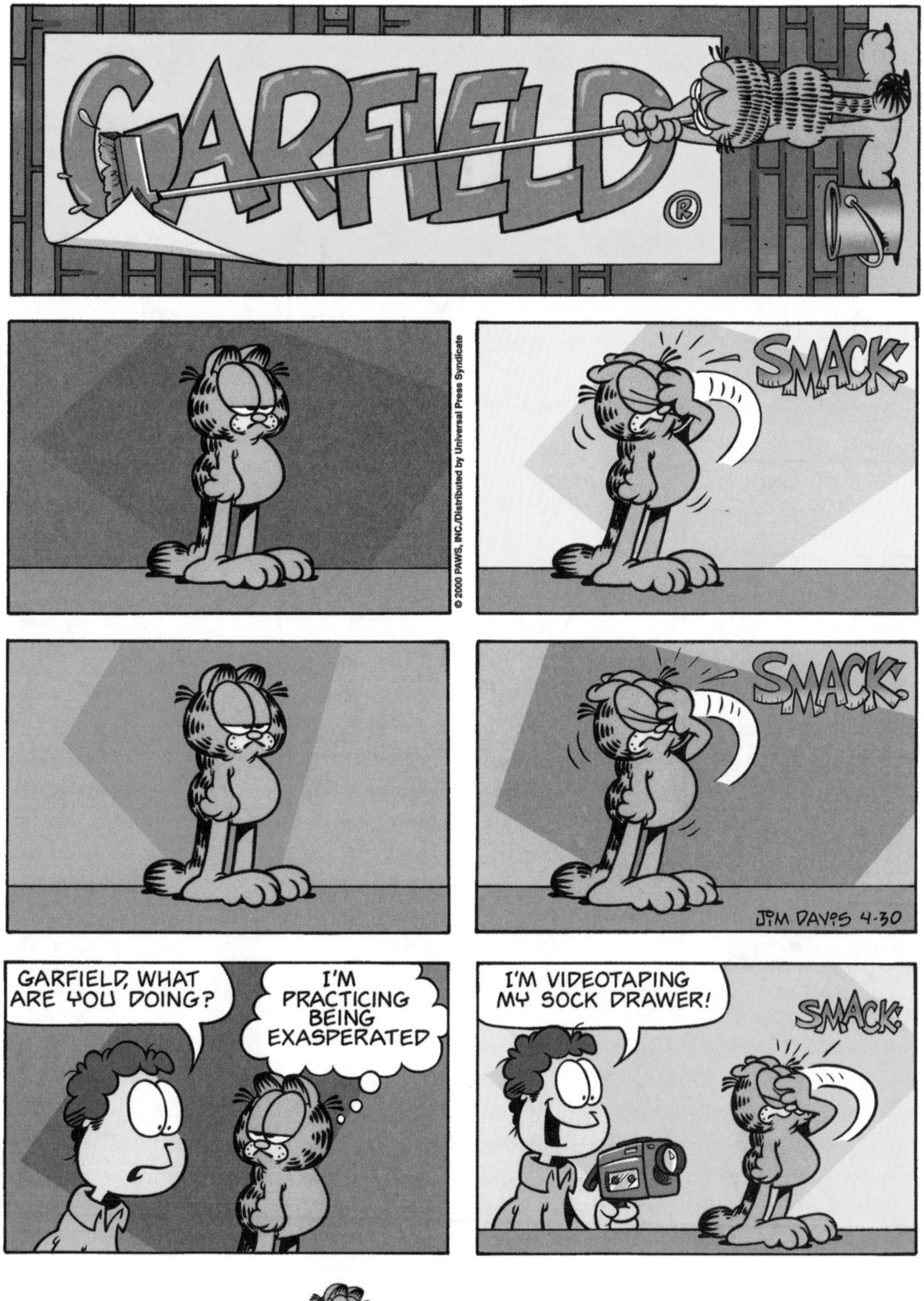
GARFIELD®
© 2000 PAWS, INC./Distributed by Universal Press Syndicate
SMACK!
SMACK!
JIM DAVIS 4-30
GARFIELD, WHAT ARE YOU DOING?
I'M PRACTICING BEING EXASPERATED
I'M VIDEOTAPING MY SOCK DRAWER!
SMACK!

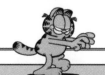

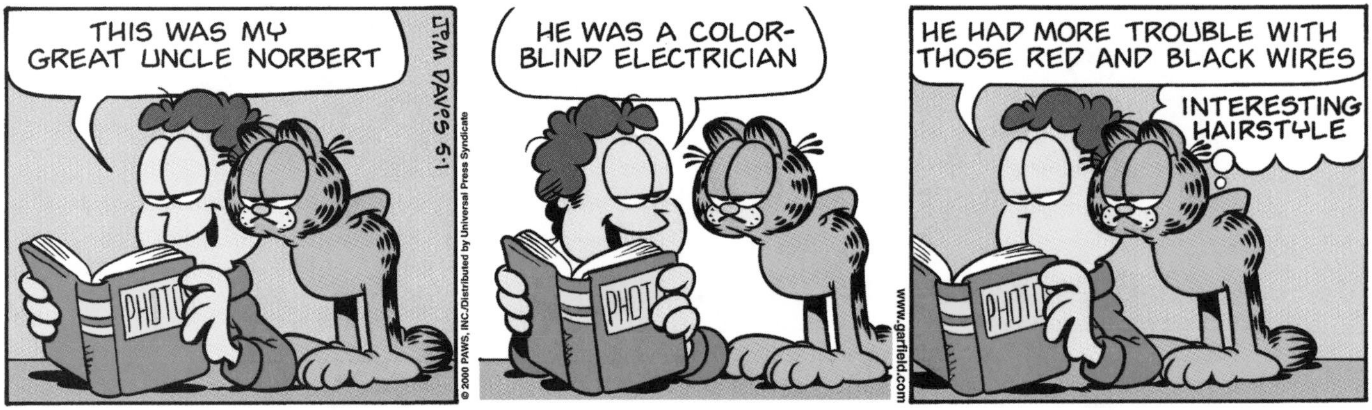
THIS WAS MY GREAT UNCLE NORBERT
JIM DAVIS 5-1
© 2000 PAWS, INC./Distributed by Universal Press Syndicate
HE WAS A COLOR-BLIND ELECTRICIAN
www.garfield.com
HE HAD MORE TROUBLE WITH THOSE RED AND BLACK WIRES
INTERESTING HAIRSTYLE

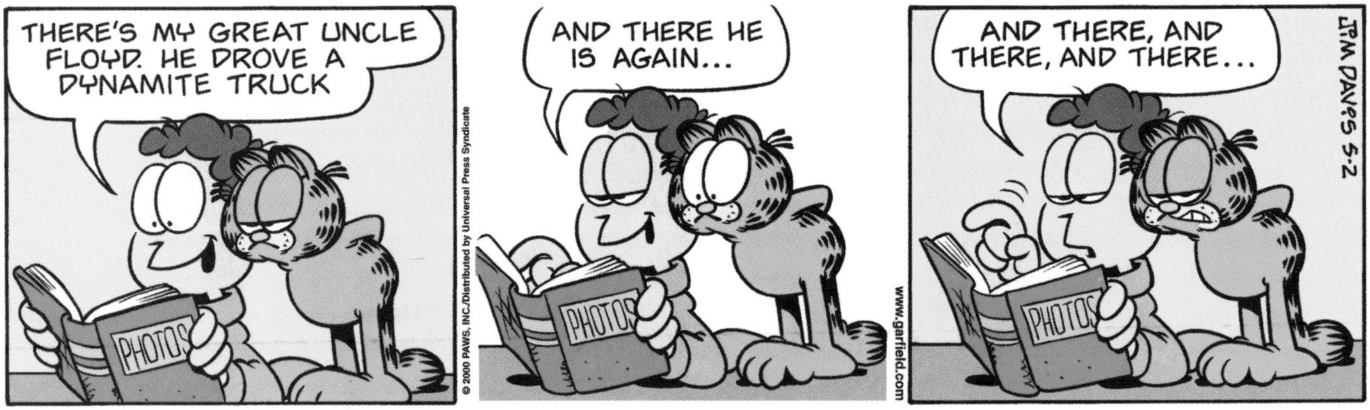
THERE'S MY GREAT UNCLE FLOYD. HE DROVE A DYNAMITE TRUCK
PHOTOS
© 2000 PAWS, INC./Distributed by Universal Press Syndicate
AND THERE HE IS AGAIN...
PHOTOS
www.garfield.com
AND THERE, AND THERE, AND THERE...
PHOTOS
JIM DAVIS 5-2

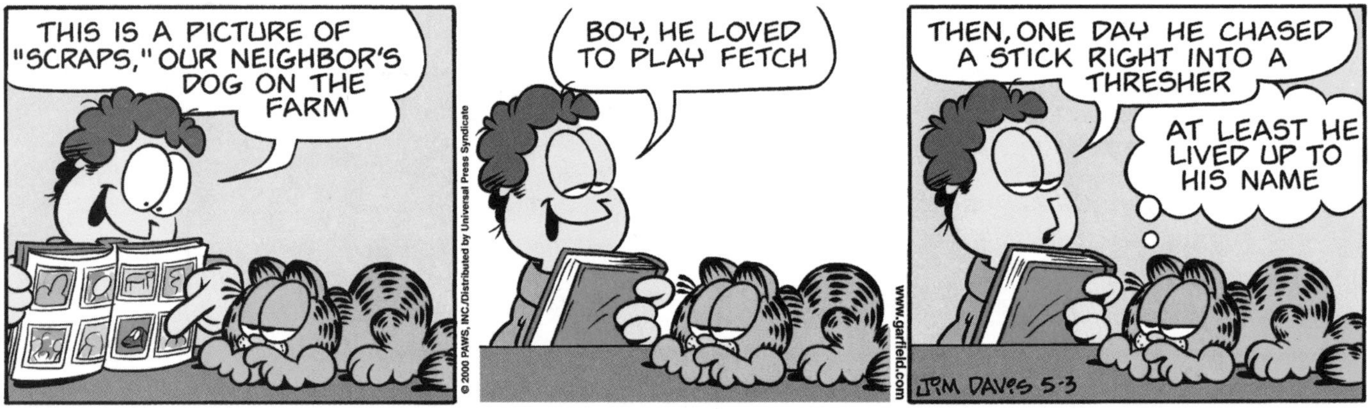
THIS IS A PICTURE OF "SCRAPS," OUR NEIGHBOR'S DOG ON THE FARM
© 2000 PAWS, INC./Distributed by Universal Press Syndicate
BOY, HE LOVED TO PLAY FETCH
www.garfield.com
THEN, ONE DAY HE CHASED A STICK RIGHT INTO A THRESHER
AT LEAST HE LIVED UP TO HIS NAME
JIM DAVIS 5-3

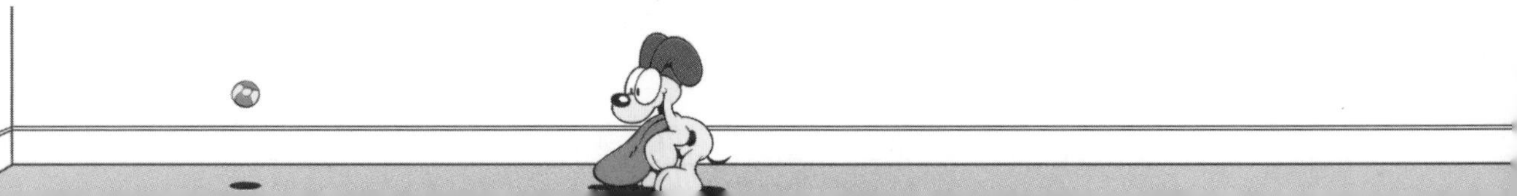

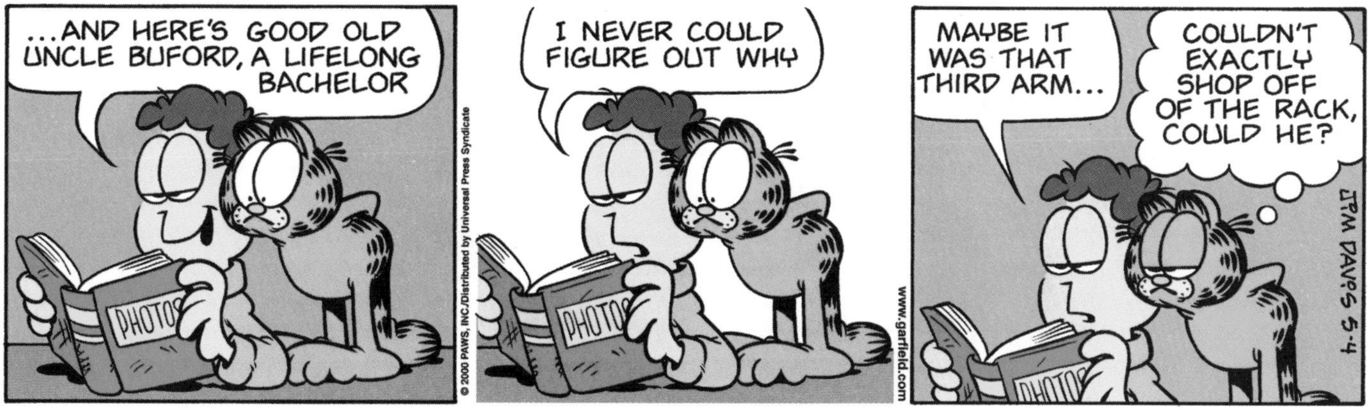
...AND HERE'S GOOD OLD UNCLE BUFORD, A LIFELONG BACHELOR
PHOTOS
© 2000 PAWS, INC./Distributed by Universal Press Syndicate
I NEVER COULD FIGURE OUT WHY
www.garfield.com
MAYBE IT WAS THAT THIRD ARM...
COULDN'T EXACTLY SHOP OFF OF THE RACK, COULD HE?
JIM DAVIS 5-4

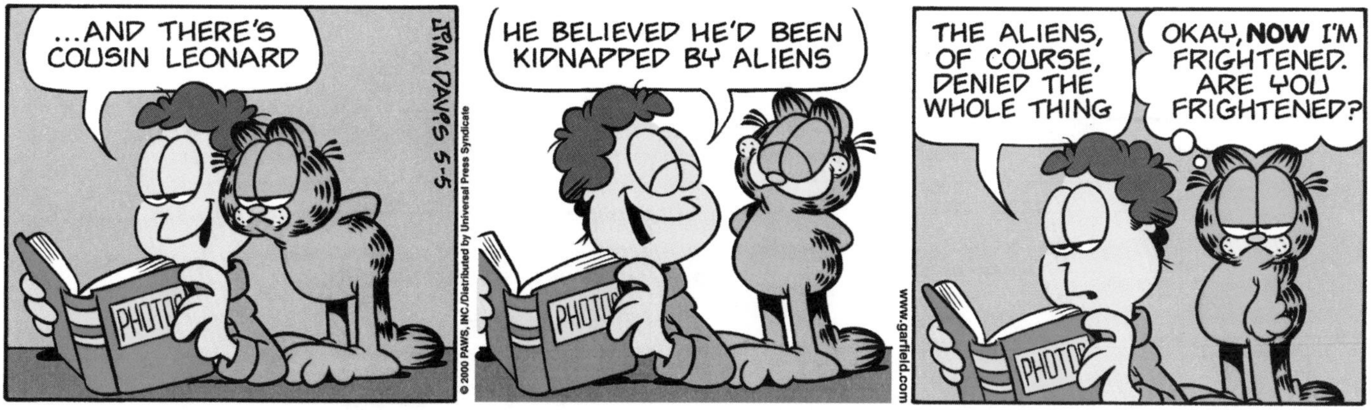
...AND THERE'S COUSIN LEONARD
PHOTOS
JIM DAVIS 5-5
© 2000 PAWS, INC./Distributed by Universal Press Syndicate
HE BELIEVED HE'D BEEN KIDNAPPED BY ALIENS
www.garfield.com
THE ALIENS, OF COURSE, DENIED THE WHOLE THING
OKAY, **NOW** I'M FRIGHTENED. ARE YOU FRIGHTENED?

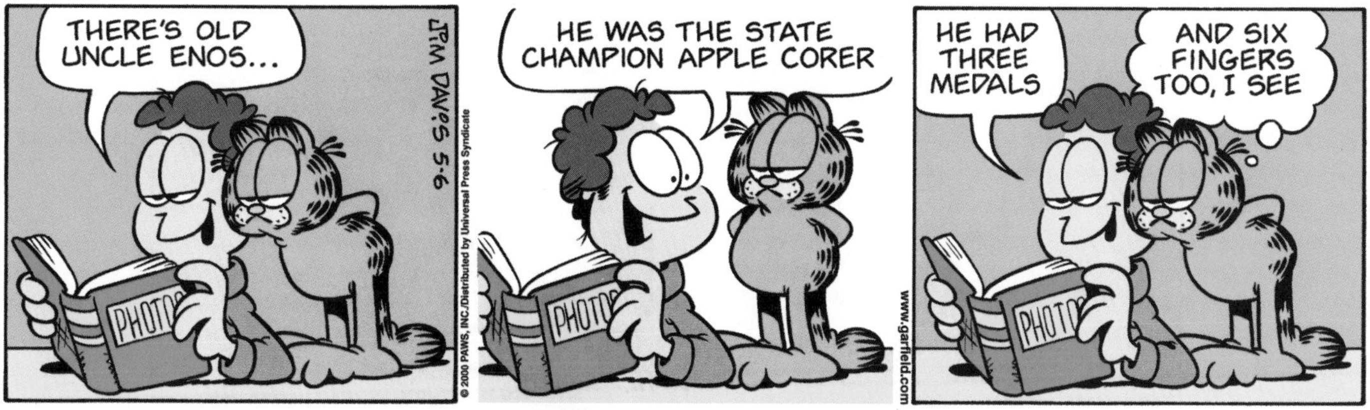
THERE'S OLD UNCLE ENOS...
PHOTOS
JIM DAVIS 5-6
© 2000 PAWS, INC./Distributed by Universal Press Syndicate
HE WAS THE STATE CHAMPION APPLE CORER
www.garfield.com
HE HAD THREE MEDALS
AND SIX FINGERS TOO, I SEE

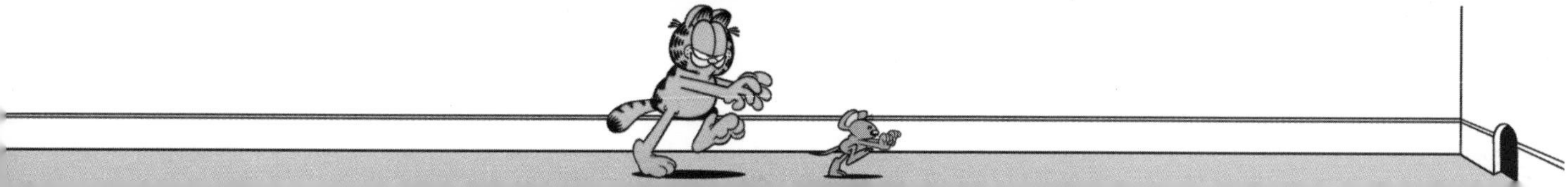

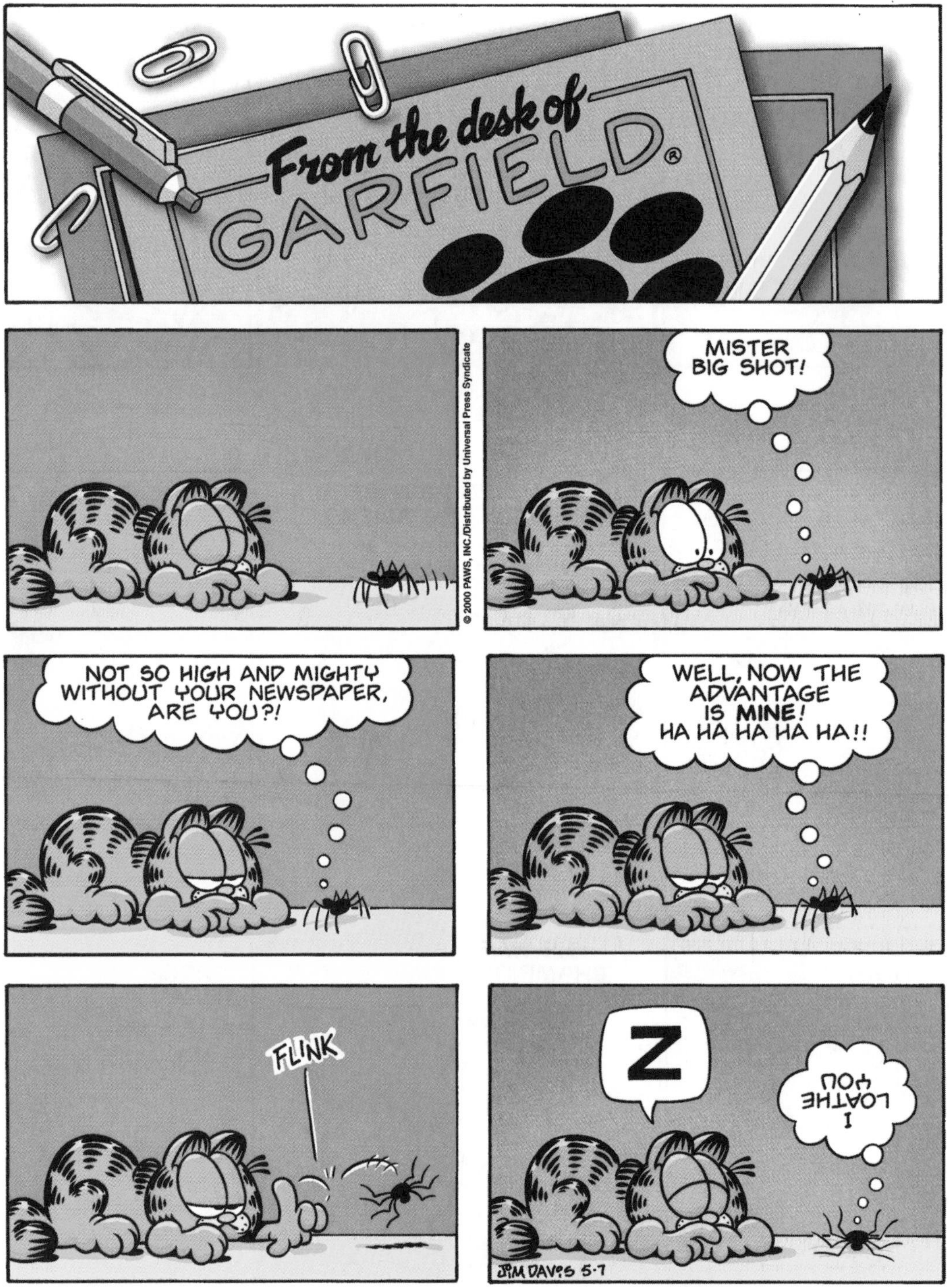
From the desk of
GARFIELD®
© 2000 PAWS, INC./Distributed by Universal Press Syndicate
MISTER BIG SHOT!
NOT SO HIGH AND MIGHTY WITHOUT YOUR NEWSPAPER, ARE YOU?!
WELL, NOW THE ADVANTAGE IS **MINE**! HA HA HA HA HA!!
FLINK
Z
I LOATHE YOU
JIM DAVIS 5-7

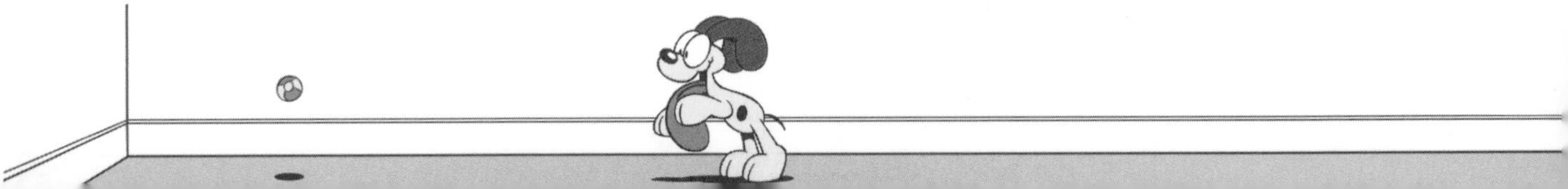

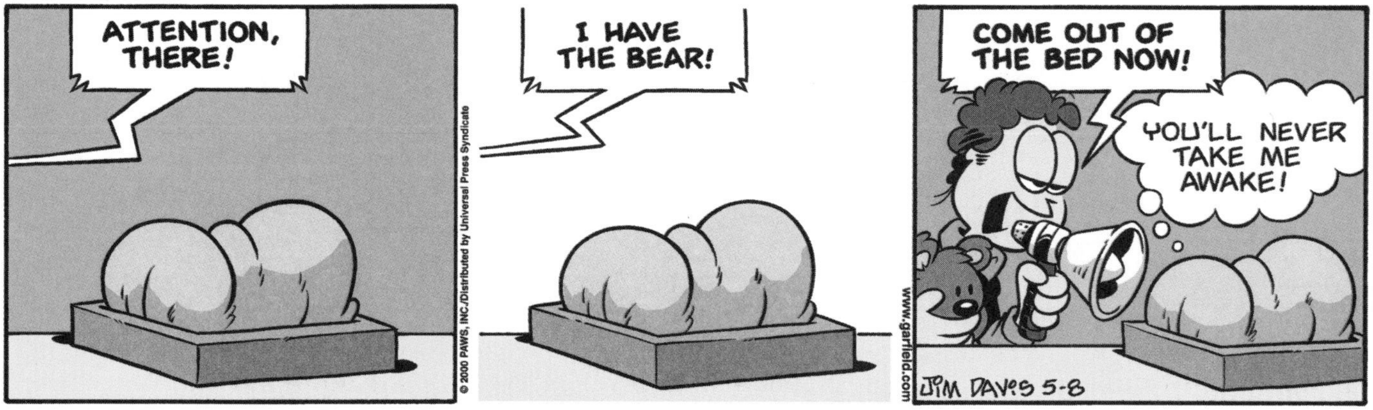
ATTENTION, THERE!
I HAVE THE BEAR!
COME OUT OF THE BED NOW!
YOU'LL NEVER TAKE ME AWAKE!
© 2000 PAWS, INC./Distributed by Universal Press Syndicate
www.garfield.com
JIM DAVIS 5-8

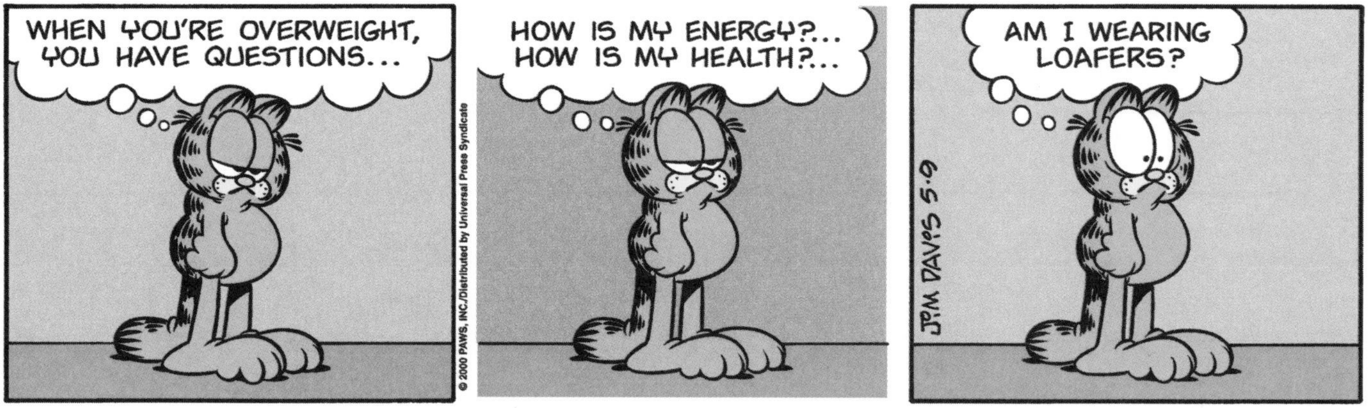
WHEN YOU'RE OVERWEIGHT, YOU HAVE QUESTIONS...
HOW IS MY ENERGY?... HOW IS MY HEALTH?...
AM I WEARING LOAFERS?
© 2000 PAWS, INC./Distributed by Universal Press Syndicate
JIM DAVIS 5-9

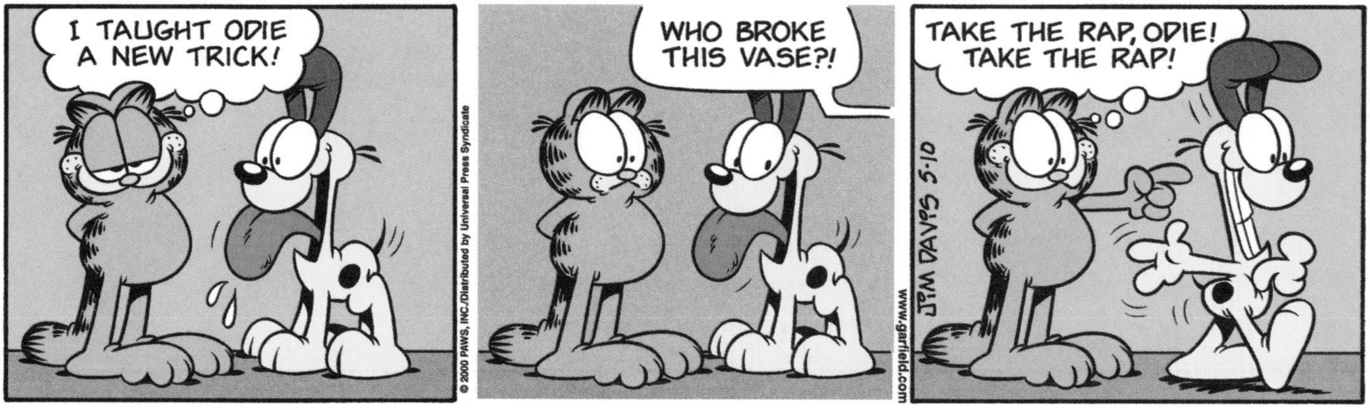
I TAUGHT ODIE A NEW TRICK!
WHO BROKE THIS VASE?!
TAKE THE RAP, ODIE! TAKE THE RAP!
© 2000 PAWS, INC./Distributed by Universal Press Syndicate
www.garfield.com
JIM DAVIS 5-10

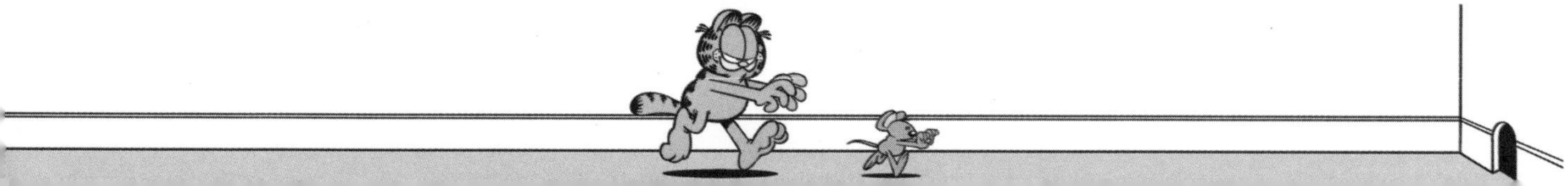

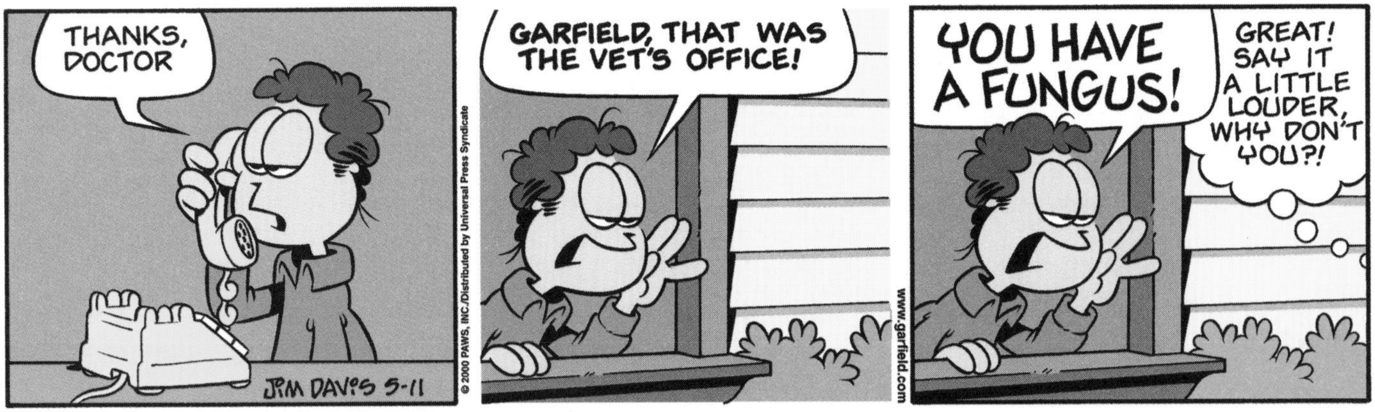
THANKS, DOCTOR
JIM DAVIS 5-11
© 2000 PAWS, INC./Distributed by Universal Press Syndicate
GARFIELD, THAT WAS THE VET'S OFFICE!
www.garfield.com
YOU HAVE A FUNGUS!
GREAT! SAY IT A LITTLE LOUDER, WHY DON'T YOU?!

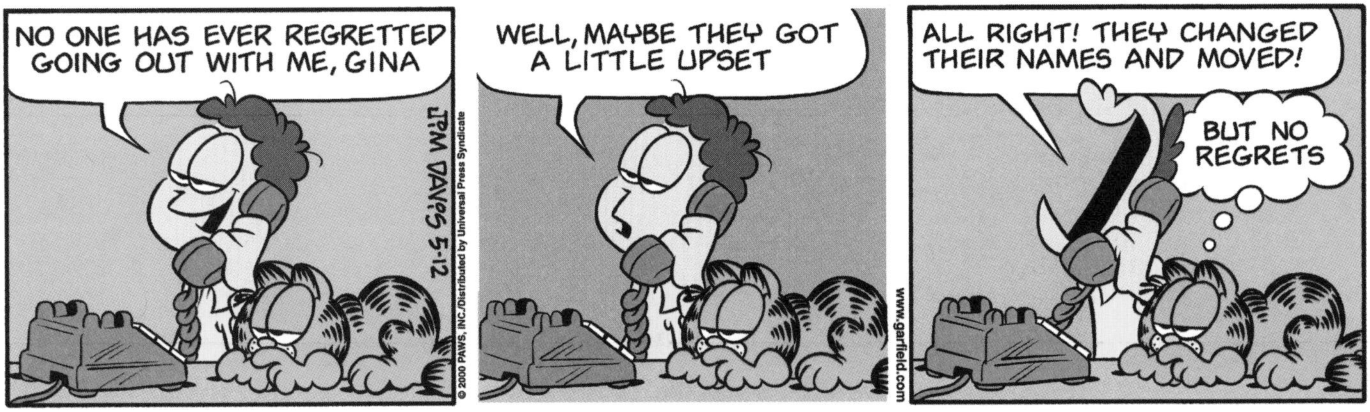
NO ONE HAS EVER REGRETTED GOING OUT WITH ME, GINA
JIM DAVIS 5-12
© 2000 PAWS, INC./Distributed by Universal Press Syndicate
WELL, MAYBE THEY GOT A LITTLE UPSET
www.garfield.com
ALL RIGHT! THEY CHANGED THEIR NAMES AND MOVED!
BUT NO REGRETS

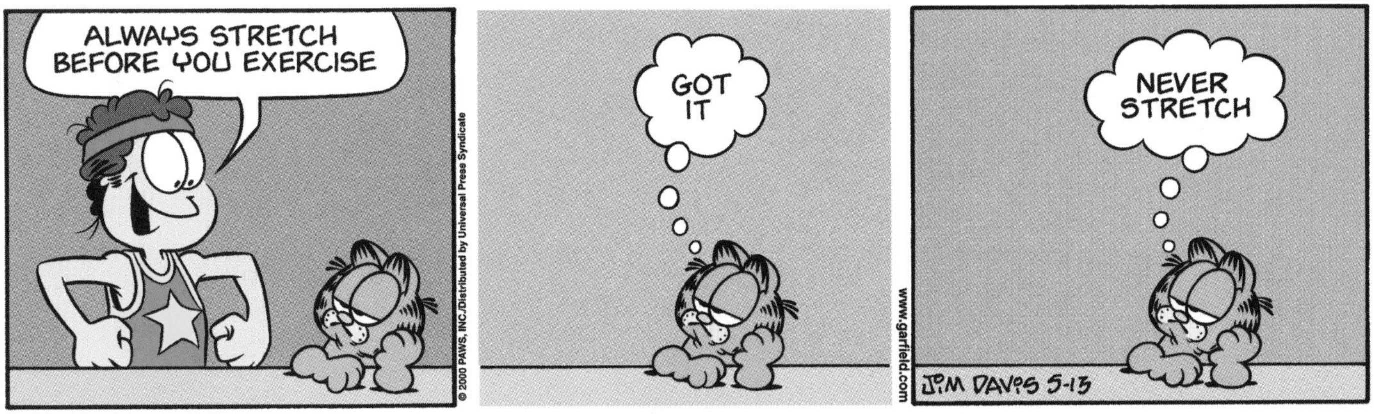
ALWAYS STRETCH BEFORE YOU EXERCISE
© 2000 PAWS, INC./Distributed by Universal Press Syndicate
GOT IT
www.garfield.com
NEVER STRETCH
JIM DAVIS 5-13

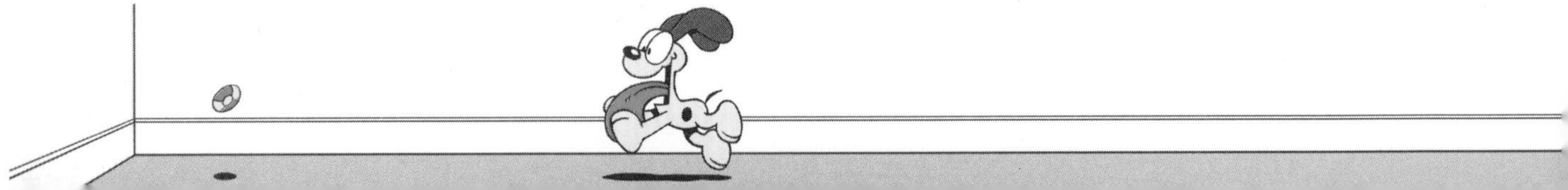

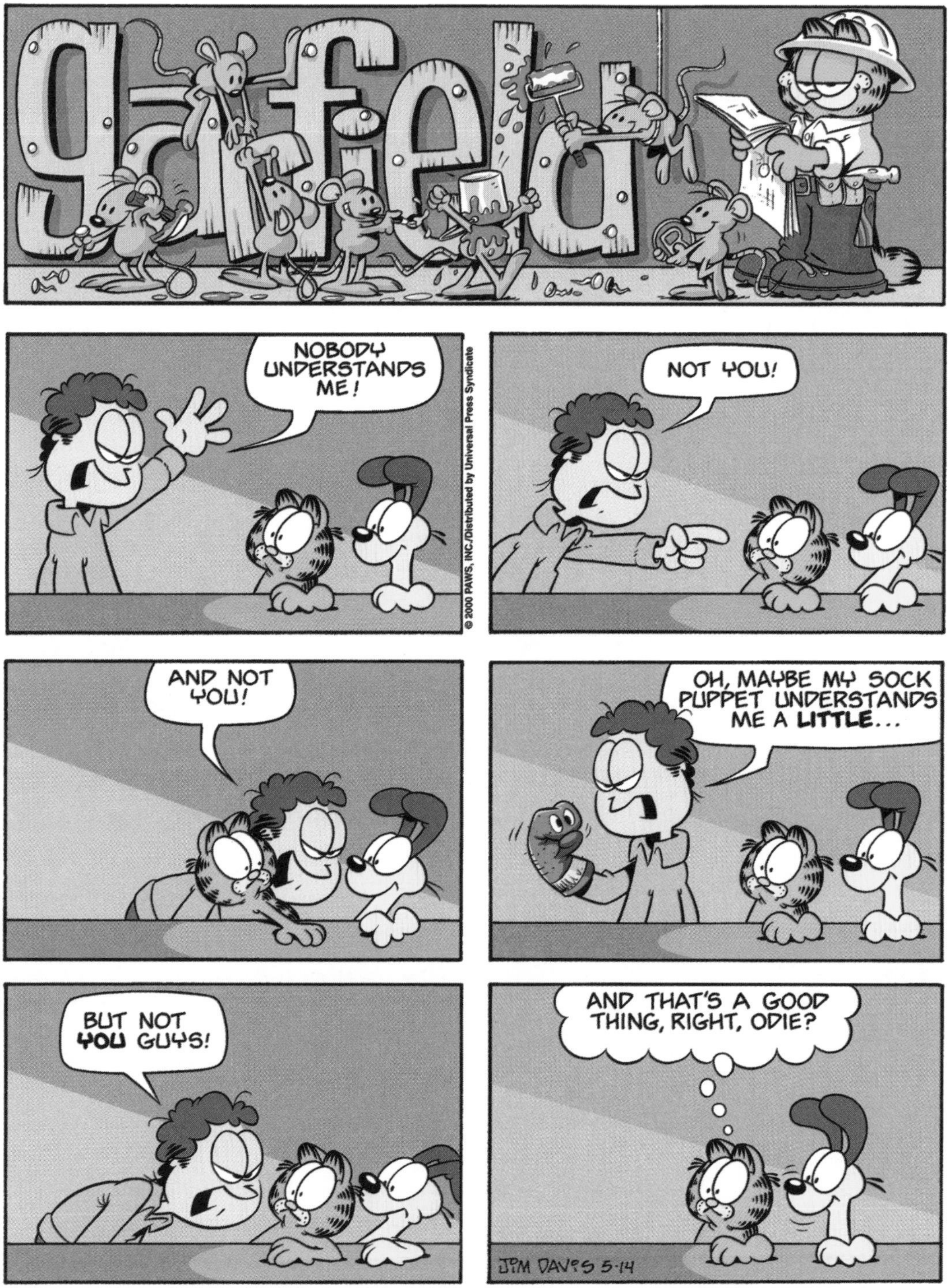
garfield
NOBODY UNDERSTANDS ME!
NOT YOU!
AND NOT YOU!
OH, MAYBE MY SOCK PUPPET UNDERSTANDS ME A **LITTLE**...
BUT NOT **YOU** GUYS!
AND THAT'S A GOOD THING, RIGHT, ODIE?
JIM DAVIS 5-14
© 2000 PAWS, INC./Distributed by Universal Press Syndicate

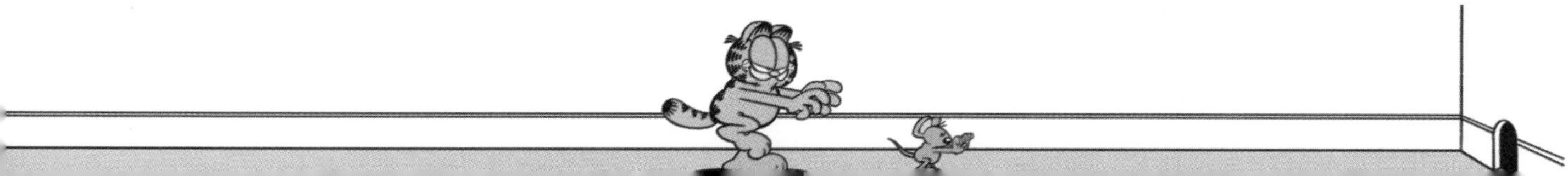

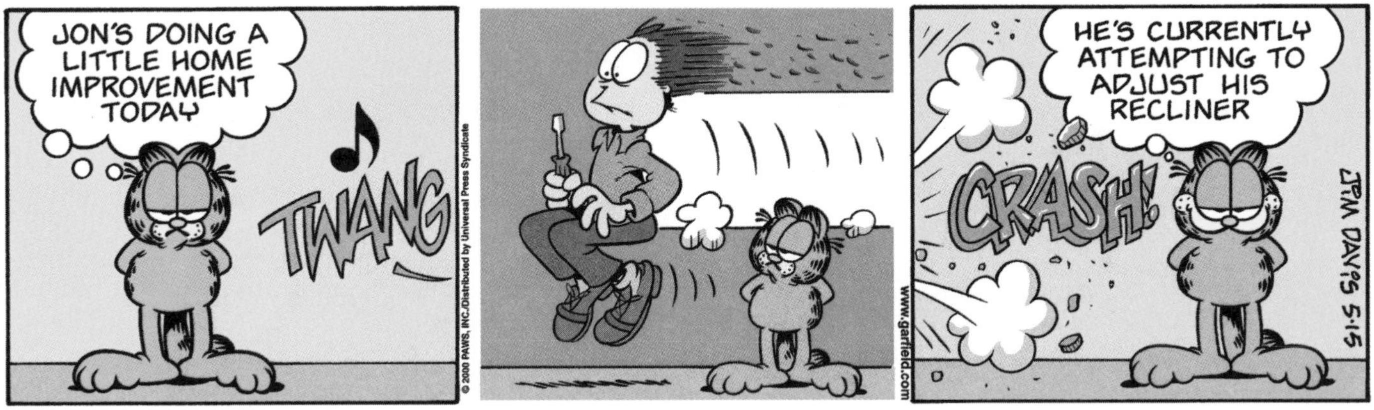
JON'S DOING A LITTLE HOME IMPROVEMENT TODAY
TWANG
© 2000 PAWS, INC./Distributed by Universal Press Syndicate
www.garfield.com
HE'S CURRENTLY ATTEMPTING TO ADJUST HIS RECLINER
CRASH!
JIM DAVIS 5-15

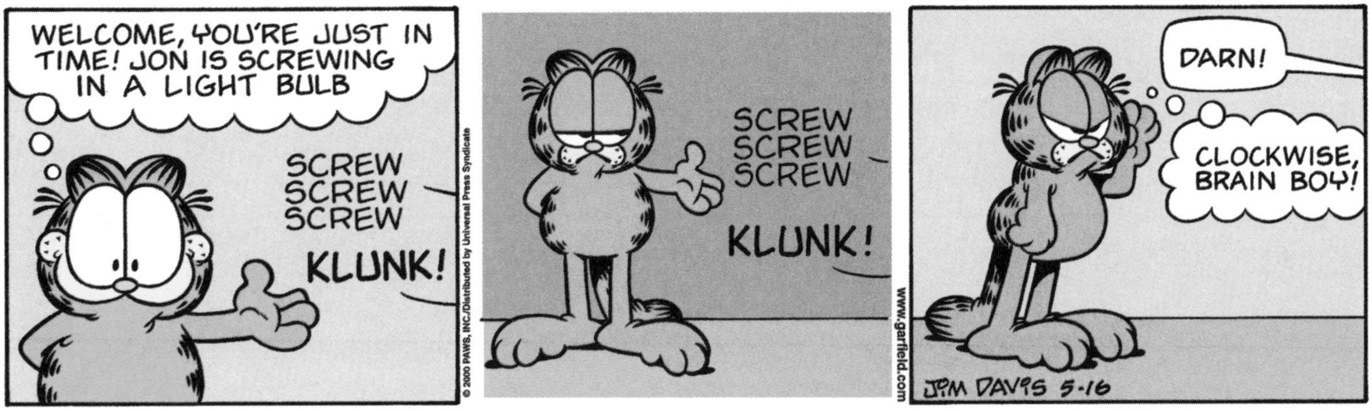
WELCOME, YOU'RE JUST IN TIME! JON IS SCREWING IN A LIGHT BULB
SCREW SCREW SCREW
KLUNK!
© 2000 PAWS, INC./Distributed by Universal Press Syndicate
SCREW SCREW SCREW
KLUNK!
www.garfield.com
DARN!
CLOCKWISE, BRAIN BOY!
JIM DAVIS 5-16

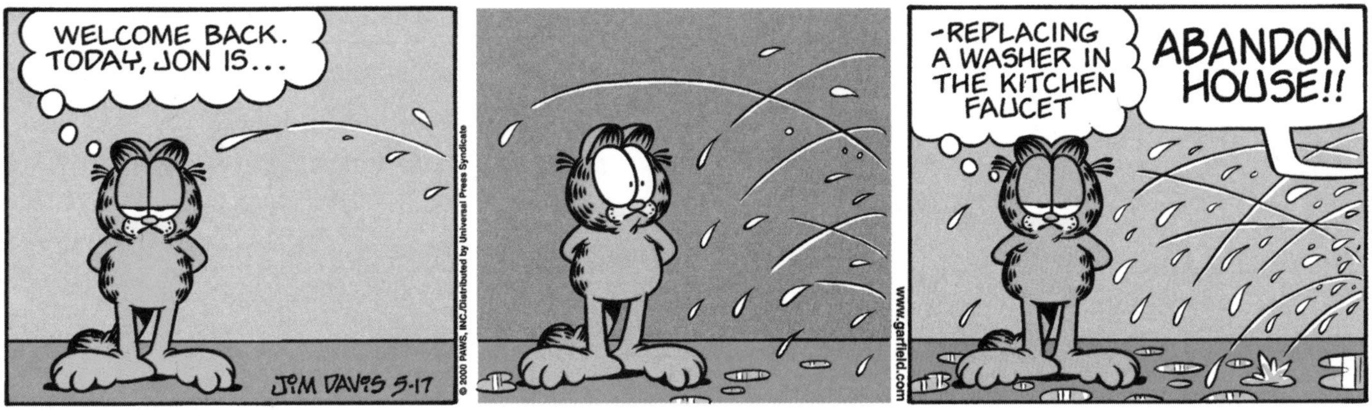
WELCOME BACK. TODAY, JON IS...
JIM DAVIS 5-17
© 2000 PAWS, INC./Distributed by Universal Press Syndicate
www.garfield.com
-REPLACING A WASHER IN THE KITCHEN FAUCET
ABANDON HOUSE!!

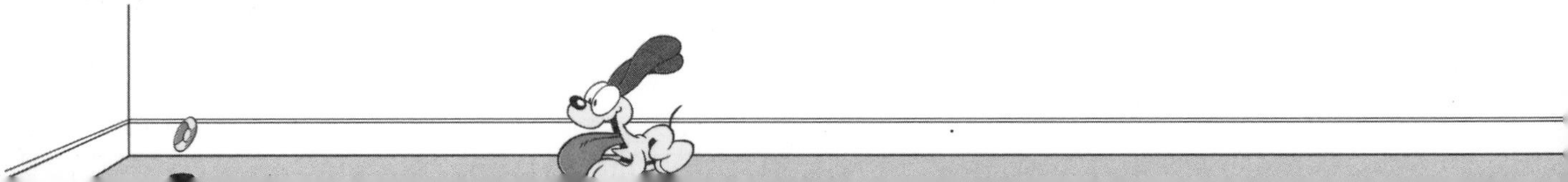

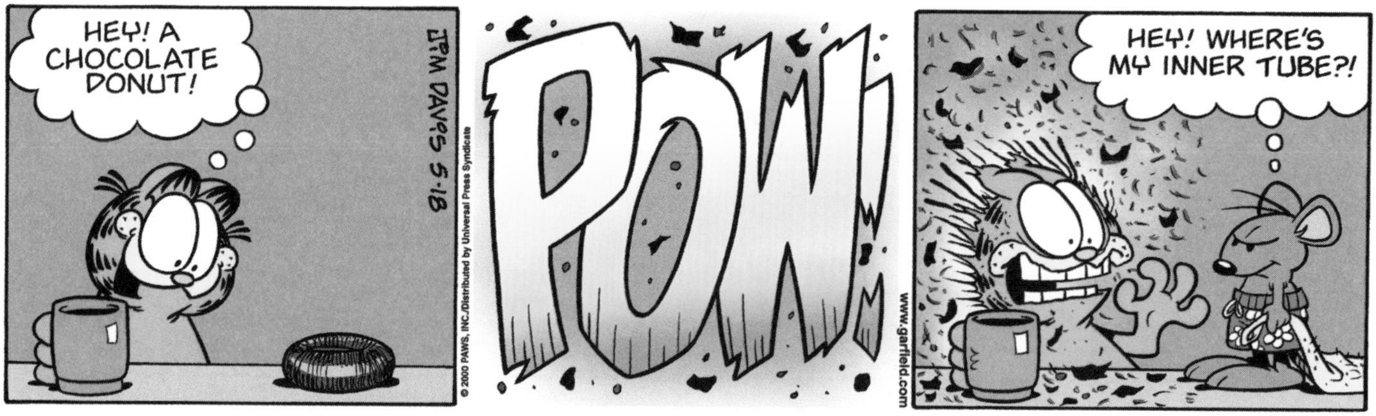
HEY! A CHOCOLATE DONUT!
JIM DAVIS 5-18
© 2000 PAWS, INC./Distributed by Universal Press Syndicate
POW!
www.garfield.com
HEY! WHERE'S MY INNER TUBE?!

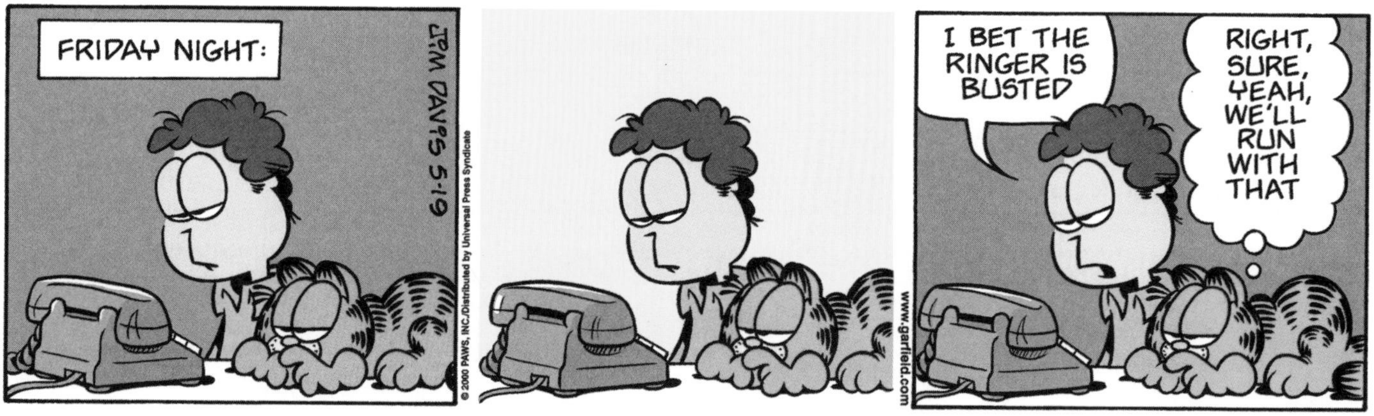
FRIDAY NIGHT:
JIM DAVIS 5-19
© 2000 PAWS, INC./Distributed by Universal Press Syndicate
www.garfield.com
I BET THE RINGER IS BUSTED
RIGHT, SURE, YEAH, WE'LL RUN WITH THAT

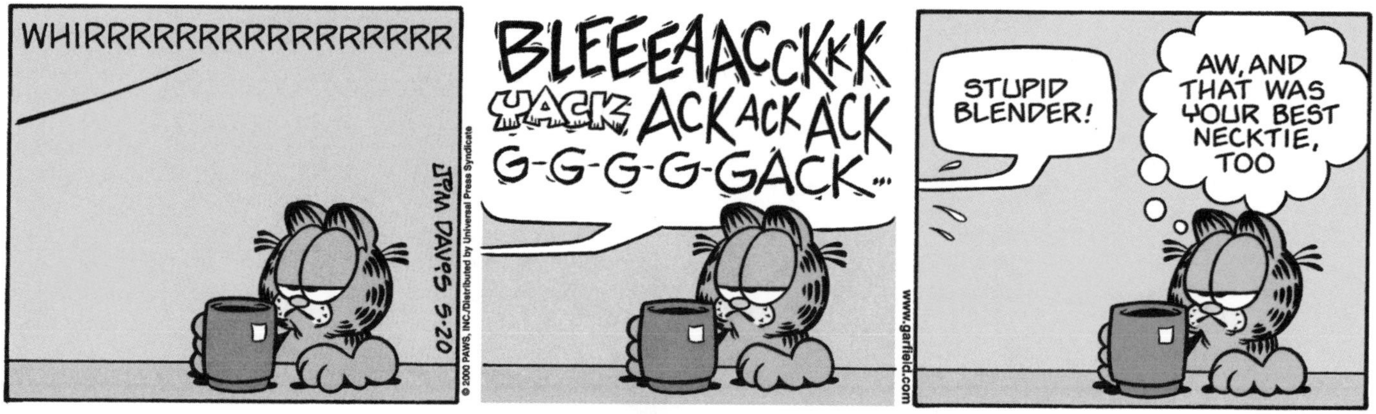
WHIRRRRRRRRRRRRRRRRR
JIM DAVIS 5-20
© 2000 PAWS, INC./Distributed by Universal Press Syndicate
BLEEEAACCKKK YACK ACK ACK ACK G-G-G-G-GACK...
www.garfield.com
STUPID BLENDER!
AW, AND THAT WAS YOUR BEST NECKTIE, TOO

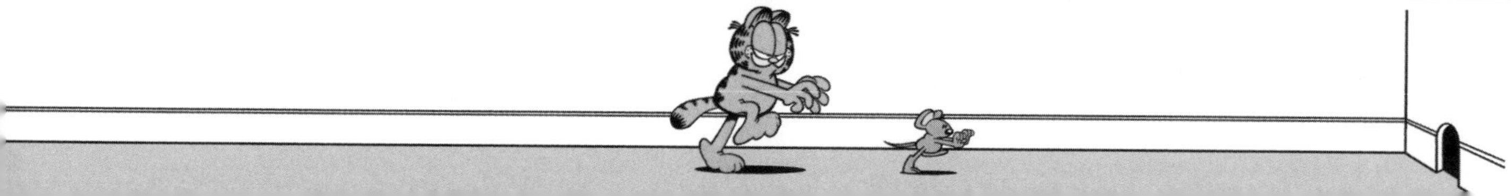

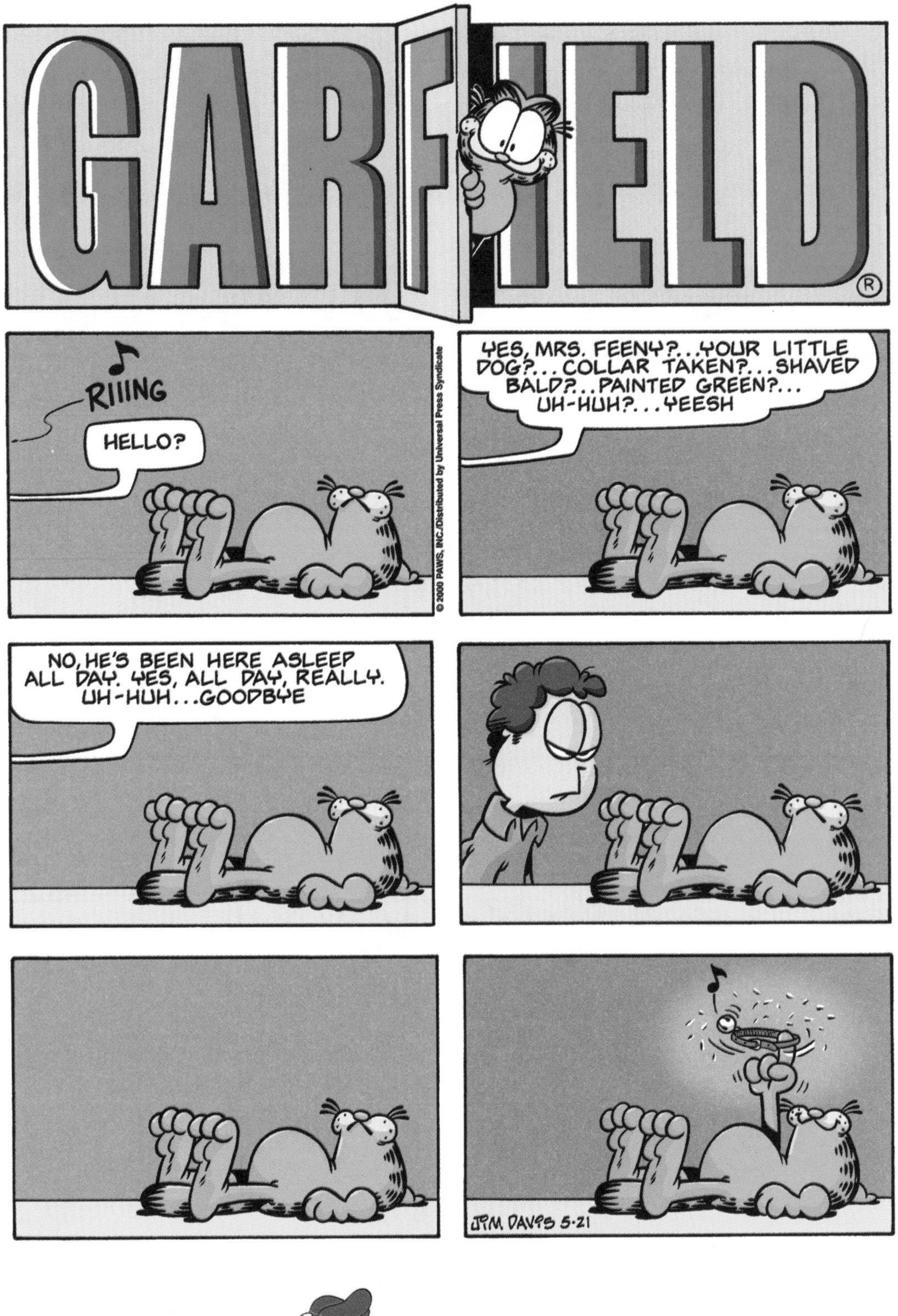
GARFIELD
RIIING
HELLO?
YES, MRS. FEENY?...YOUR LITTLE DOG?...COLLAR TAKEN?...SHAVED BALD?...PAINTED GREEN?... UH-HUH?...YEESH
NO, HE'S BEEN HERE ASLEEP ALL DAY. YES, ALL DAY, REALLY. UH-HUH...GOODBYE
© 2000 PAWS, INC./Distributed by Universal Press Syndicate
JIM DAVIS 5-21

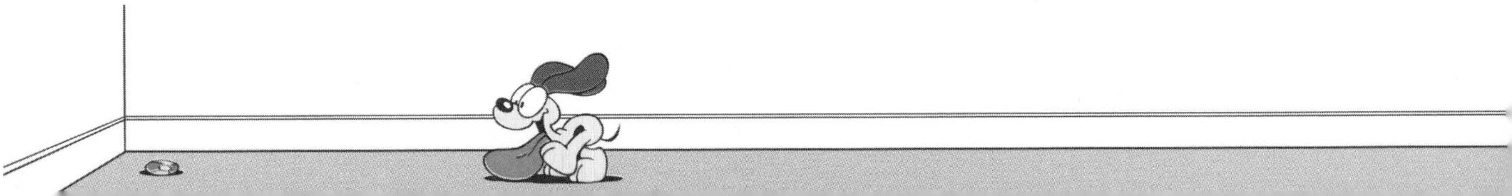

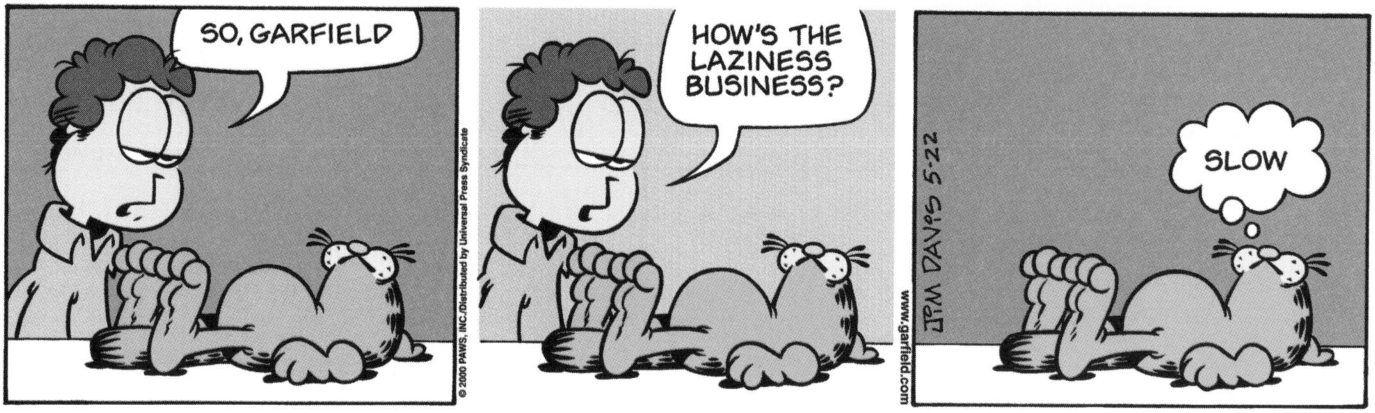
SO, GARFIELD
HOW'S THE LAZINESS BUSINESS?
SLOW
© 2000 PAWS, INC./Distributed by Universal Press Syndicate
www.garfield.com
JIM DAVIS 5-22

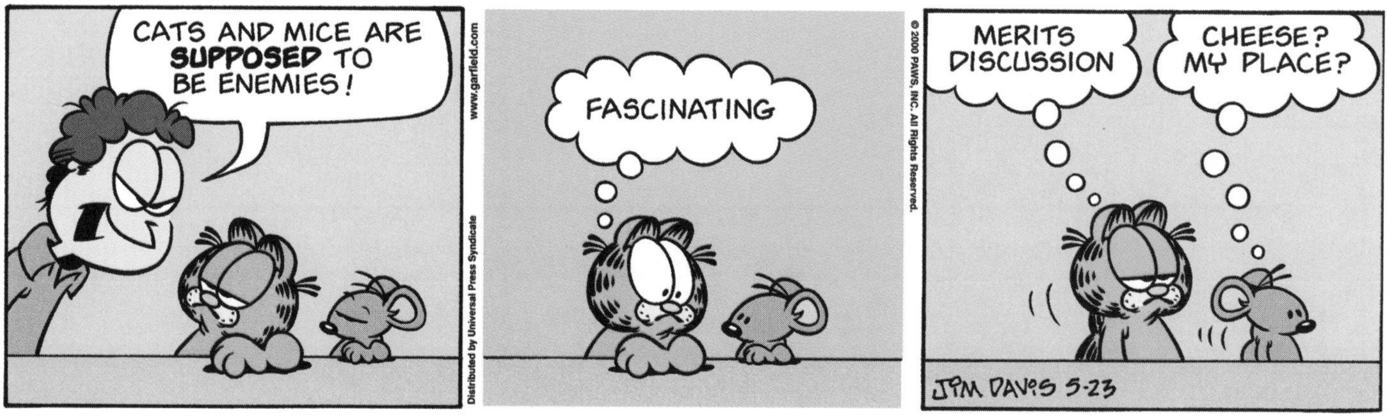
CATS AND MICE ARE **SUPPOSED** TO BE ENEMIES!
FASCINATING
MERITS DISCUSSION
CHEESE? MY PLACE?
www.garfield.com
Distributed by Universal Press Syndicate
© 2000 PAWS, INC. All Rights Reserved.
JIM DAVIS 5-23

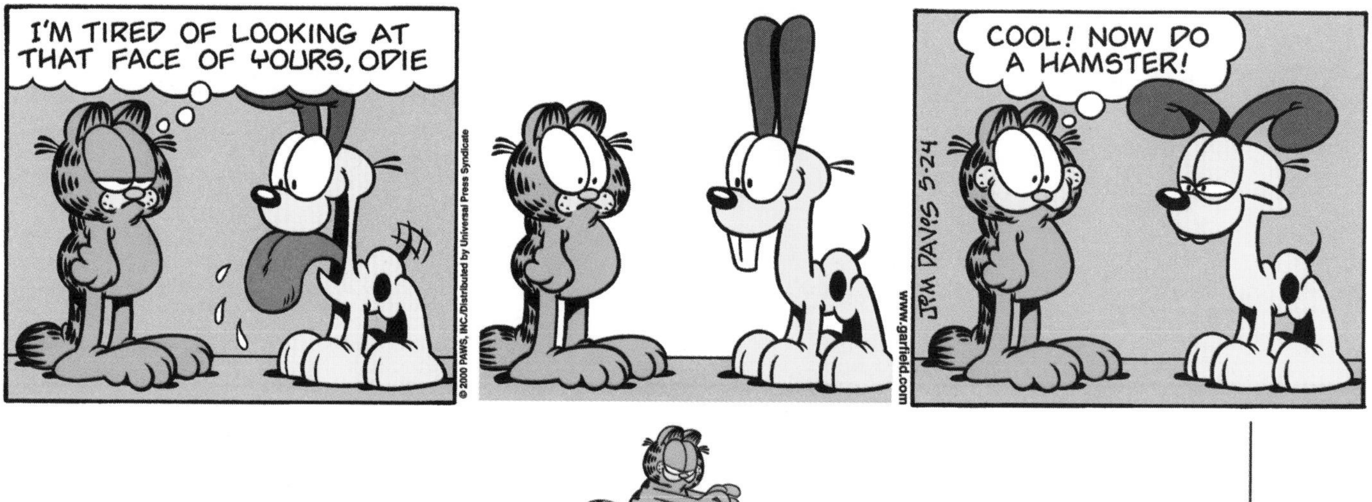
I'M TIRED OF LOOKING AT THAT FACE OF YOURS, ODIE
COOL! NOW DO A HAMSTER!
© 2000 PAWS, INC./Distributed by Universal Press Syndicate
www.garfield.com
JIM DAVIS 5-24

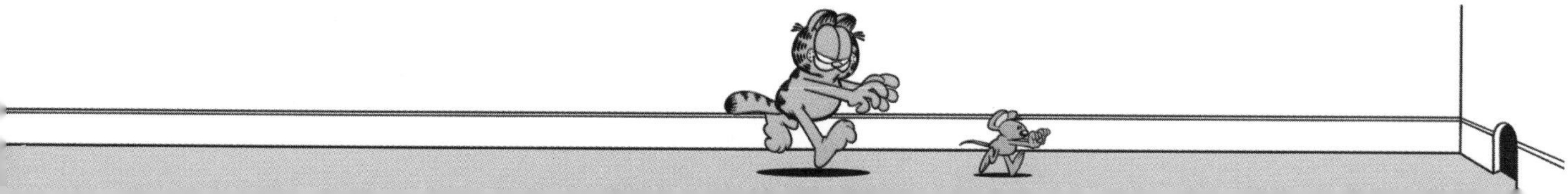

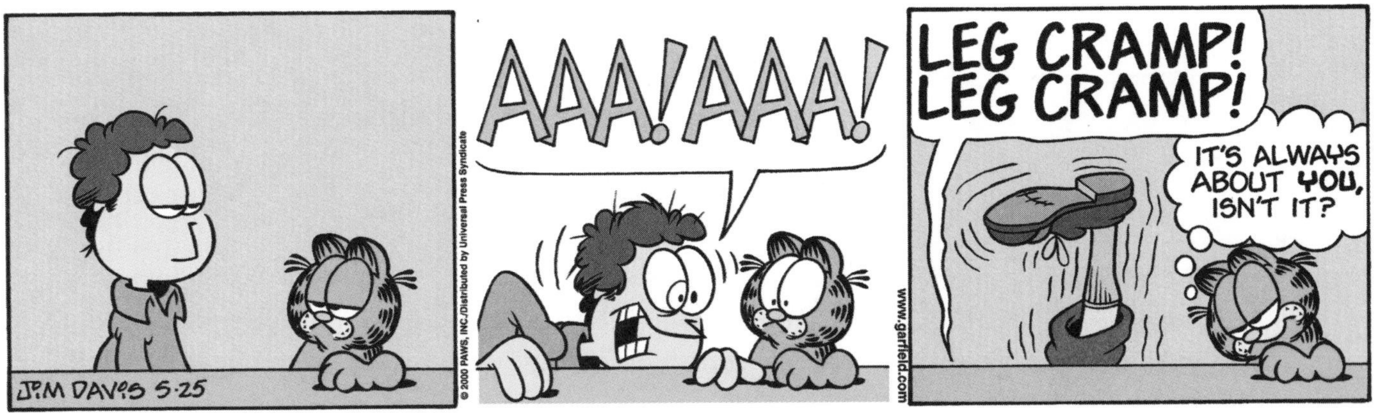
JIM DAVIS 5-25
© 2000 PAWS, INC./Distributed by Universal Press Syndicate
AAA! AAA!
LEG CRAMP! LEG CRAMP!
IT'S ALWAYS ABOUT **YOU**, ISN'T IT?
www.garfield.com

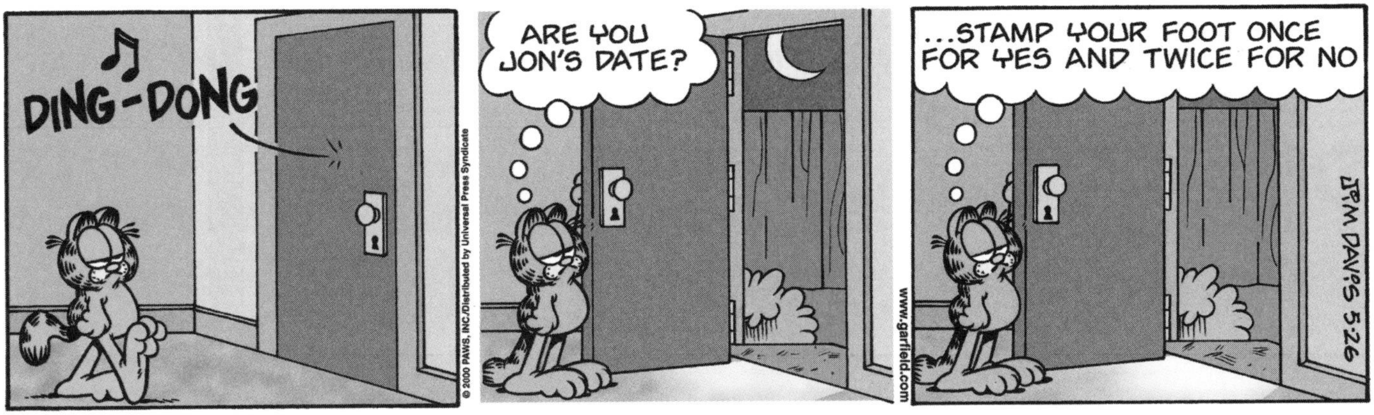
DING-DONG
© 2000 PAWS, INC./Distributed by Universal Press Syndicate
ARE YOU JON'S DATE?
www.garfield.com
...STAMP YOUR FOOT ONCE FOR YES AND TWICE FOR NO
JIM DAVIS 5-26

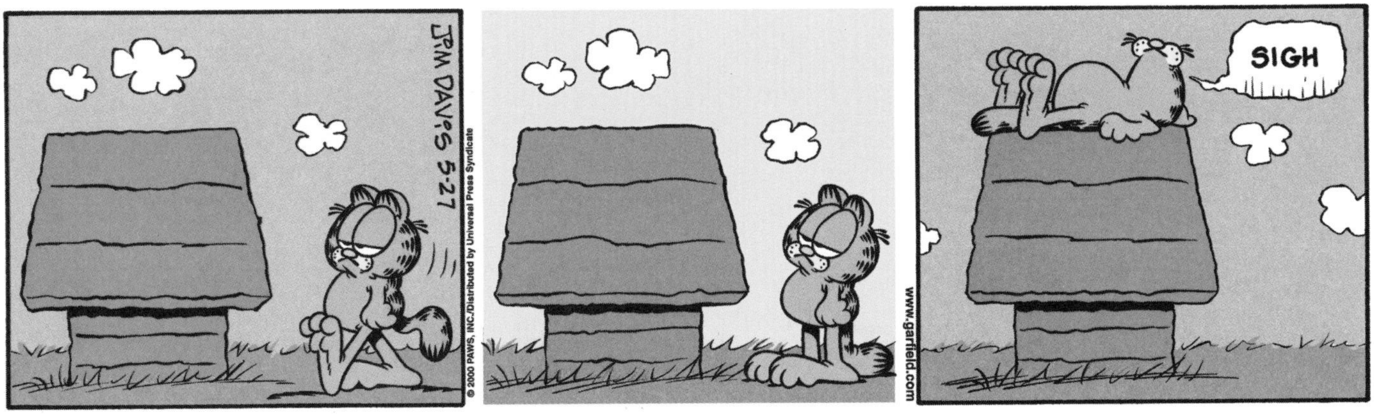
JIM DAVIS 5-27
© 2000 PAWS, INC./Distributed by Universal Press Syndicate
www.garfield.com
SIGH

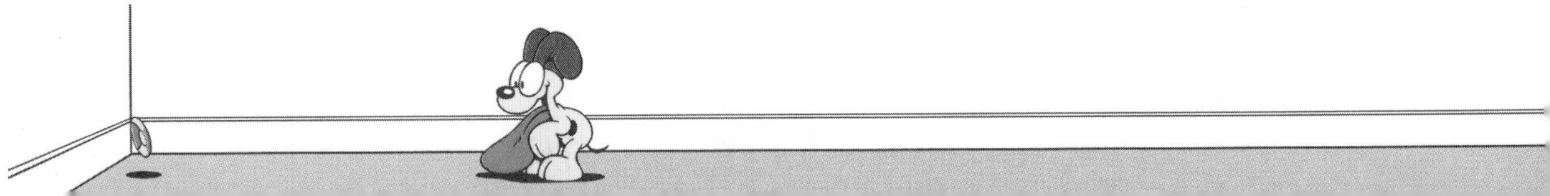

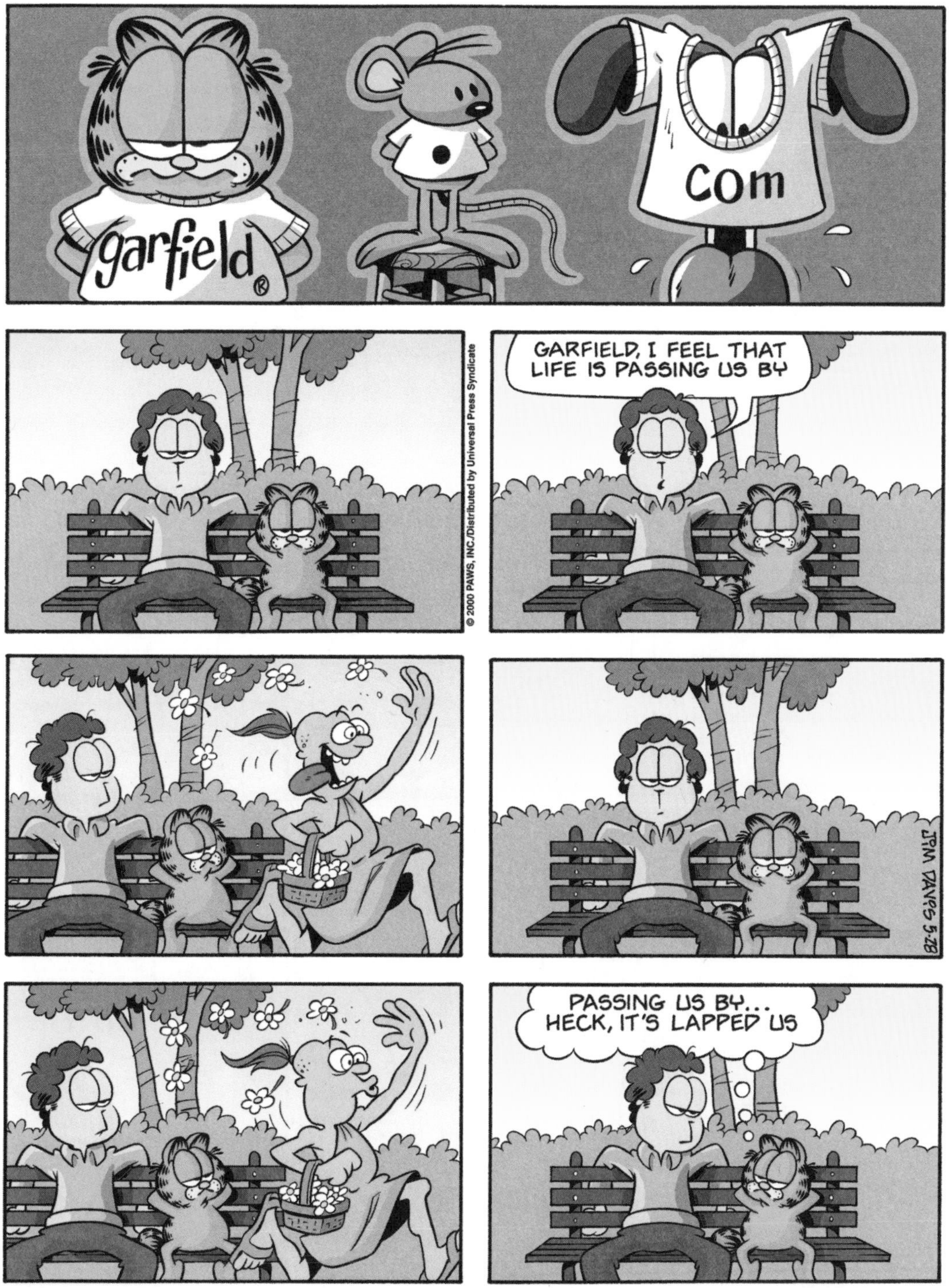
garfield®
com
© 2000 PAWS, INC./Distributed by Universal Press Syndicate
GARFIELD, I FEEL THAT LIFE IS PASSING US BY
JIM DAVIS 5-28
PASSING US BY... HECK, IT'S LAPPED US

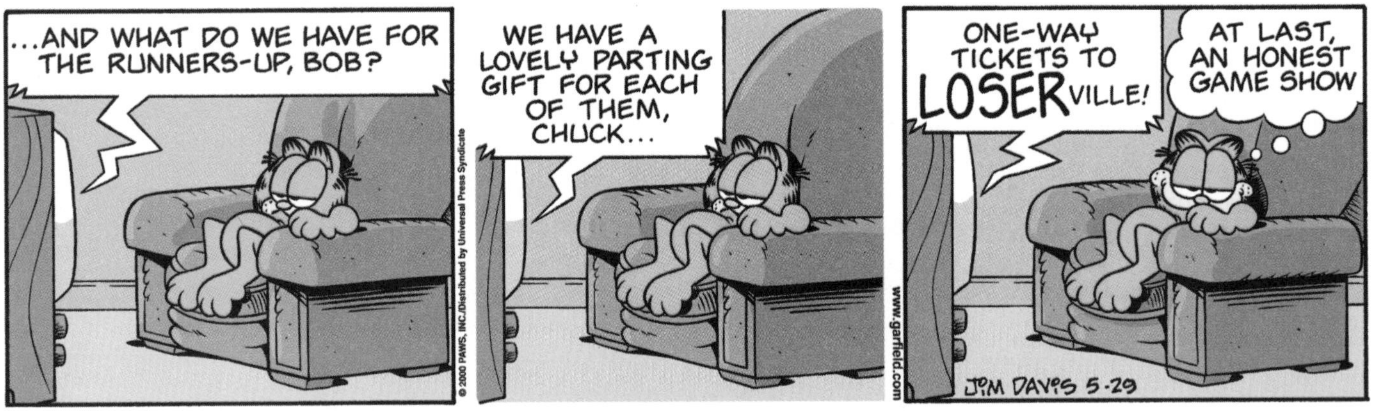
...AND WHAT DO WE HAVE FOR THE RUNNERS-UP, BOB?
WE HAVE A LOVELY PARTING GIFT FOR EACH OF THEM, CHUCK...
ONE-WAY TICKETS TO LOSERVILLE!
AT LAST, AN HONEST GAME SHOW
© 2000 PAWS, INC./Distributed by Universal Press Syndicate
www.garfield.com
JIM DAVIS 5-29

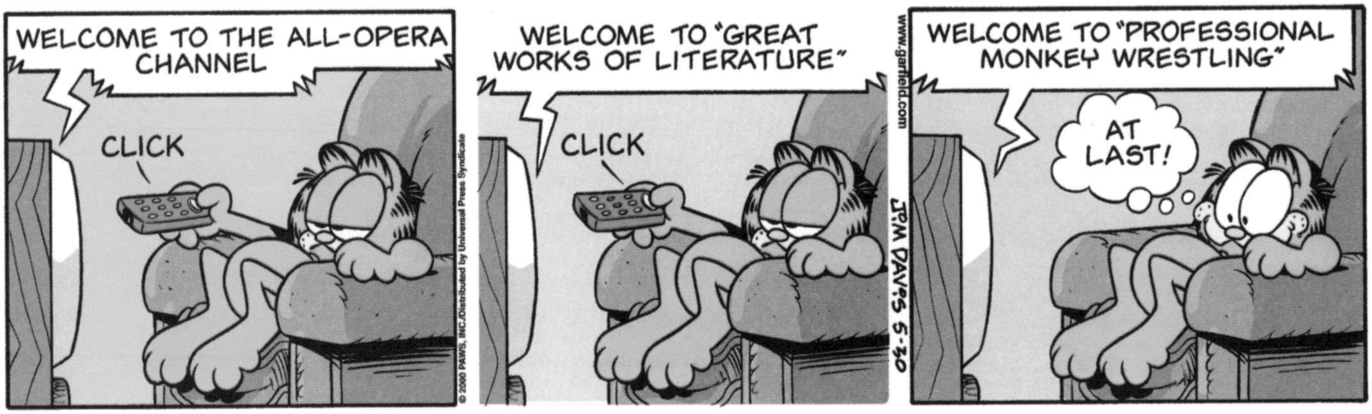
WELCOME TO THE ALL-OPERA CHANNEL
CLICK
WELCOME TO "GREAT WORKS OF LITERATURE"
CLICK
WELCOME TO "PROFESSIONAL MONKEY WRESTLING"
AT LAST!
© 2000 PAWS, INC./Distributed by Universal Press Syndicate
www.garfield.com
JIM DAVIS 5-30

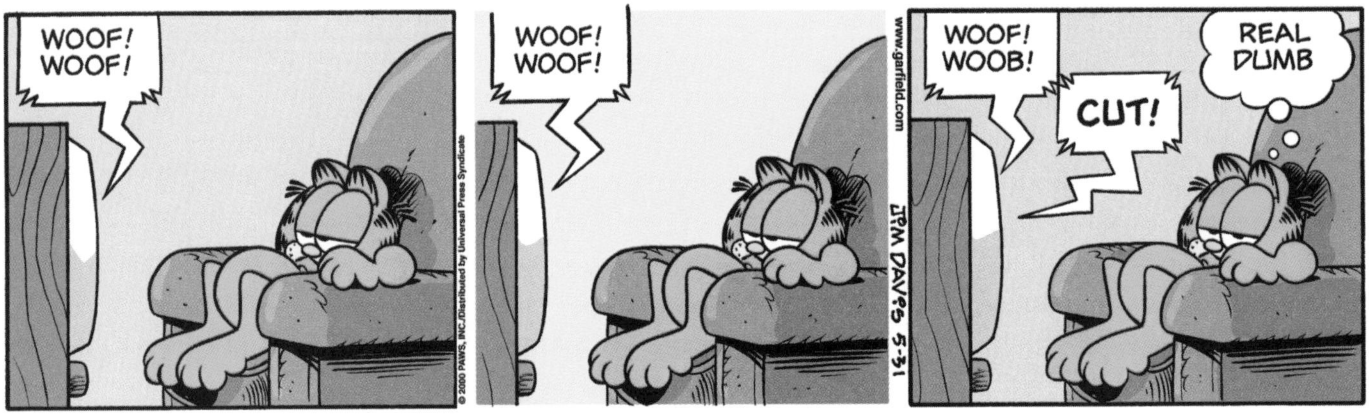
WOOF! WOOF!
WOOF! WOOF!
WOOF! WOOB!
CUT!
REAL DUMB
© 2000 PAWS, INC./Distributed by Universal Press Syndicate
www.garfield.com
JIM DAVIS 5-31

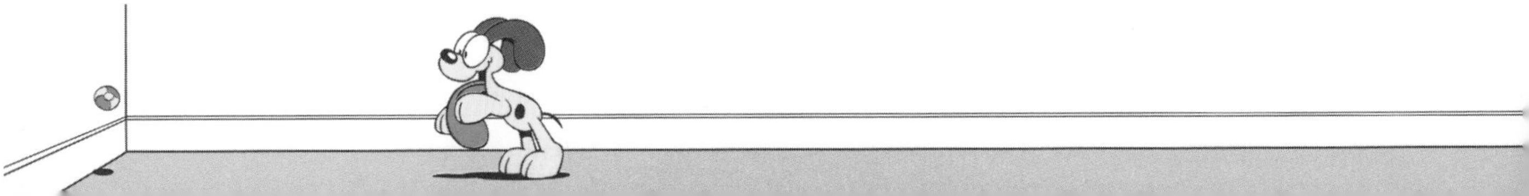

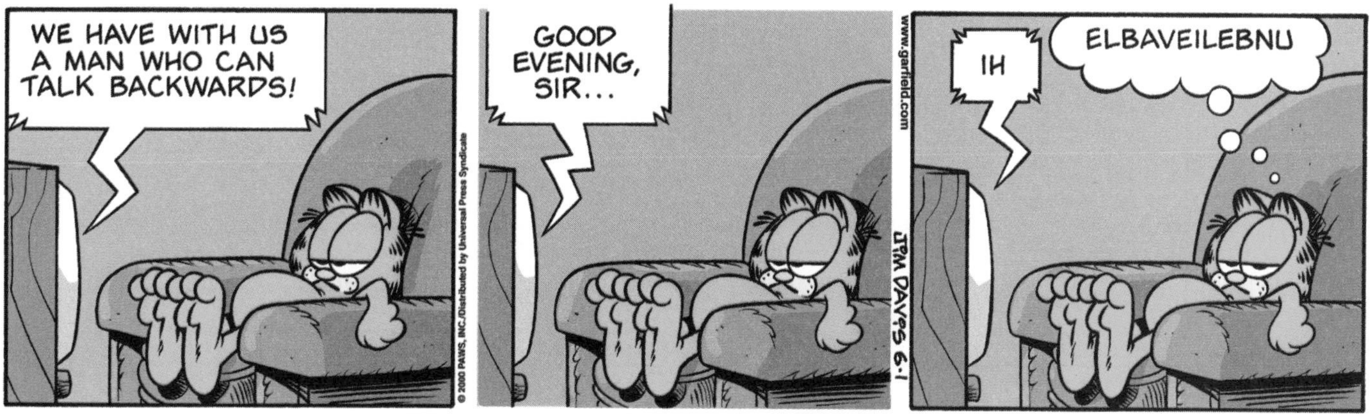
WE HAVE WITH US A MAN WHO CAN TALK BACKWARDS!
GOOD EVENING, SIR...
IH
ELBAVEILEBNU
© 2000 PAWS, INC./Distributed by Universal Press Syndicate
www.garfield.com
JIM DAVIS 6-1

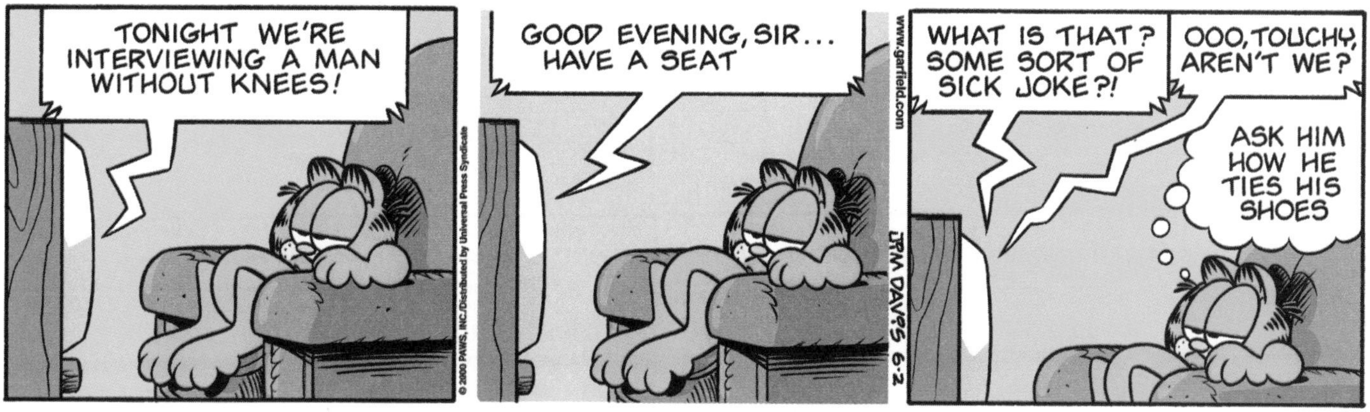
TONIGHT WE'RE INTERVIEWING A MAN WITHOUT KNEES!
GOOD EVENING, SIR... HAVE A SEAT
WHAT IS THAT? SOME SORT OF SICK JOKE?!
OOO, TOUCHY, AREN'T WE?
ASK HIM HOW HE TIES HIS SHOES
© 2000 PAWS, INC./Distributed by Universal Press Syndicate
www.garfield.com
JIM DAVIS 6-2

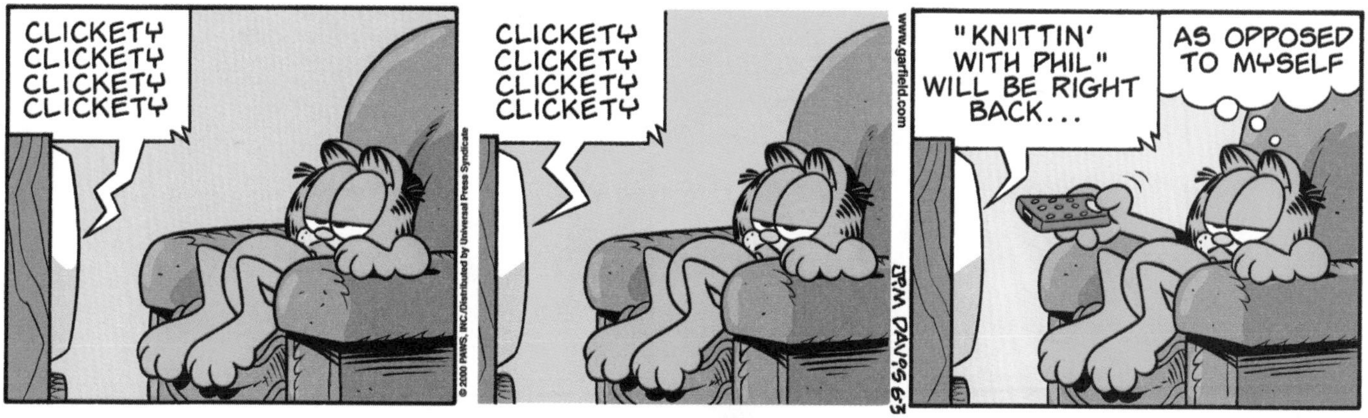
CLICKETY CLICKETY CLICKETY CLICKETY
CLICKETY CLICKETY CLICKETY CLICKETY
"KNITTIN' WITH PHIL" WILL BE RIGHT BACK...
AS OPPOSED TO MYSELF
© 2000 PAWS, INC./Distributed by Universal Press Syndicate
www.garfield.com
JIM DAVIS 6-3

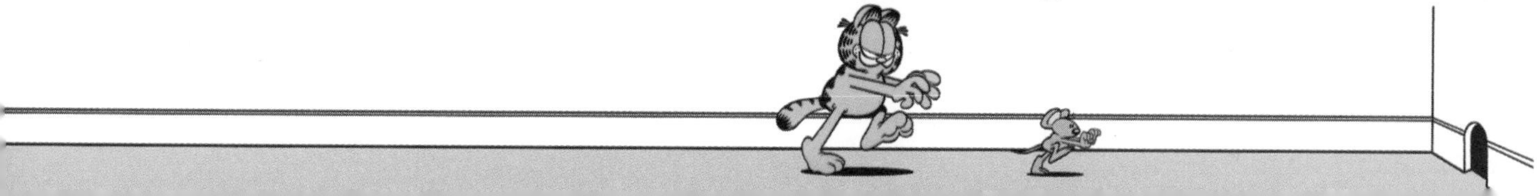

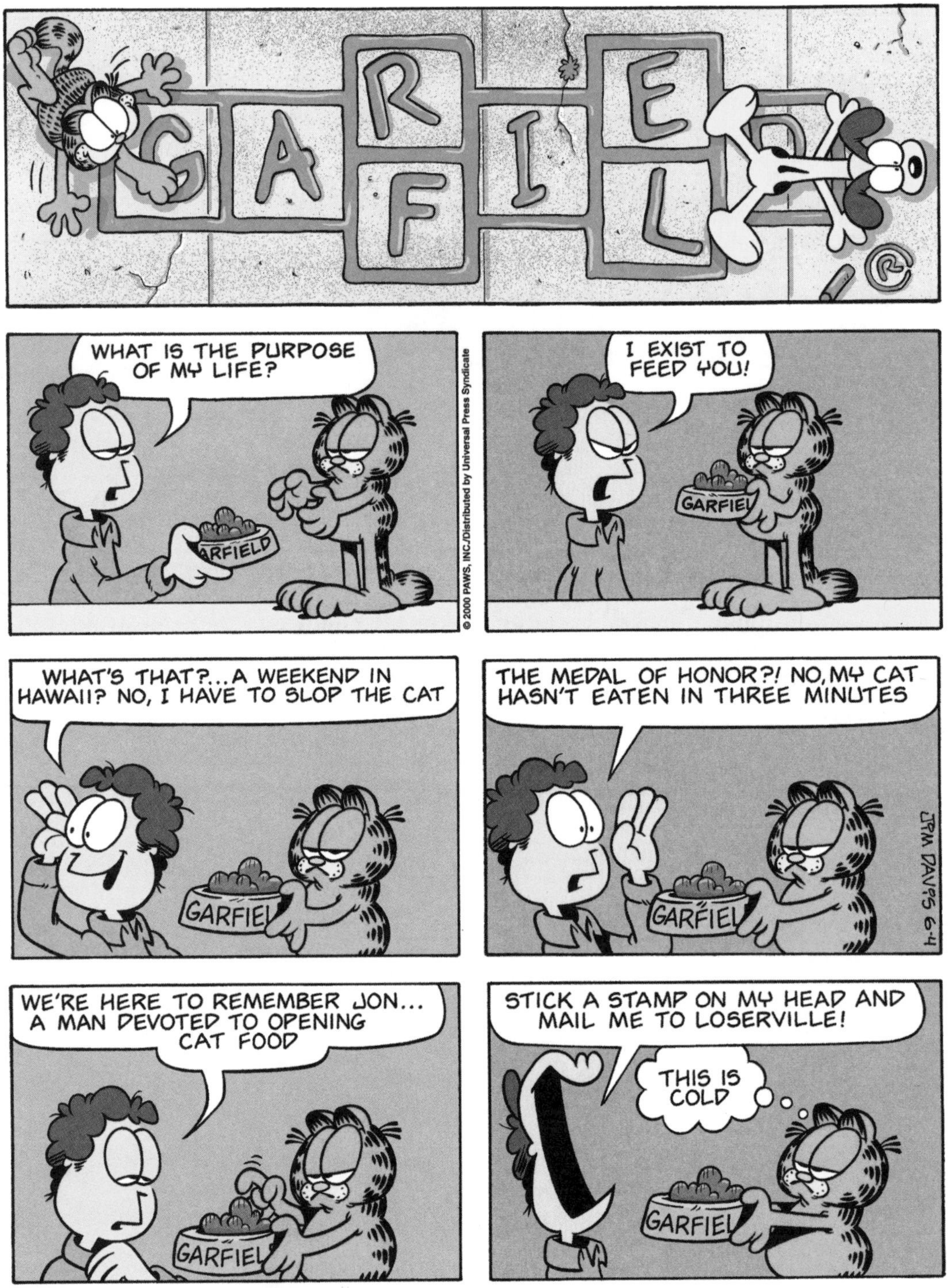
GARFIELD ®
WHAT IS THE PURPOSE OF MY LIFE?
© 2000 PAWS, INC./Distributed by Universal Press Syndicate
GARFIELD
I EXIST TO FEED YOU!
GARFIEL
WHAT'S THAT?...A WEEKEND IN HAWAII? NO, I HAVE TO SLOP THE CAT
GARFIEL
THE MEDAL OF HONOR?! NO, MY CAT HASN'T EATEN IN THREE MINUTES
GARFIEL
JIM DAVIS 6-4
WE'RE HERE TO REMEMBER JON... A MAN DEVOTED TO OPENING CAT FOOD
GARFIEL
STICK A STAMP ON MY HEAD AND MAIL ME TO LOSERVILLE!
THIS IS COLD
GARFIEL

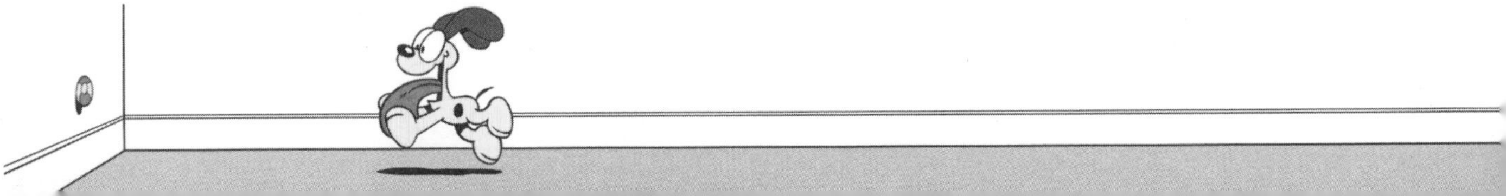

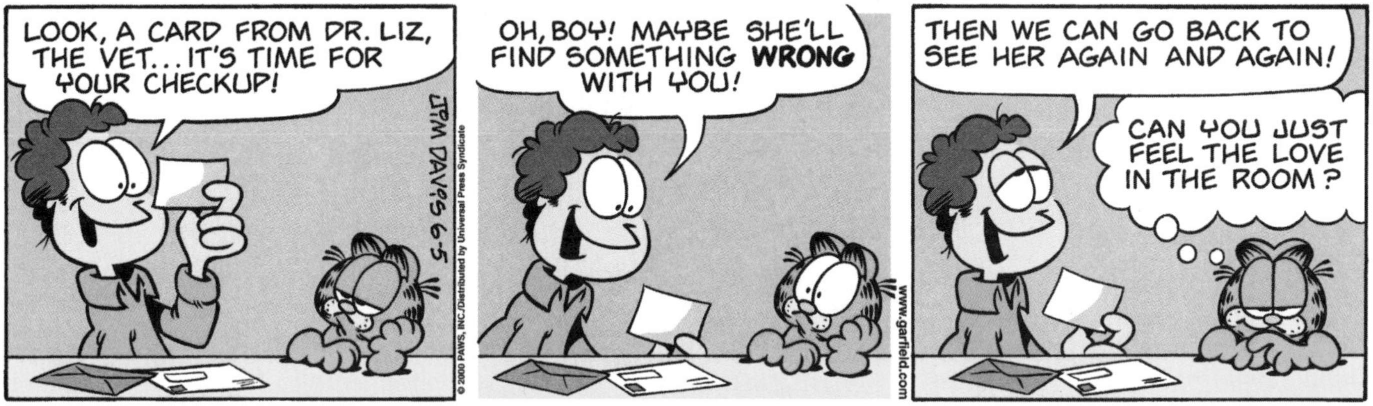
LOOK, A CARD FROM DR. LIZ, THE VET... IT'S TIME FOR YOUR CHECKUP!
JIM DAVIS 6-5
© 2000 PAWS, INC./Distributed by Universal Press Syndicate
OH, BOY! MAYBE SHE'LL FIND SOMETHING **WRONG** WITH YOU!
www.garfield.com
THEN WE CAN GO BACK TO SEE HER AGAIN AND AGAIN!
CAN YOU JUST FEEL THE LOVE IN THE ROOM?

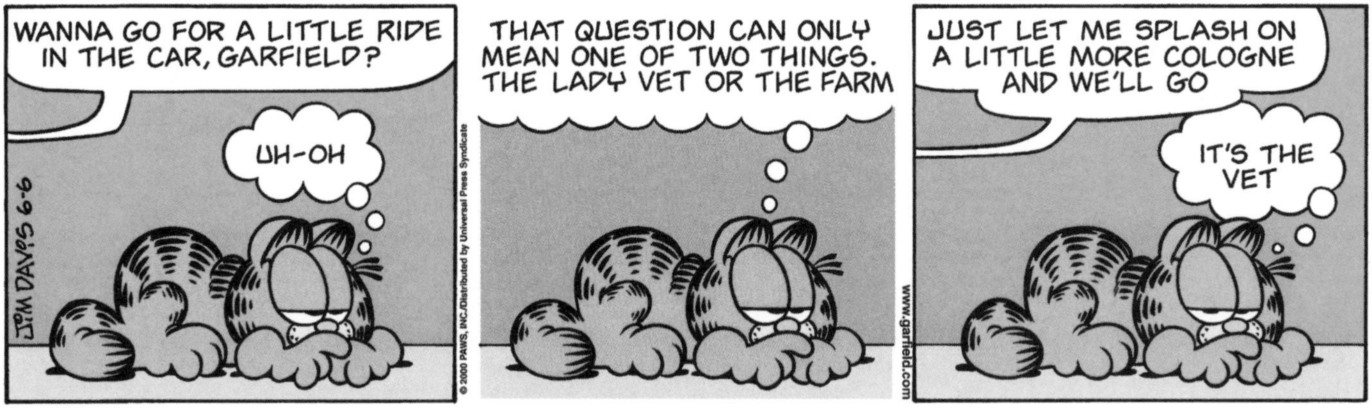
WANNA GO FOR A LITTLE RIDE IN THE CAR, GARFIELD?
UH-OH
JIM DAVIS 6-6
© 2000 PAWS, INC./Distributed by Universal Press Syndicate
THAT QUESTION CAN ONLY MEAN ONE OF TWO THINGS. THE LADY VET OR THE FARM
www.garfield.com
JUST LET ME SPLASH ON A LITTLE MORE COLOGNE AND WE'LL GO
IT'S THE VET

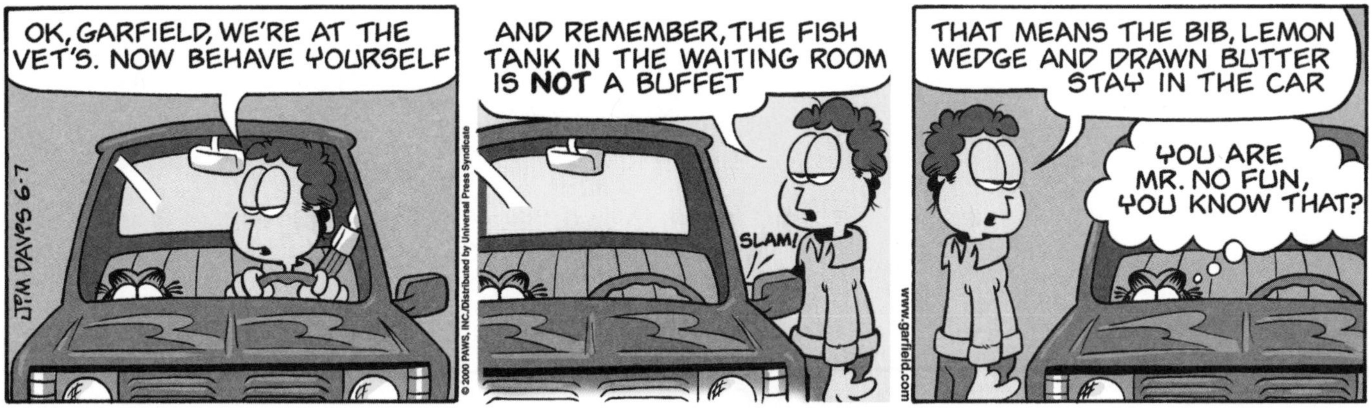
OK, GARFIELD, WE'RE AT THE VET'S. NOW BEHAVE YOURSELF
JIM DAVIS 6-7
© 2000 PAWS, INC./Distributed by Universal Press Syndicate
AND REMEMBER, THE FISH TANK IN THE WAITING ROOM IS **NOT** A BUFFET
SLAM!
www.garfield.com
THAT MEANS THE BIB, LEMON WEDGE AND DRAWN BUTTER STAY IN THE CAR
YOU ARE MR. NO FUN, YOU KNOW THAT?

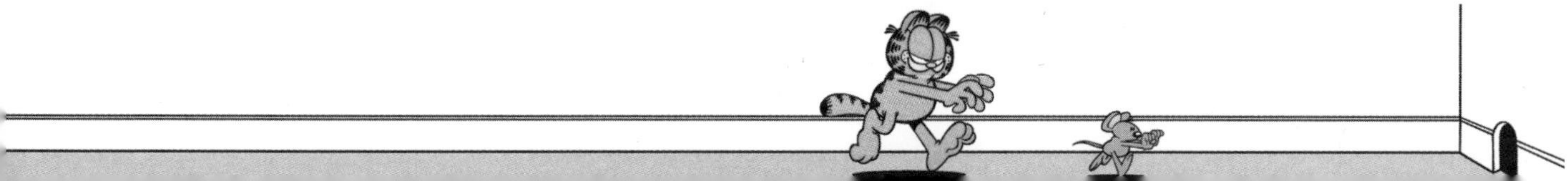

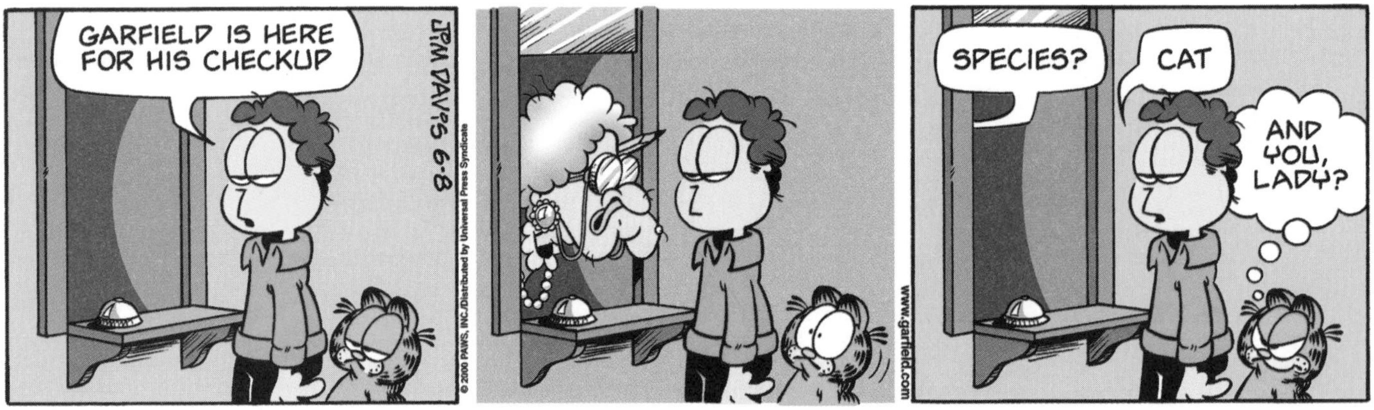
GARFIELD IS HERE FOR HIS CHECKUP
JIM DAVIS 6-8
© 2000 PAWS, INC./Distributed by Universal Press Syndicate
www.garfield.com
SPECIES?
CAT
AND YOU, LADY?

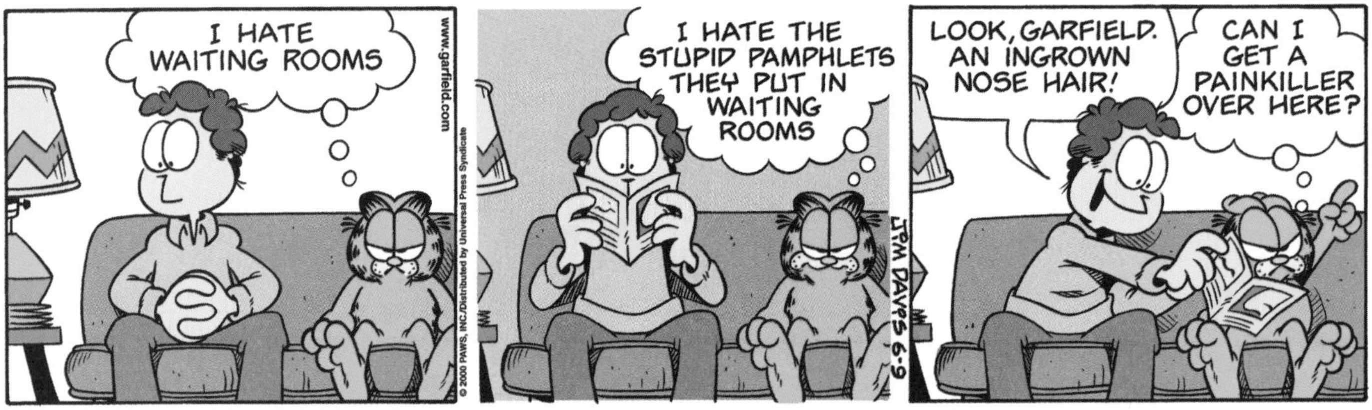
I HATE WAITING ROOMS
www.garfield.com
© 2000 PAWS, INC./Distributed by Universal Press Syndicate
I HATE THE STUPID PAMPHLETS THEY PUT IN WAITING ROOMS
JIM DAVIS 6-9
LOOK, GARFIELD. AN INGROWN NOSE HAIR!
CAN I GET A PAINKILLER OVER HERE?

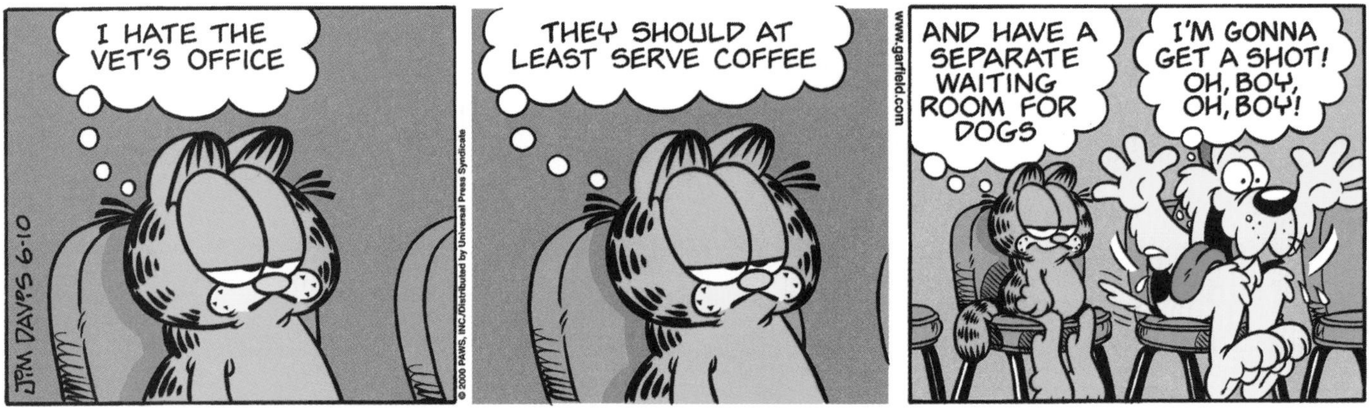
I HATE THE VET'S OFFICE
JIM DAVIS 6-10
© 2000 PAWS, INC./Distributed by Universal Press Syndicate
THEY SHOULD AT LEAST SERVE COFFEE
www.garfield.com
AND HAVE A SEPARATE WAITING ROOM FOR DOGS
I'M GONNA GET A SHOT! OH, BOY, OH, BOY!

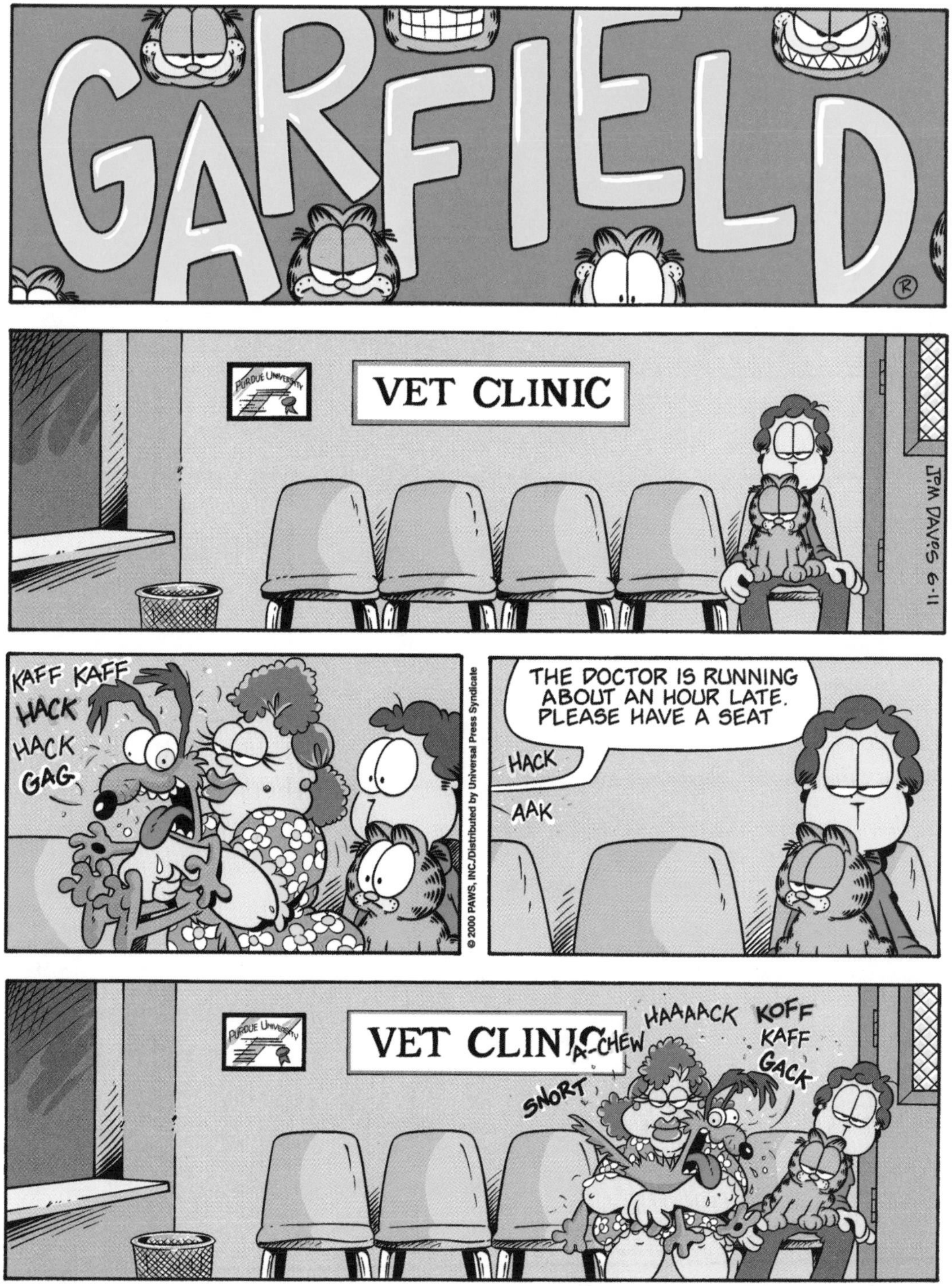
GARFIELD®
PURDUE UNIVERSITY
VET CLINIC
JIM DAVIS 6-11
KAFF KAFF
HACK
HACK
GAG
© 2000 PAWS, INC./Distributed by Universal Press Syndicate
THE DOCTOR IS RUNNING ABOUT AN HOUR LATE. PLEASE HAVE A SEAT
HACK
AAK
PURDUE UNIVERSITY
VET CLINIC
A-CHEW
HAAAACK
KOFF
KAFF
GACK
SNORT

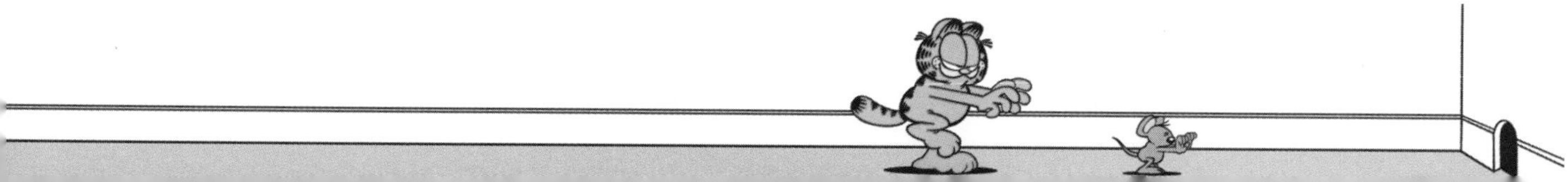

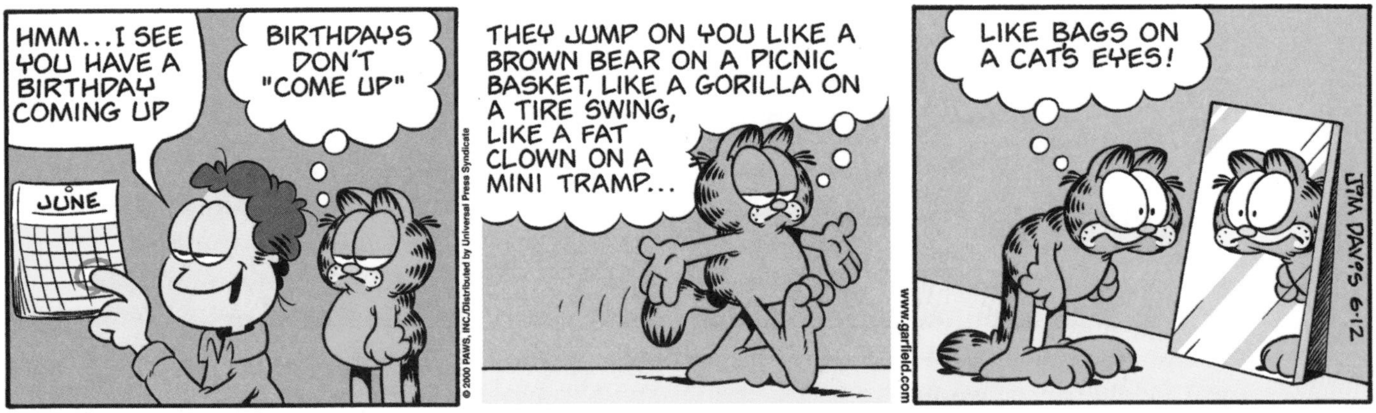
HMM...I SEE YOU HAVE A BIRTHDAY COMING UP
JUNE
BIRTHDAYS DON'T "COME UP"
© 2000 PAWS, INC./Distributed by Universal Press Syndicate
THEY JUMP ON YOU LIKE A BROWN BEAR ON A PICNIC BASKET, LIKE A GORILLA ON A TIRE SWING, LIKE A FAT CLOWN ON A MINI TRAMP...
www.garfield.com
LIKE BAGS ON A CAT'S EYES!
JIM DAVIS 6·12

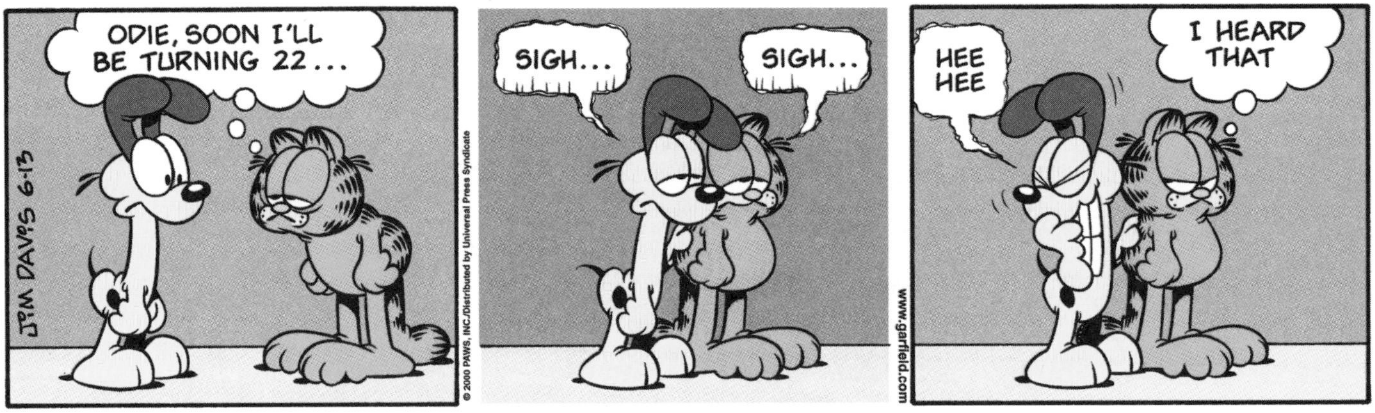
ODIE, SOON I'LL BE TURNING 22...
JIM DAVIS 6·13
© 2000 PAWS, INC./Distributed by Universal Press Syndicate
SIGH...
SIGH...
www.garfield.com
HEE HEE
I HEARD THAT

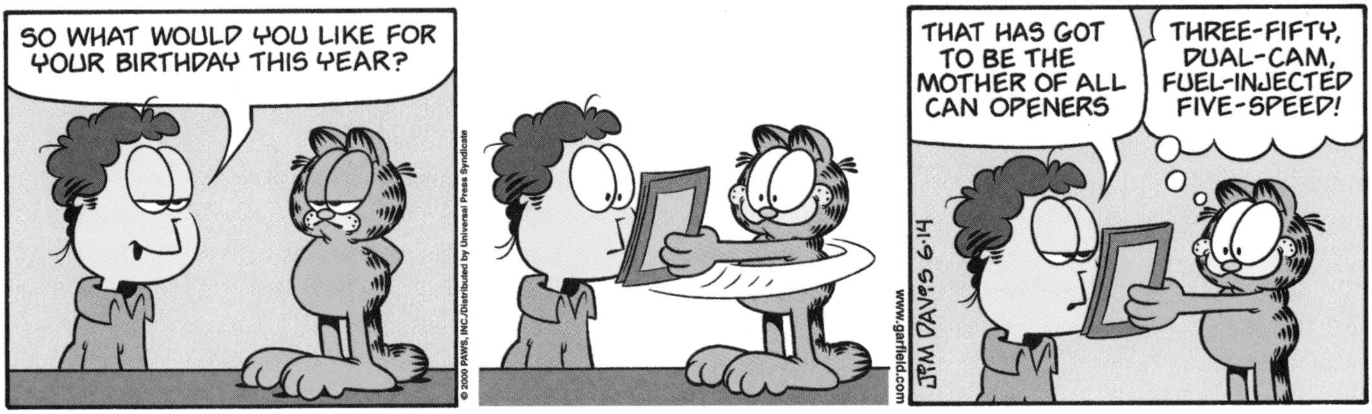
SO WHAT WOULD YOU LIKE FOR YOUR BIRTHDAY THIS YEAR?
© 2000 PAWS, INC./Distributed by Universal Press Syndicate
www.garfield.com
JIM DAVIS 6·14
THAT HAS GOT TO BE THE MOTHER OF ALL CAN OPENERS
THREE-FIFTY, DUAL-CAM, FUEL-INJECTED FIVE-SPEED!

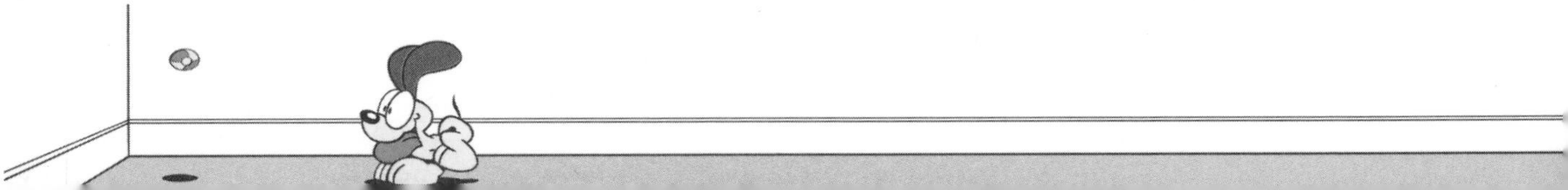

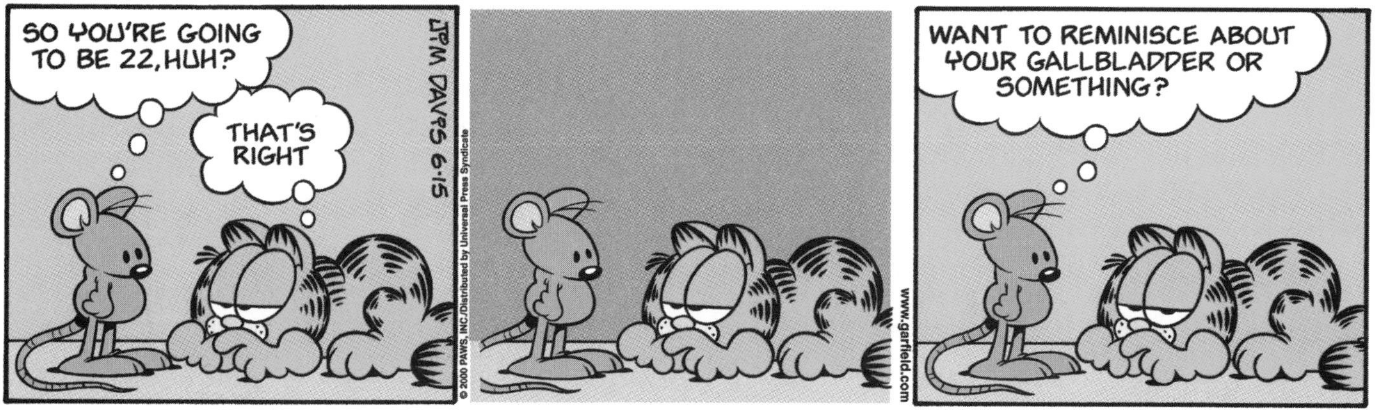
SO YOU'RE GOING TO BE 22, HUH?
THAT'S RIGHT
JIM DAVIS 6-15
© 2000 PAWS, INC./Distributed by Universal Press Syndicate
WANT TO REMINISCE ABOUT YOUR GALLBLADDER OR SOMETHING?
www.garfield.com

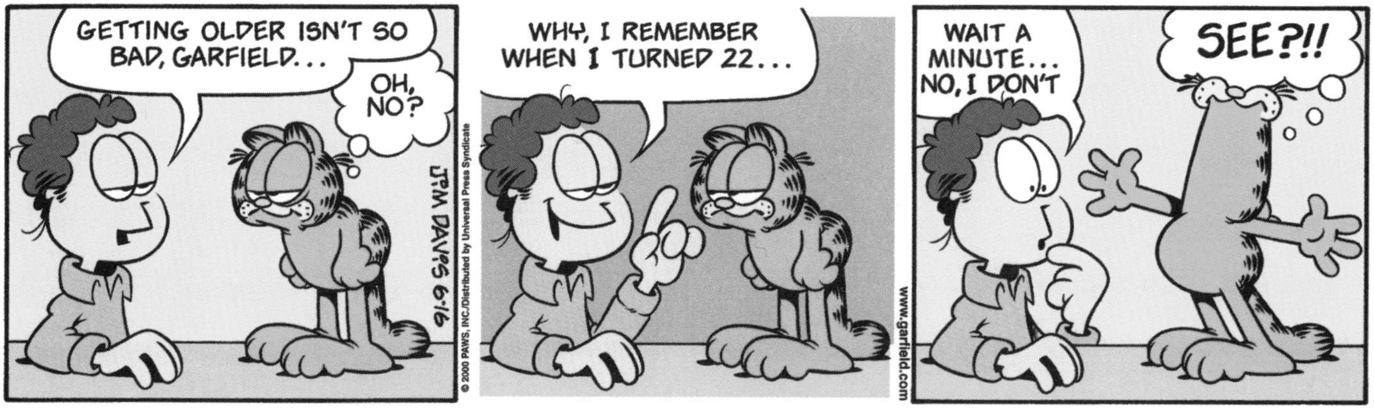
GETTING OLDER ISN'T SO BAD, GARFIELD...
OH, NO?
JIM DAVIS 6-16
© 2000 PAWS, INC./Distributed by Universal Press Syndicate
WHY, I REMEMBER WHEN I TURNED 22...
WAIT A MINUTE... NO, I DON'T
SEE?!!
www.garfield.com

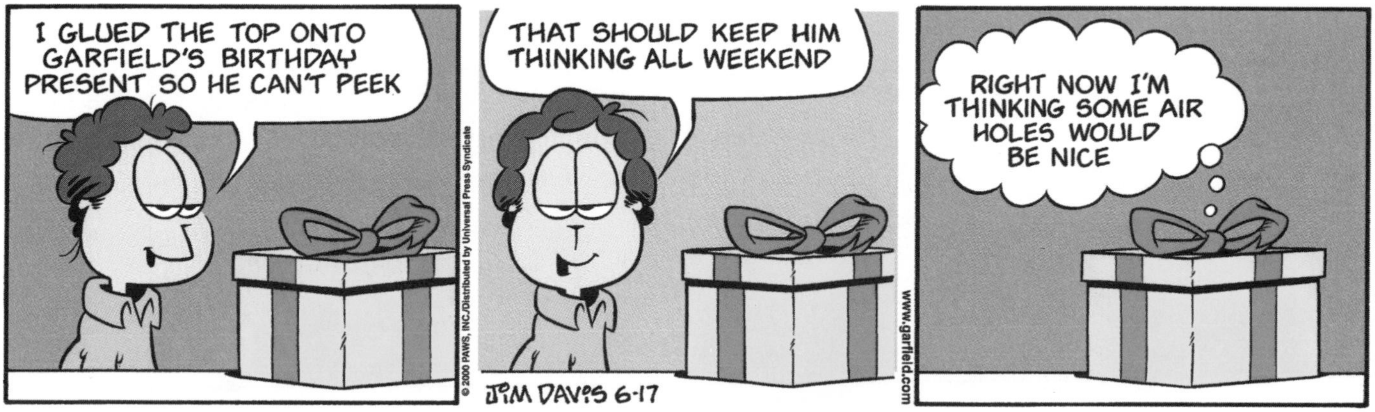
I GLUED THE TOP ONTO GARFIELD'S BIRTHDAY PRESENT SO HE CAN'T PEEK
© 2000 PAWS, INC./Distributed by Universal Press Syndicate
THAT SHOULD KEEP HIM THINKING ALL WEEKEND
JIM DAVIS 6-17
RIGHT NOW I'M THINKING SOME AIR HOLES WOULD BE NICE
www.garfield.com

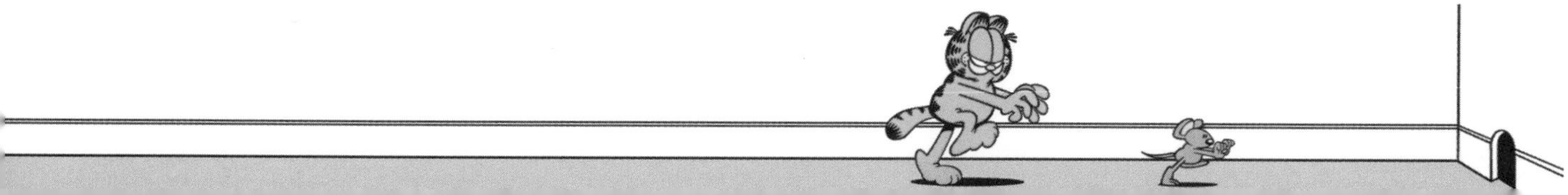

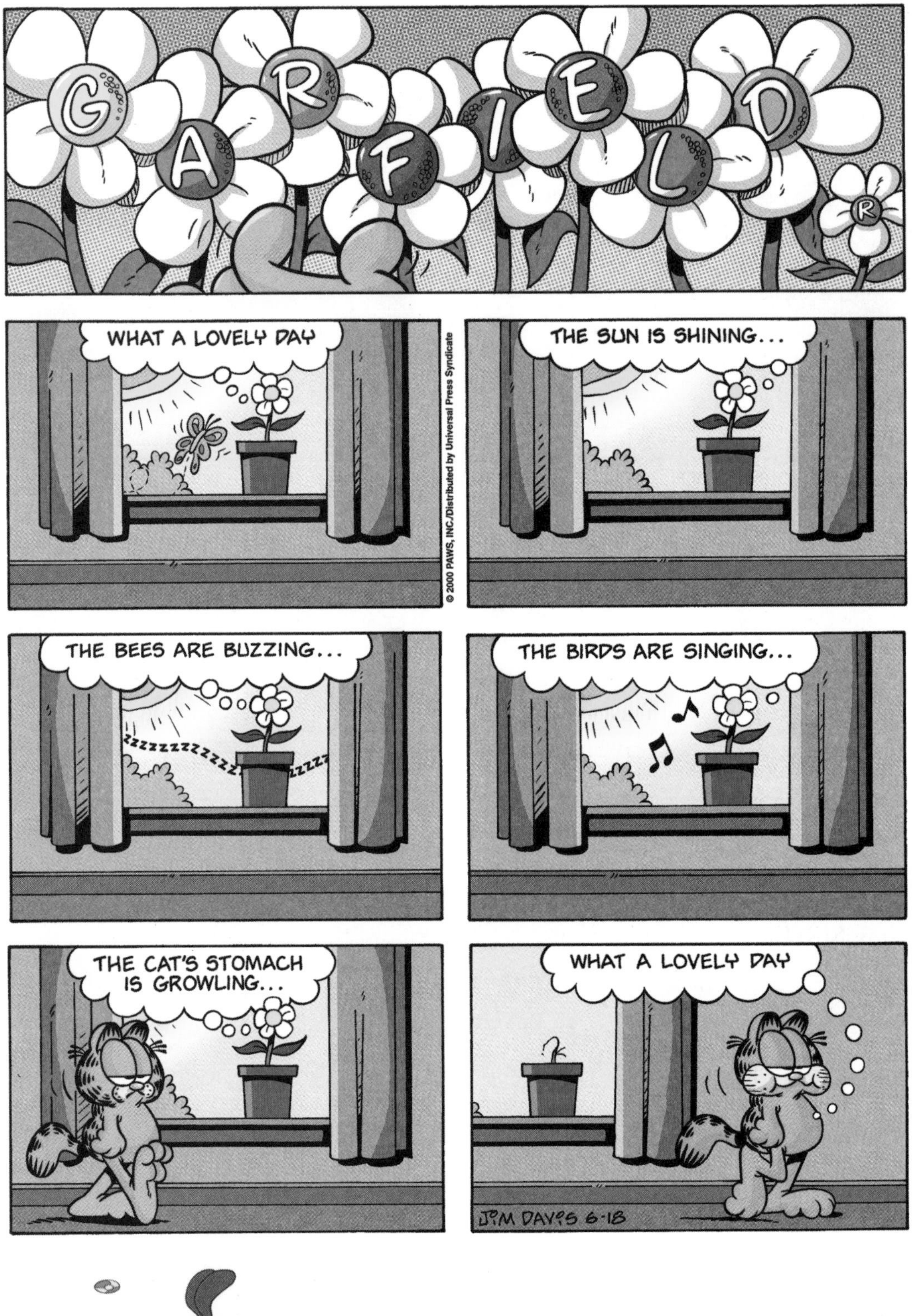
GARFIELD
WHAT A LOVELY DAY
THE SUN IS SHINING...
THE BEES ARE BUZZING...
ZZZZZZZZZZZZZZ
THE BIRDS ARE SINGING...
THE CAT'S STOMACH IS GROWLING...
WHAT A LOVELY DAY
JIM DAVIS 6-18
© 2000 PAWS, INC./Distributed by Universal Press Syndicate

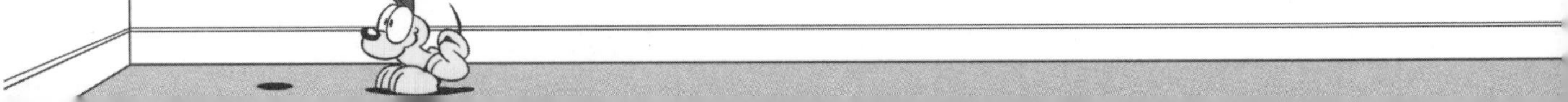

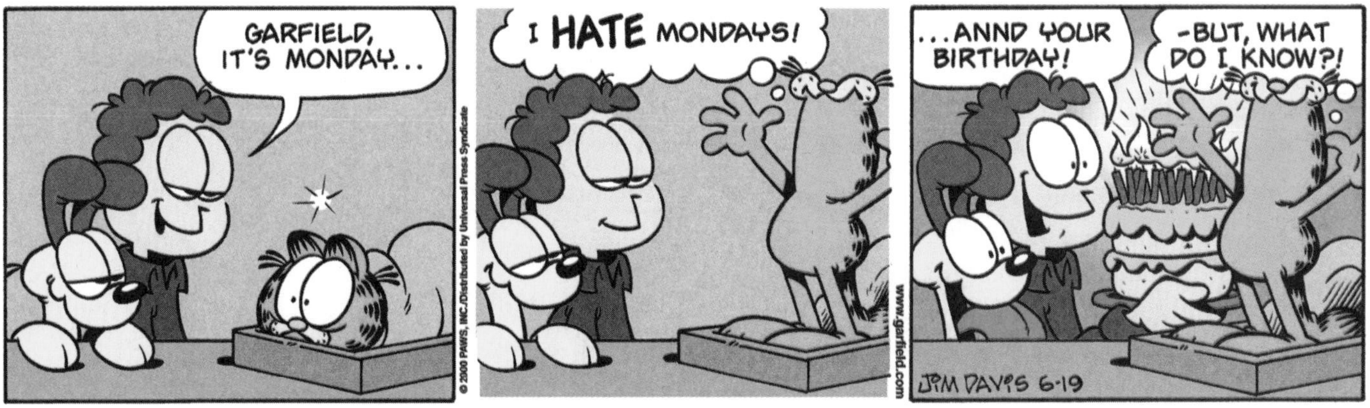
GARFIELD, IT'S MONDAY...
I HATE MONDAYS!
...ANND YOUR BIRTHDAY!
-BUT, WHAT DO I KNOW?!
JIM DAVIS 6-19

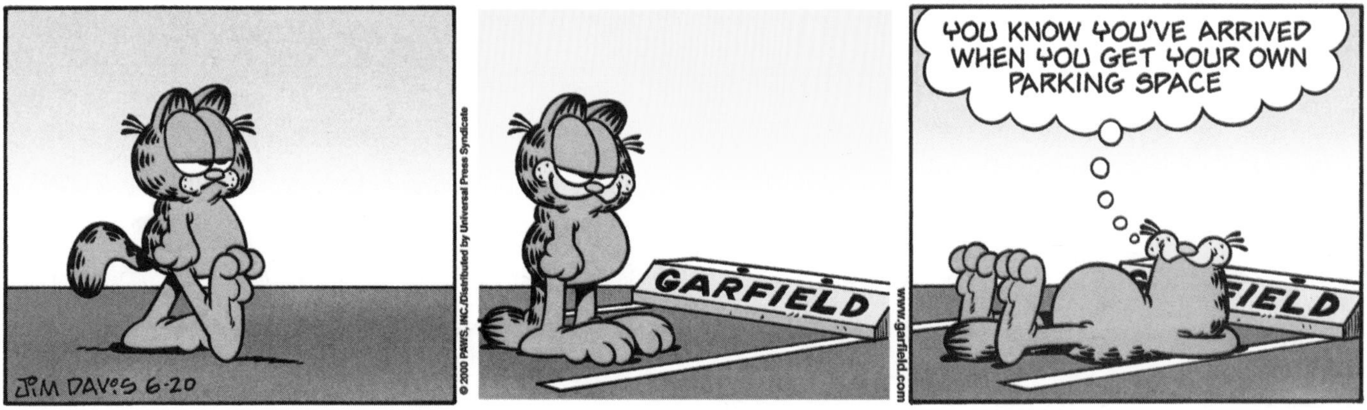
JIM DAVIS 6-20
GARFIELD
YOU KNOW YOU'VE ARRIVED WHEN YOU GET YOUR OWN PARKING SPACE

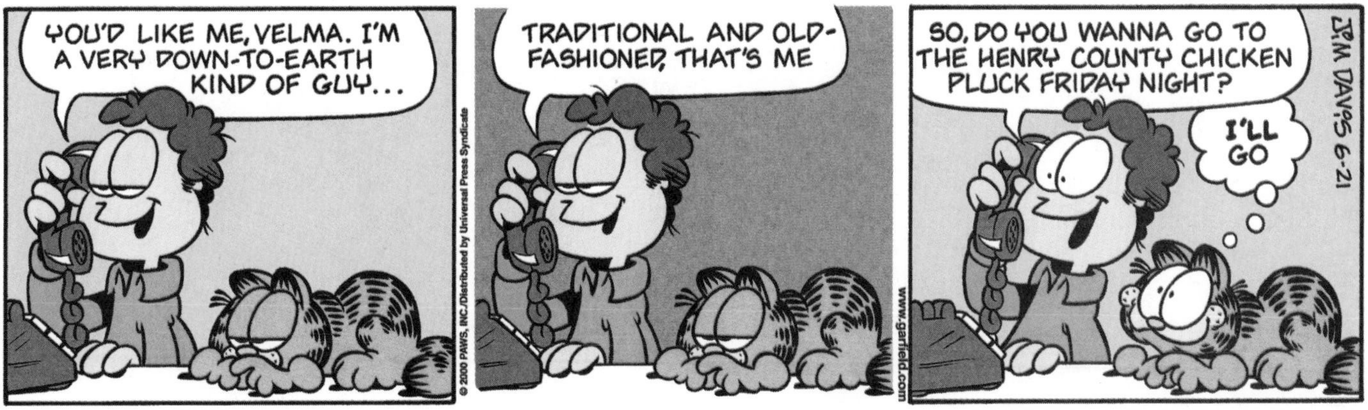
YOU'D LIKE ME, VELMA. I'M A VERY DOWN-TO-EARTH KIND OF GUY...
TRADITIONAL AND OLD-FASHIONED, THAT'S ME
SO, DO YOU WANNA GO TO THE HENRY COUNTY CHICKEN PLUCK FRIDAY NIGHT?
I'LL GO
JIM DAVIS 6-21

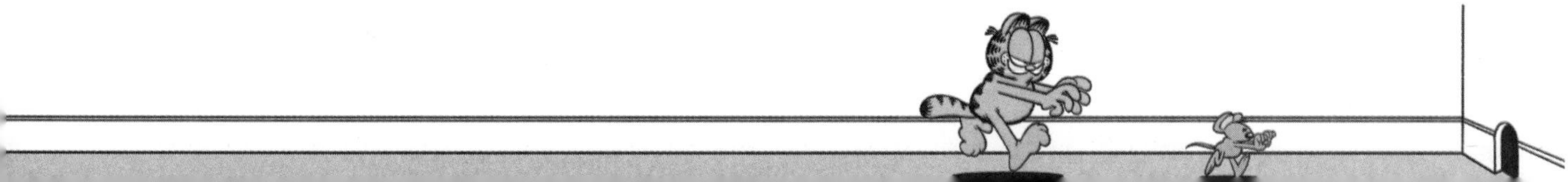

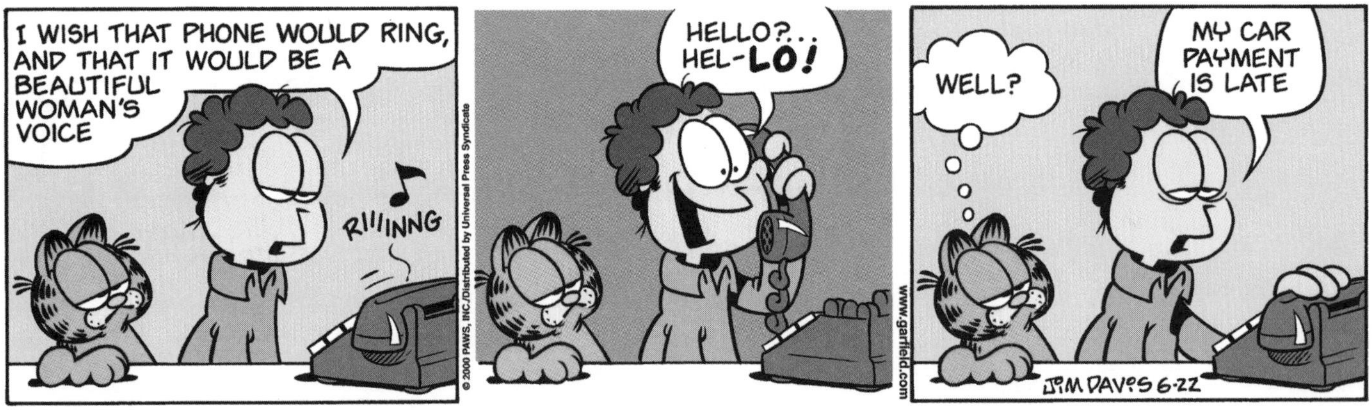
I WISH THAT PHONE WOULD RING, AND THAT IT WOULD BE A BEAUTIFUL WOMAN'S VOICE
RIIIINNG
HELLO?... HEL-LO!
WELL?
MY CAR PAYMENT IS LATE
JIM DAVIS 6-22
© 2000 PAWS, INC./Distributed by Universal Press Syndicate
www.garfield.com

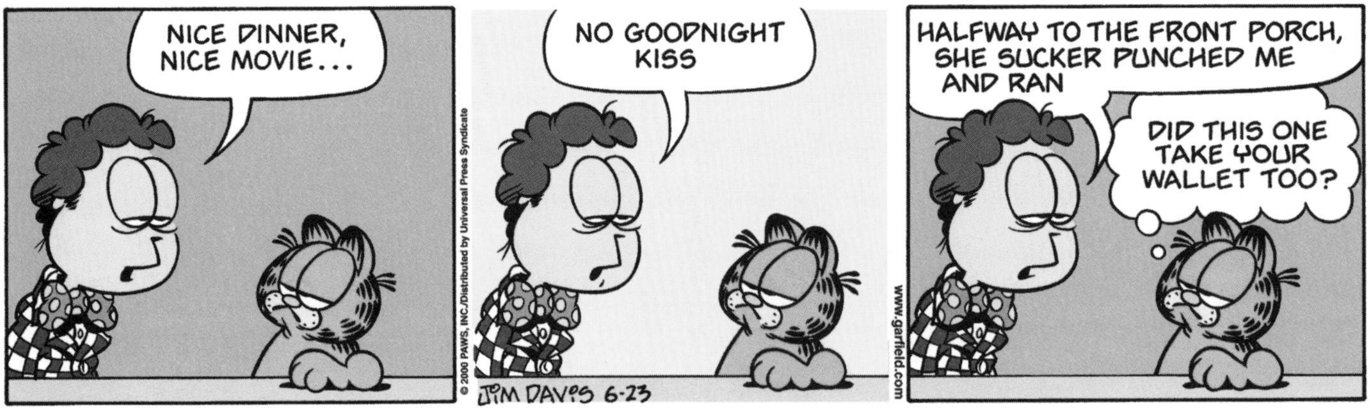
NICE DINNER, NICE MOVIE...
NO GOODNIGHT KISS
HALFWAY TO THE FRONT PORCH, SHE SUCKER PUNCHED ME AND RAN
DID THIS ONE TAKE YOUR WALLET TOO?
JIM DAVIS 6-23
© 2000 PAWS, INC./Distributed by Universal Press Syndicate
www.garfield.com

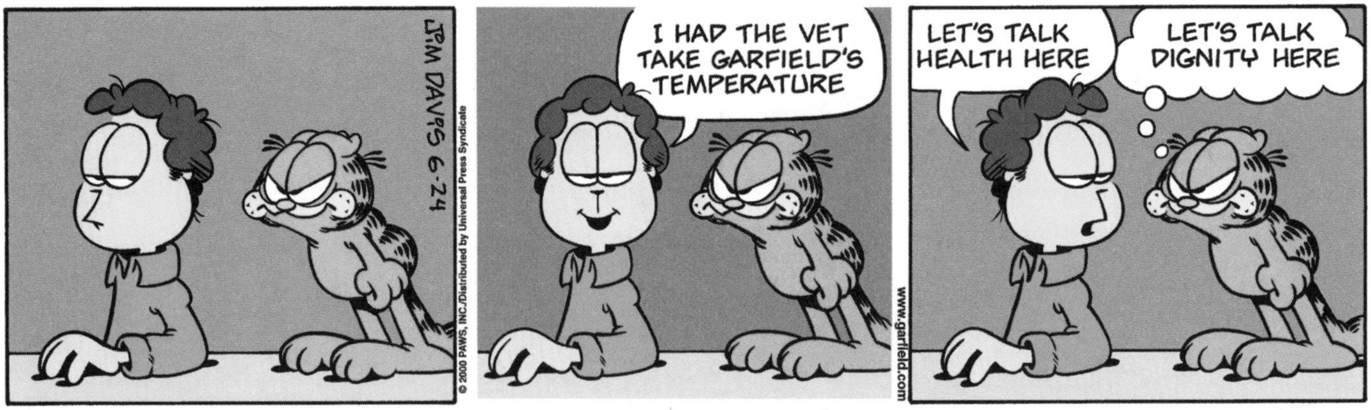
JIM DAVIS 6-24
I HAD THE VET TAKE GARFIELD'S TEMPERATURE
LET'S TALK HEALTH HERE
LET'S TALK DIGNITY HERE
© 2000 PAWS, INC./Distributed by Universal Press Syndicate
www.garfield.com

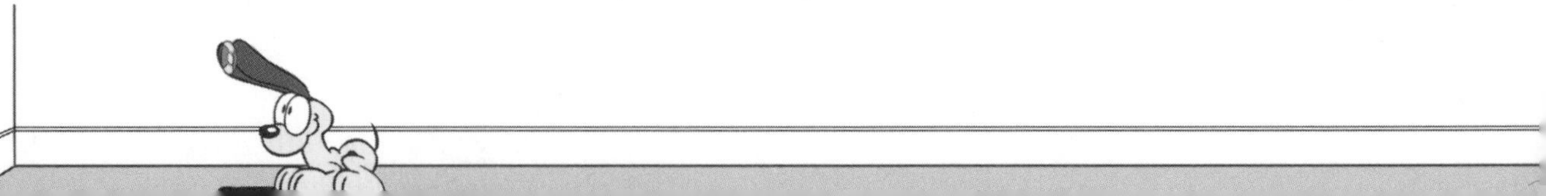

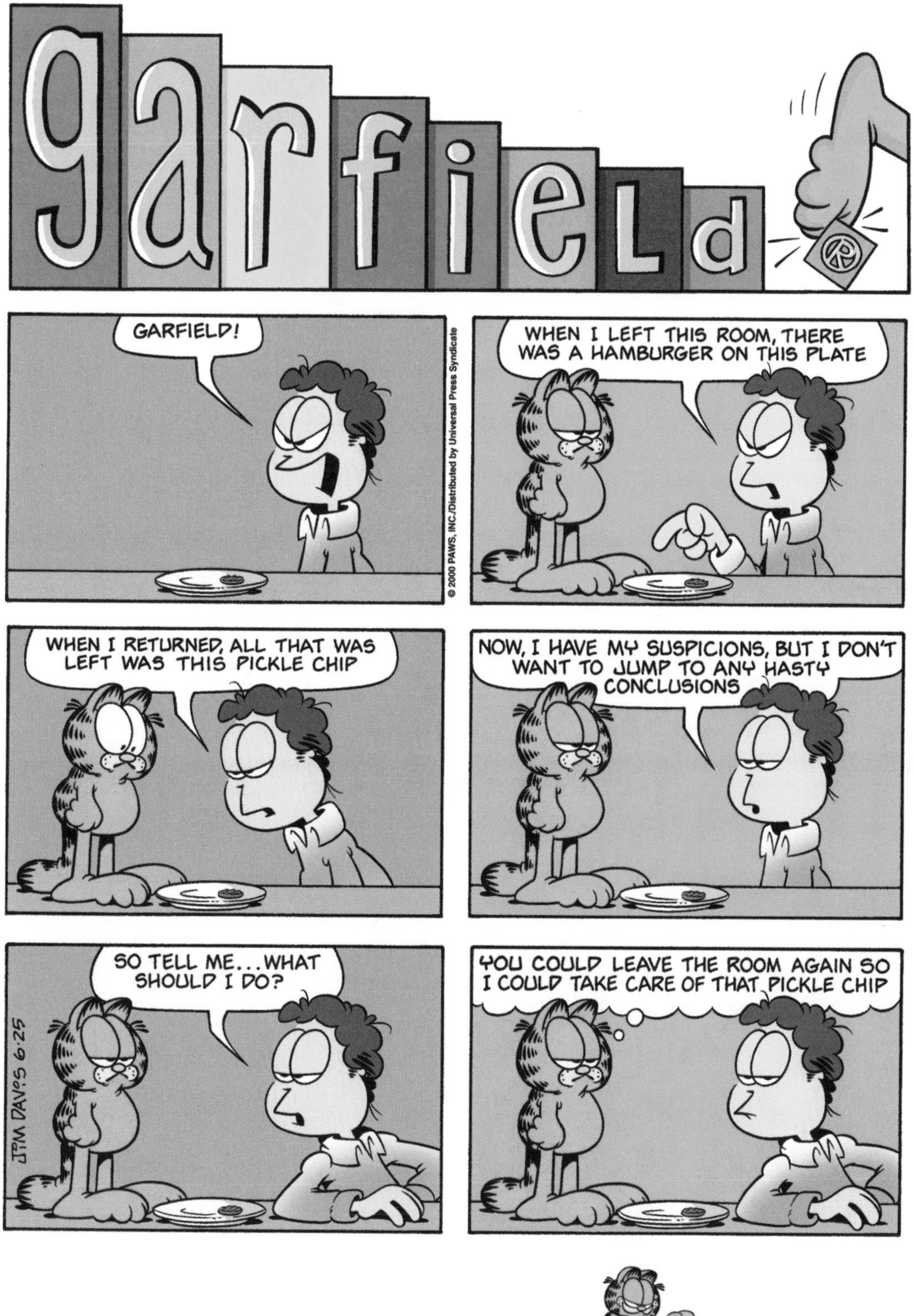
garfield
GARFIELD!
© 2000 PAWS, INC./Distributed by Universal Press Syndicate
WHEN I LEFT THIS ROOM, THERE WAS A HAMBURGER ON THIS PLATE
WHEN I RETURNED, ALL THAT WAS LEFT WAS THIS PICKLE CHIP
NOW, I HAVE MY SUSPICIONS, BUT I DON'T WANT TO JUMP TO ANY HASTY CONCLUSIONS
SO TELL ME...WHAT SHOULD I DO?
JIM DAVIS 6·25
YOU COULD LEAVE THE ROOM AGAIN SO I COULD TAKE CARE OF THAT PICKLE CHIP

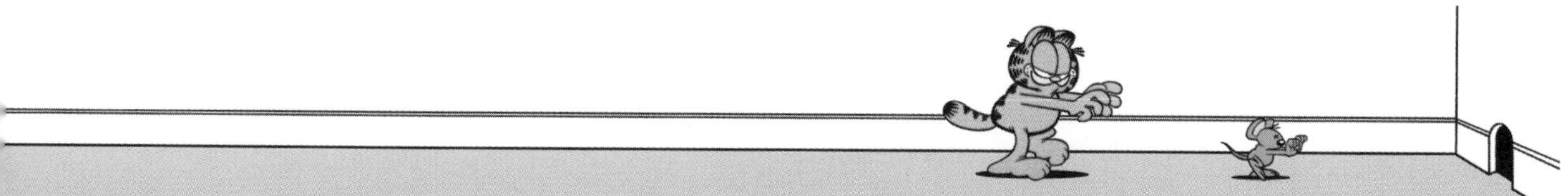

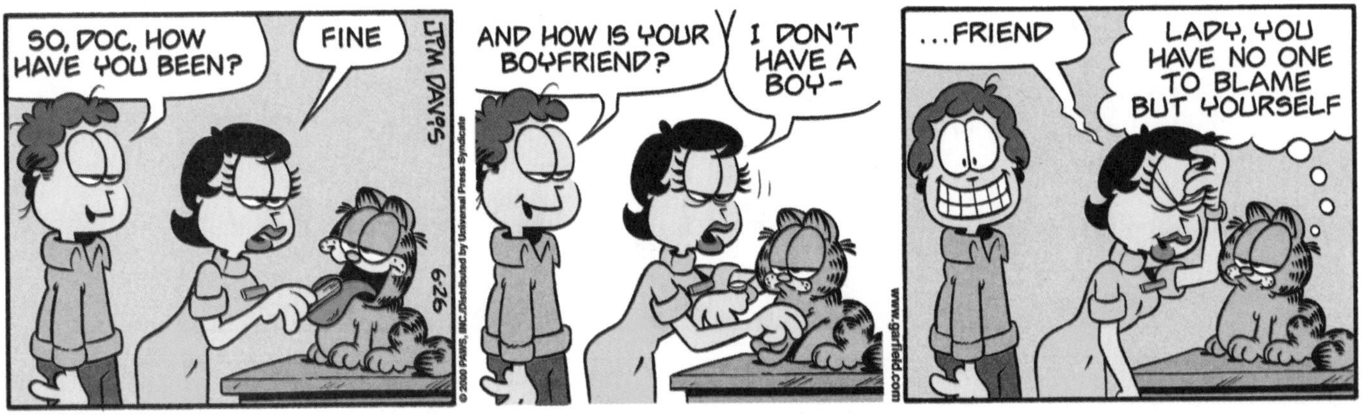
SO, DOC, HOW HAVE YOU BEEN?
FINE
AND HOW IS YOUR BOYFRIEND?
I DON'T HAVE A BOY-
...FRIEND
LADY, YOU HAVE NO ONE TO BLAME BUT YOURSELF

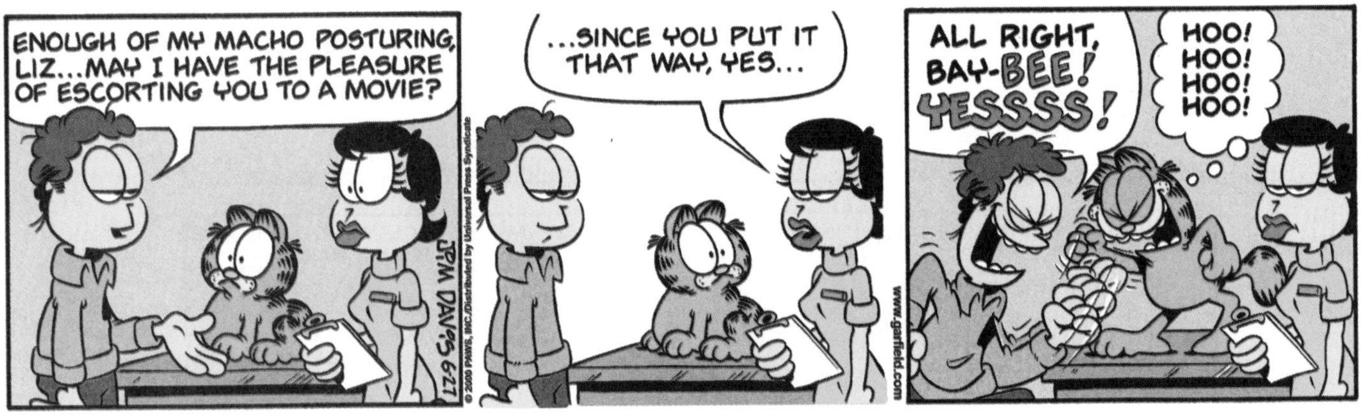
ENOUGH OF MY MACHO POSTURING, LIZ...MAY I HAVE THE PLEASURE OF ESCORTING YOU TO A MOVIE?
...SINCE YOU PUT IT THAT WAY, YES...
ALL RIGHT, BAY-BEE! YESSSS!
HOO! HOO! HOO! HOO!

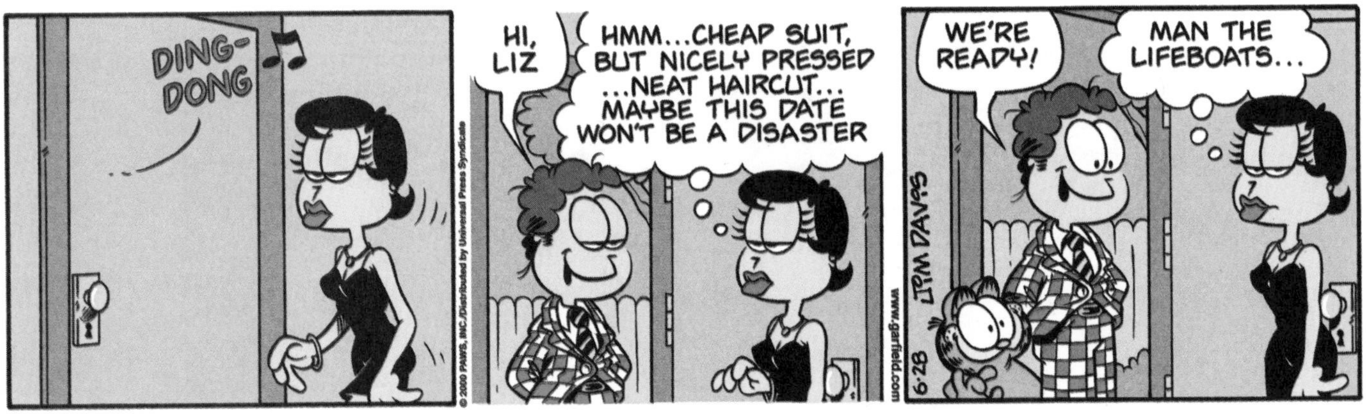
DING-DONG
HI, LIZ
HMM...CHEAP SUIT, BUT NICELY PRESSED ...NEAT HAIRCUT... MAYBE THIS DATE WON'T BE A DISASTER
WE'RE READY!
MAN THE LIFEBOATS...

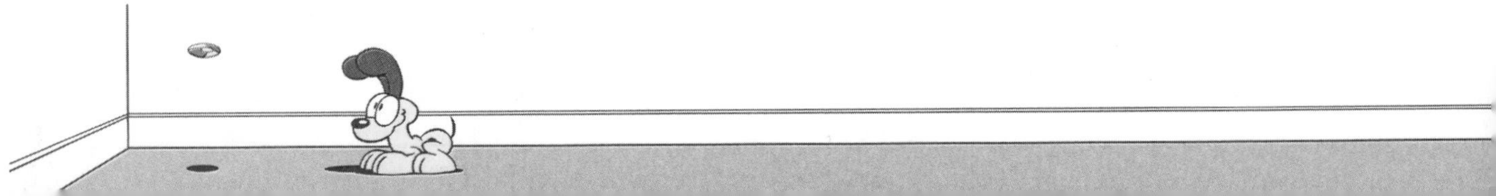

DO YOU LIKE THE CORSAGE, LIZ?

6-29

JIM DAVIS

IT'S BEAUTIFUL, JON, BUT...

HOW AM I SUPPOSED TO SEE THE MOVIE?

I COULD NIBBLE SOME EYE HOLES FOR YOU

www.garfield.com

ARE YOU SURE YOU'RE GOING TO GET AWAY WITH THIS, JON?

OH, YEAH...WE GO TO THE MOVIES HERE ALL THE TIME

6-30 JIM DAVIS

TWO, PLEASE

HEY, MORTY! THE FREAK WITH THE TAIL IS BACK!

www.garfield.com

SO, JON, WHAT MOVIE ARE WE SEEING?

7-1 JIM DAVIS

"SLUDGE MONSTER VII: THE OOZING"

WOULD YOU LIKE A BUCKET OF POPCORN?

NO, JUST THE BUCKET, PLEASE

www.garfield.com

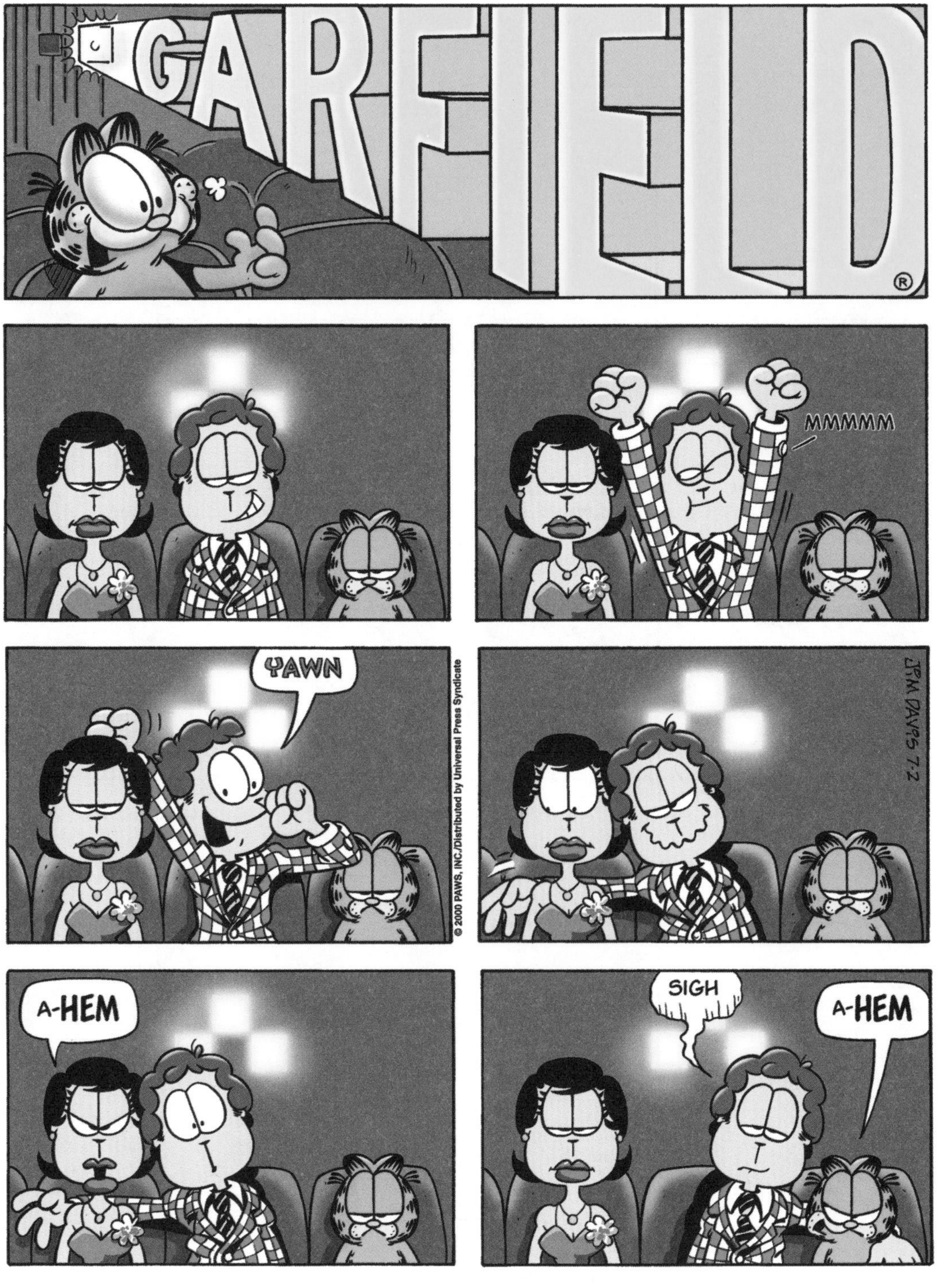
GARFIELD
MMMMM
YAWN
© 2000 PAWS, INC./Distributed by Universal Press Syndicate
JPM DAVIS 7-2
A-HEM
SIGH
A-HEM

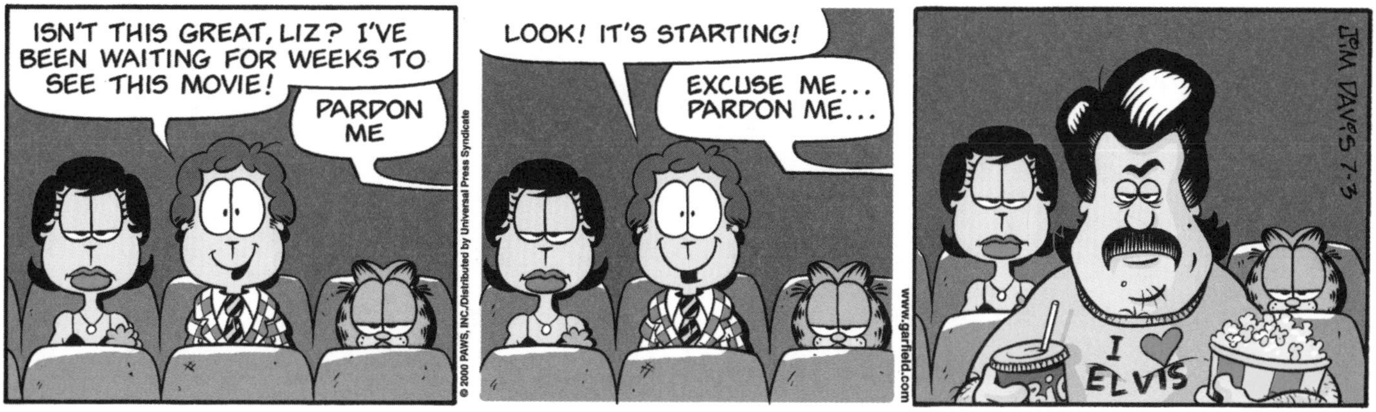
ISN'T THIS GREAT, LIZ? I'VE BEEN WAITING FOR WEEKS TO SEE THIS MOVIE!
PARDON ME
© 2000 PAWS, INC./Distributed by Universal Press Syndicate
LOOK! IT'S STARTING!
EXCUSE ME... PARDON ME...
www.garfield.com
JPM DAVIS 7-3
I ♥ ELVIS

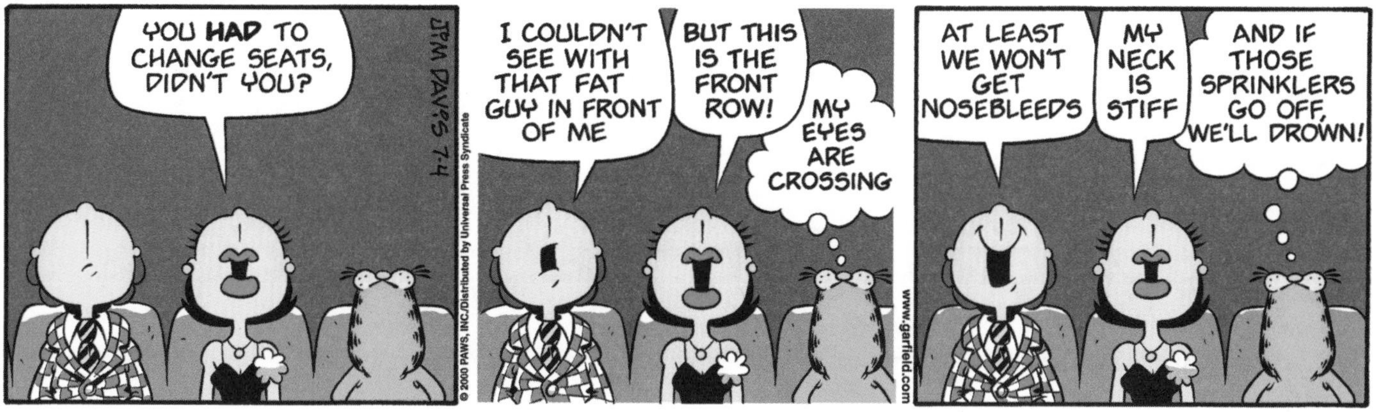
YOU **HAD** TO CHANGE SEATS, DIDN'T YOU?
JPM DAVIS 7-4
© 2000 PAWS, INC./Distributed by Universal Press Syndicate
I COULDN'T SEE WITH THAT FAT GUY IN FRONT OF ME
BUT THIS IS THE FRONT ROW!
MY EYES ARE CROSSING
www.garfield.com
AT LEAST WE WON'T GET NOSEBLEEDS
MY NECK IS STIFF
AND IF THOSE SPRINKLERS GO OFF, WE'LL DROWN!

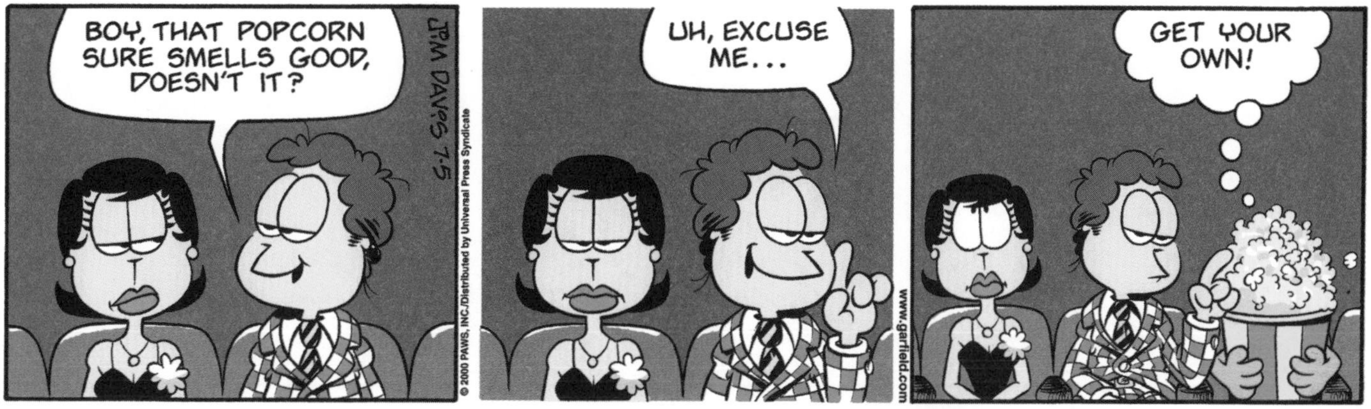
BOY, THAT POPCORN SURE SMELLS GOOD, DOESN'T IT?
JPM DAVIS 7-5
© 2000 PAWS, INC./Distributed by Universal Press Syndicate
UH, EXCUSE ME...
www.garfield.com
GET YOUR OWN!

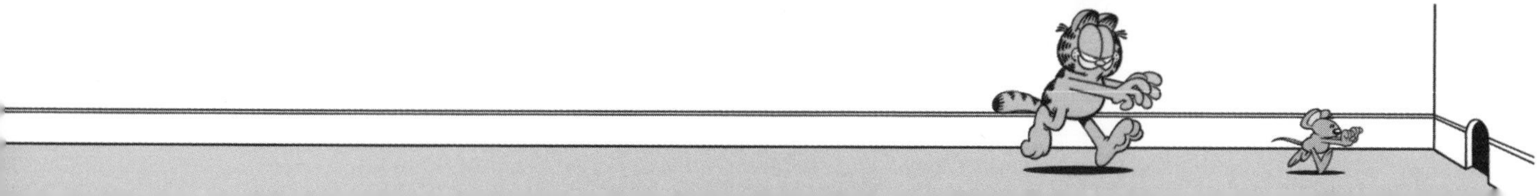

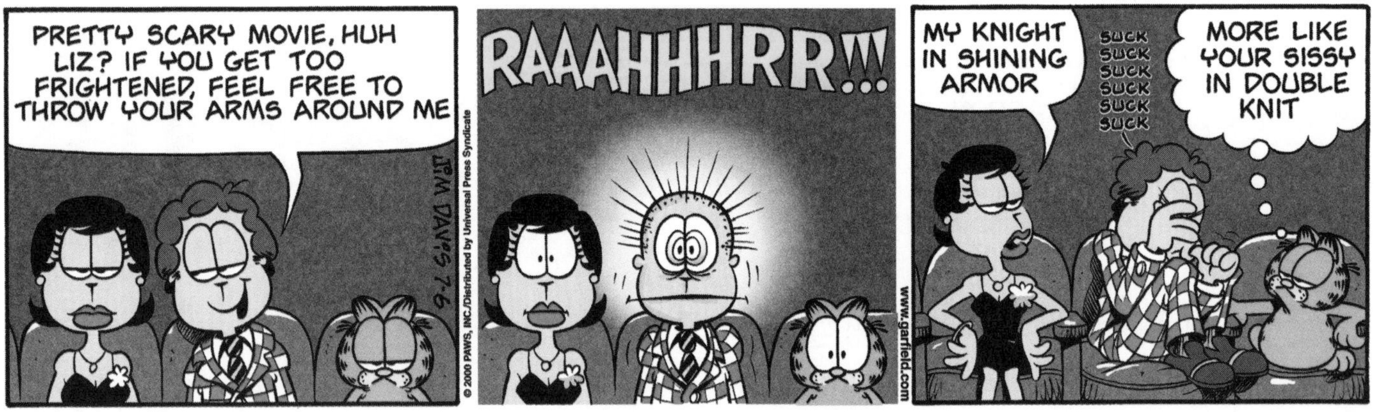
PRETTY SCARY MOVIE, HUH LIZ? IF YOU GET TOO FRIGHTENED, FEEL FREE TO THROW YOUR ARMS AROUND ME
JIM DAVIS 7-6
© 2000 PAWS, INC./Distributed by Universal Press Syndicate
RAAAHHHRR!!!
www.garfield.com
MY KNIGHT IN SHINING ARMOR
SUCK SUCK SUCK SUCK SUCK SUCK
MORE LIKE YOUR SISSY IN DOUBLE KNIT

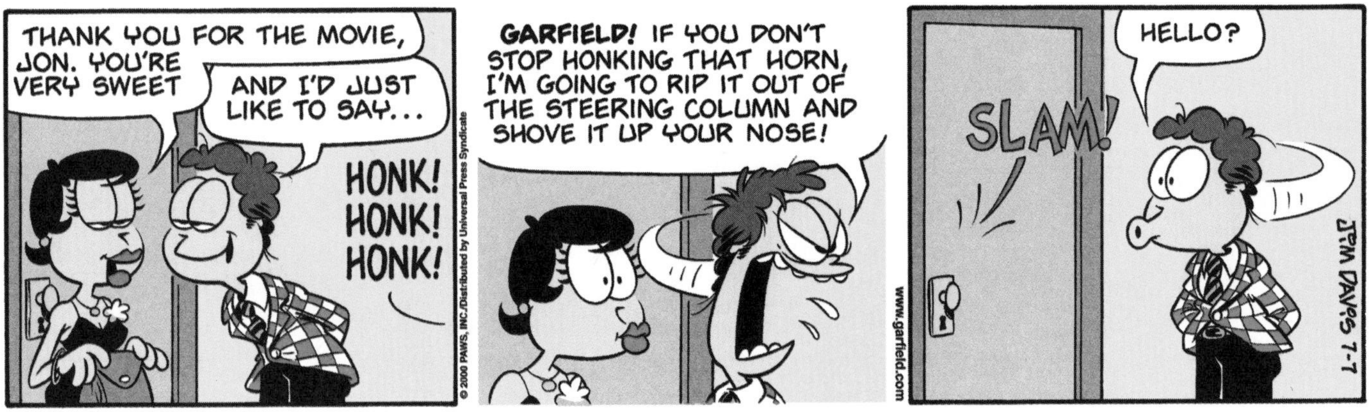
THANK YOU FOR THE MOVIE, JON. YOU'RE VERY SWEET
AND I'D JUST LIKE TO SAY...
HONK! HONK! HONK!
© 2000 PAWS, INC./Distributed by Universal Press Syndicate
GARFIELD! IF YOU DON'T STOP HONKING THAT HORN, I'M GOING TO RIP IT OUT OF THE STEERING COLUMN AND SHOVE IT UP YOUR NOSE!
www.garfield.com
SLAM!
HELLO?
JIM DAVIS 7-7

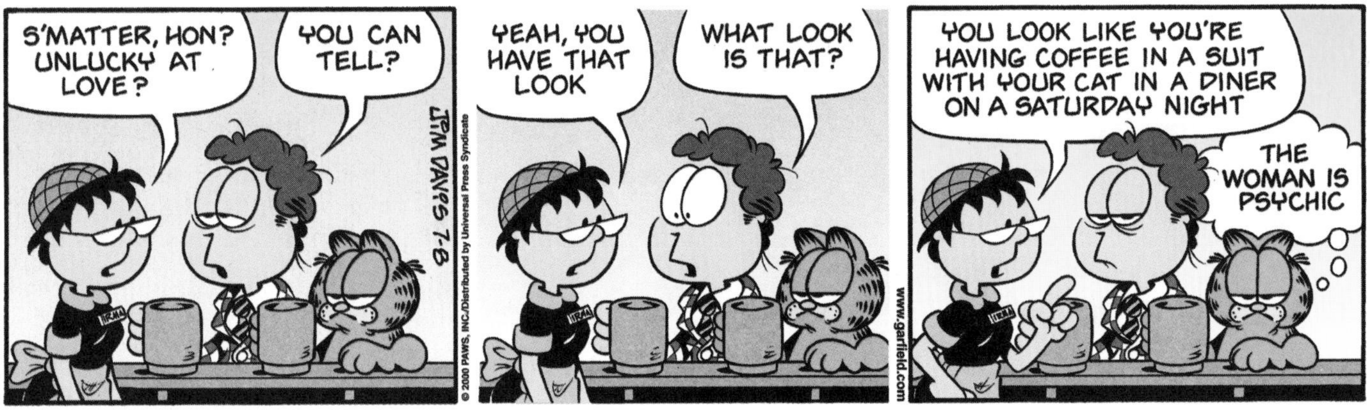
S'MATTER, HON? UNLUCKY AT LOVE?
YOU CAN TELL?
JIM DAVIS 7-8
© 2000 PAWS, INC./Distributed by Universal Press Syndicate
YEAH, YOU HAVE THAT LOOK
WHAT LOOK IS THAT?
www.garfield.com
YOU LOOK LIKE YOU'RE HAVING COFFEE IN A SUIT WITH YOUR CAT IN A DINER ON A SATURDAY NIGHT
THE WOMAN IS PSYCHIC

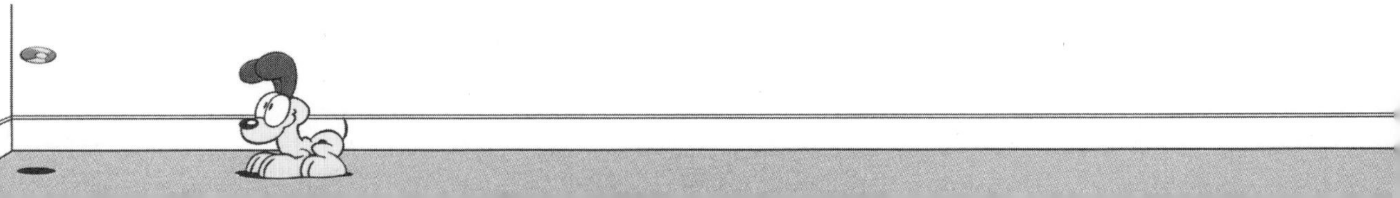

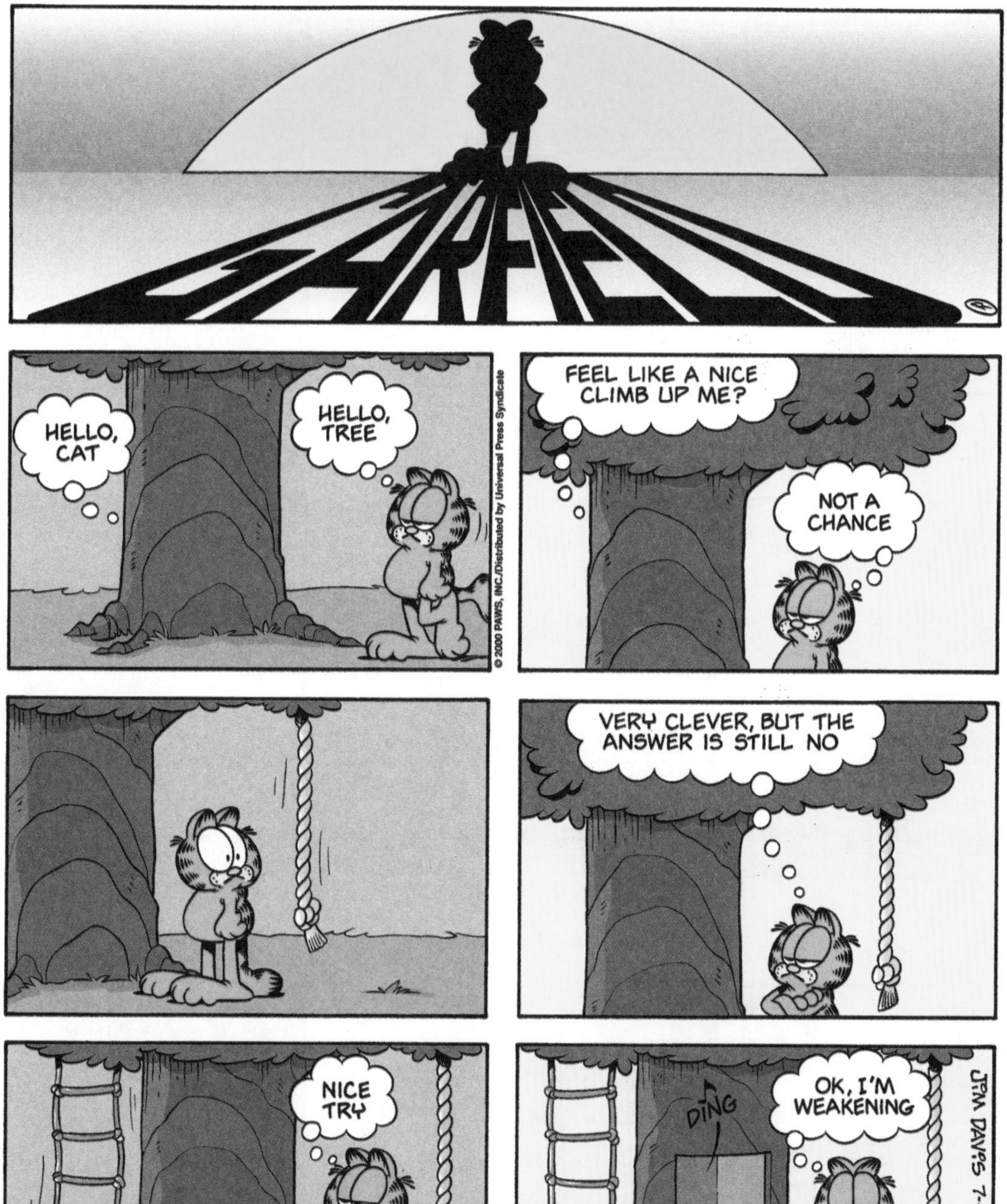
GARFIELD
HELLO, CAT
HELLO, TREE
© 2000 PAWS, INC./Distributed by Universal Press Syndicate
FEEL LIKE A NICE CLIMB UP ME?
NOT A CHANCE
VERY CLEVER, BUT THE ANSWER IS STILL NO
NICE TRY
DING
OK, I'M WEAKENING
JIM DAVIS 7-9

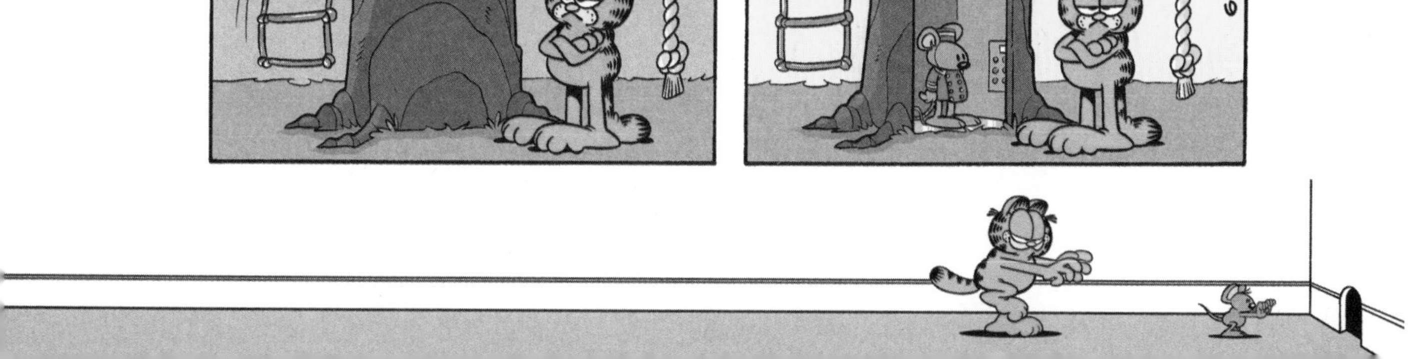

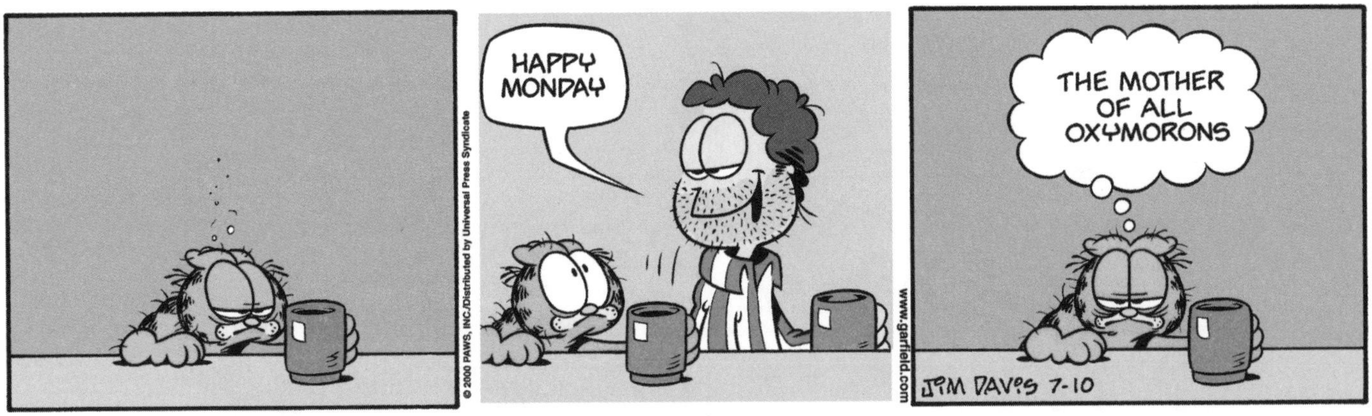
HAPPY MONDAY
THE MOTHER OF ALL OXYMORONS
© 2000 PAWS, INC./Distributed by Universal Press Syndicate
www.garfield.com
JIM DAVIS 7-10

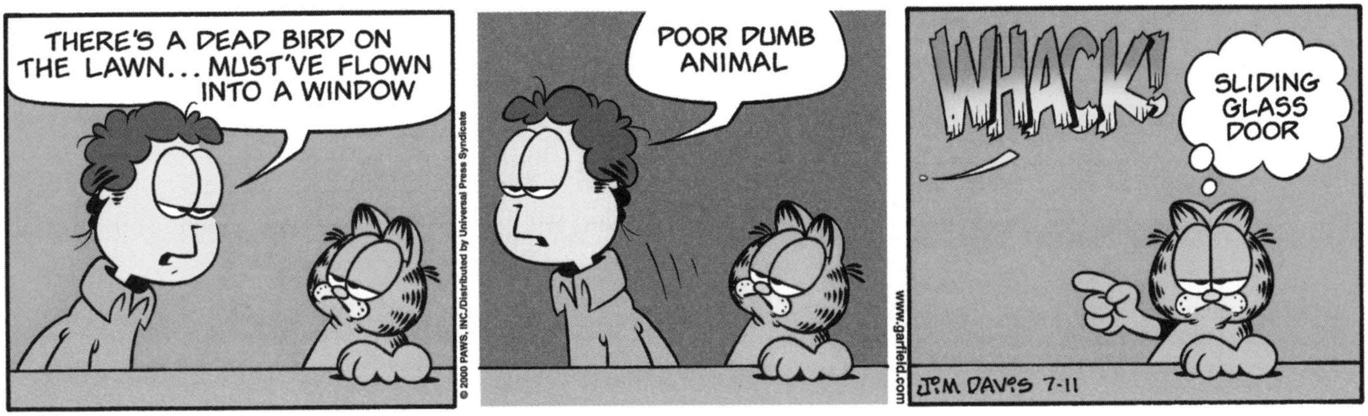
THERE'S A DEAD BIRD ON THE LAWN... MUST'VE FLOWN INTO A WINDOW
POOR DUMB ANIMAL
WHACK!
SLIDING GLASS DOOR
© 2000 PAWS, INC./Distributed by Universal Press Syndicate
www.garfield.com
JIM DAVIS 7-11

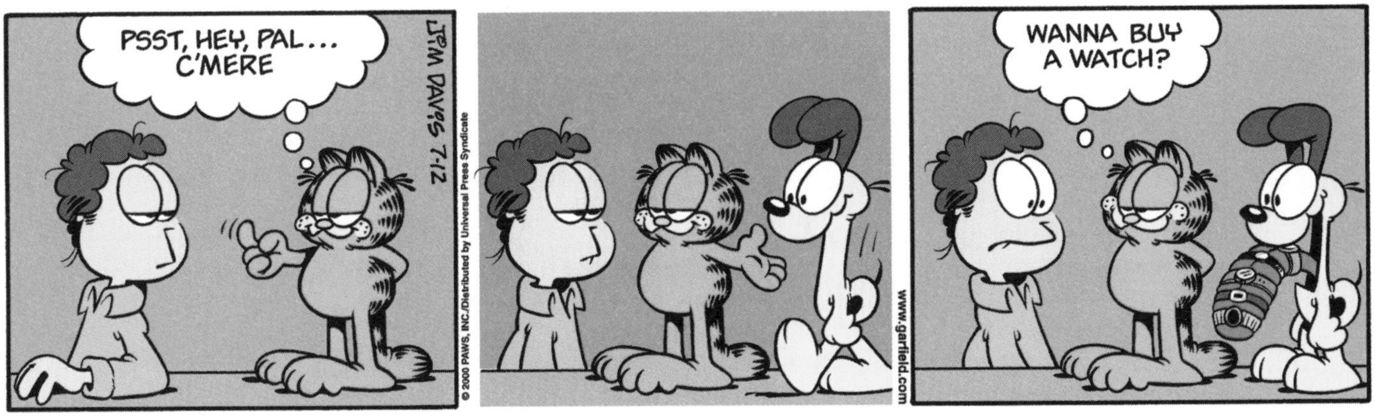
PSST, HEY, PAL... C'MERE
JIM DAVIS 7-12
© 2000 PAWS, INC./Distributed by Universal Press Syndicate
www.garfield.com
WANNA BUY A WATCH?

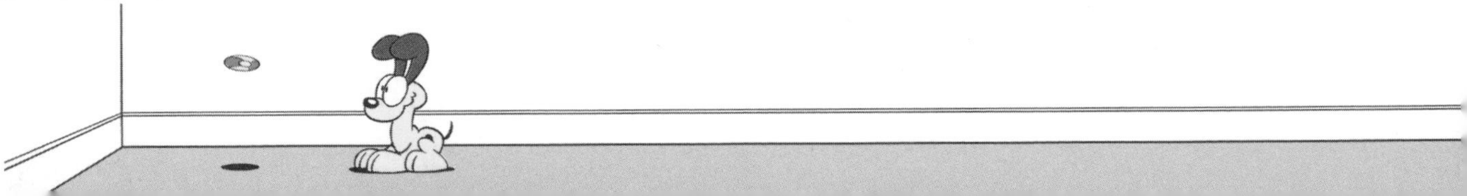

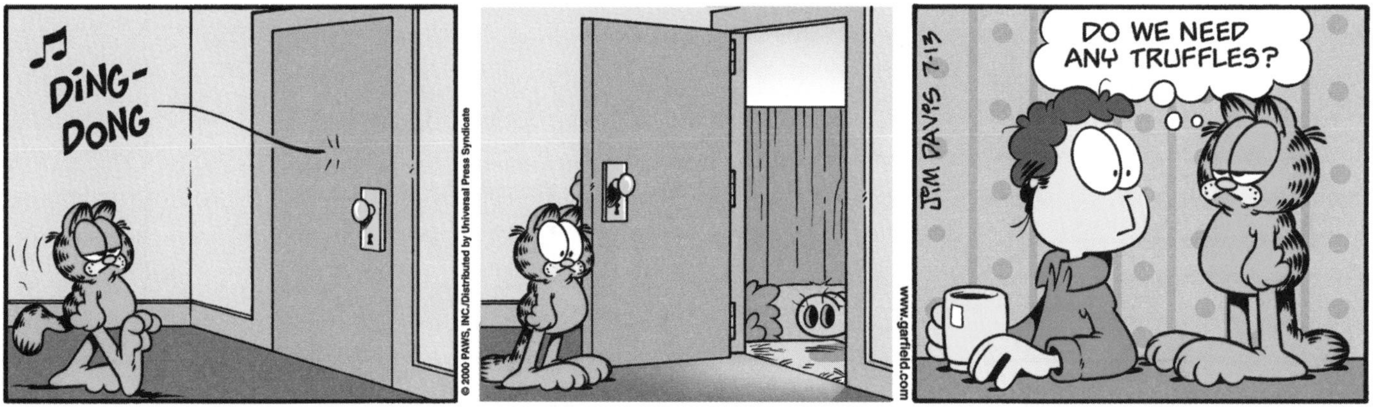
DING-
DONG
© 2000 PAWS, INC./Distributed by Universal Press Syndicate
www.garfield.com
JIM DAVIS 7-13
DO WE NEED ANY TRUFFLES?

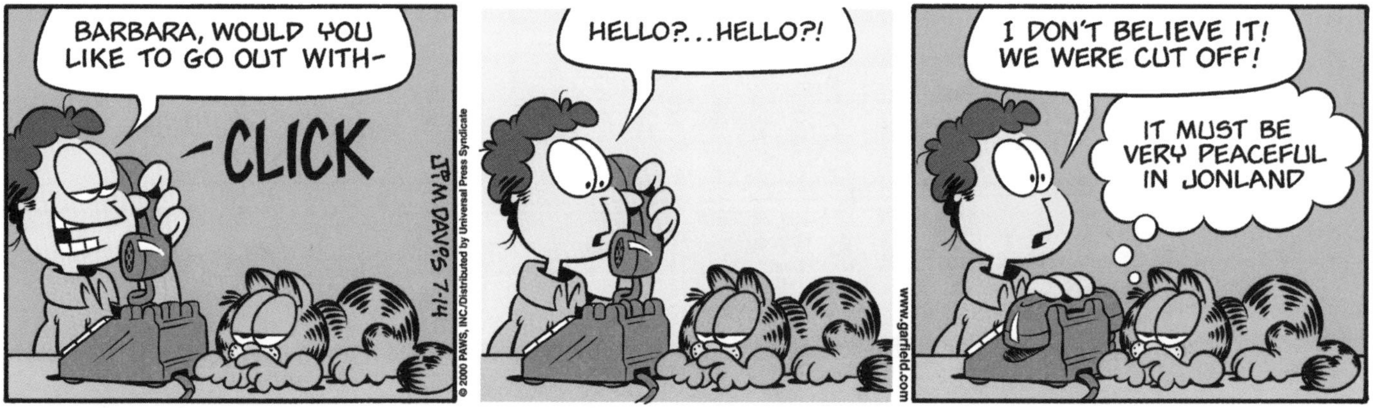
BARBARA, WOULD YOU LIKE TO GO OUT WITH-
-CLICK
JIM DAVIS 7-14
© 2000 PAWS, INC./Distributed by Universal Press Syndicate
HELLO?...HELLO?!
www.garfield.com
I DON'T BELIEVE IT! WE WERE CUT OFF!
IT MUST BE VERY PEACEFUL IN JONLAND

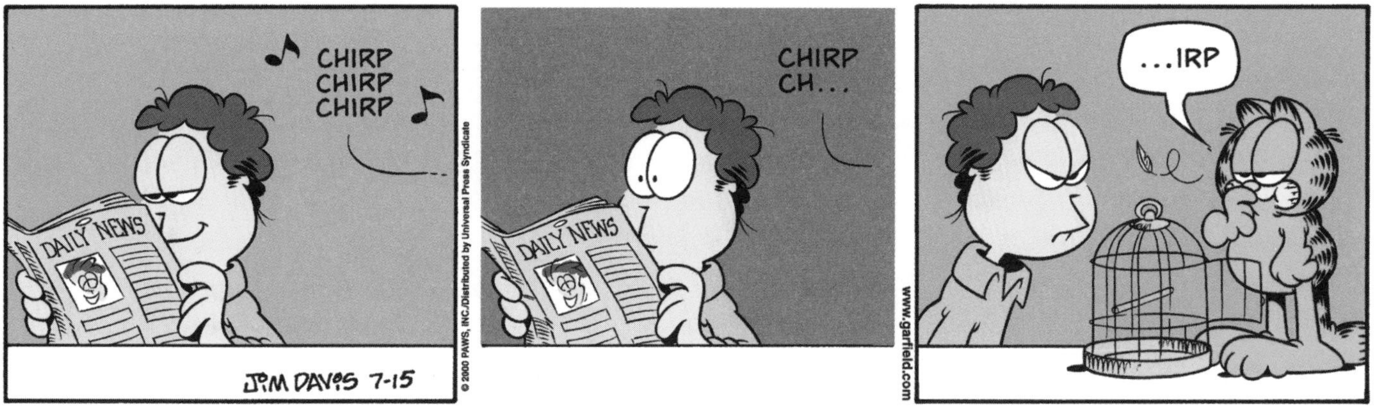
CHIRP
CHIRP
CHIRP
DAILY NEWS
JIM DAVIS 7-15
© 2000 PAWS, INC./Distributed by Universal Press Syndicate
CHIRP
CH...
DAILY NEWS
www.garfield.com
...IRP

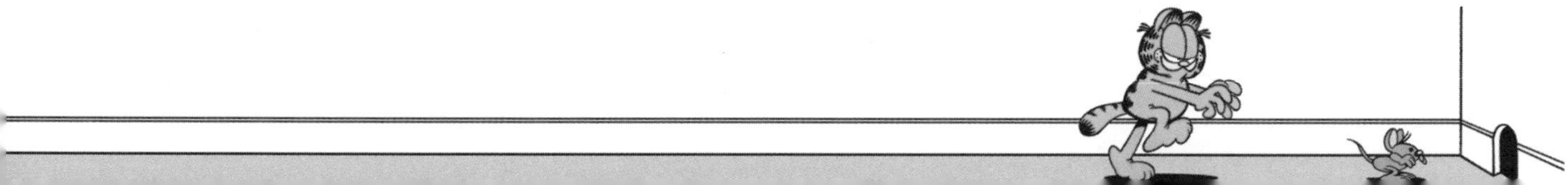

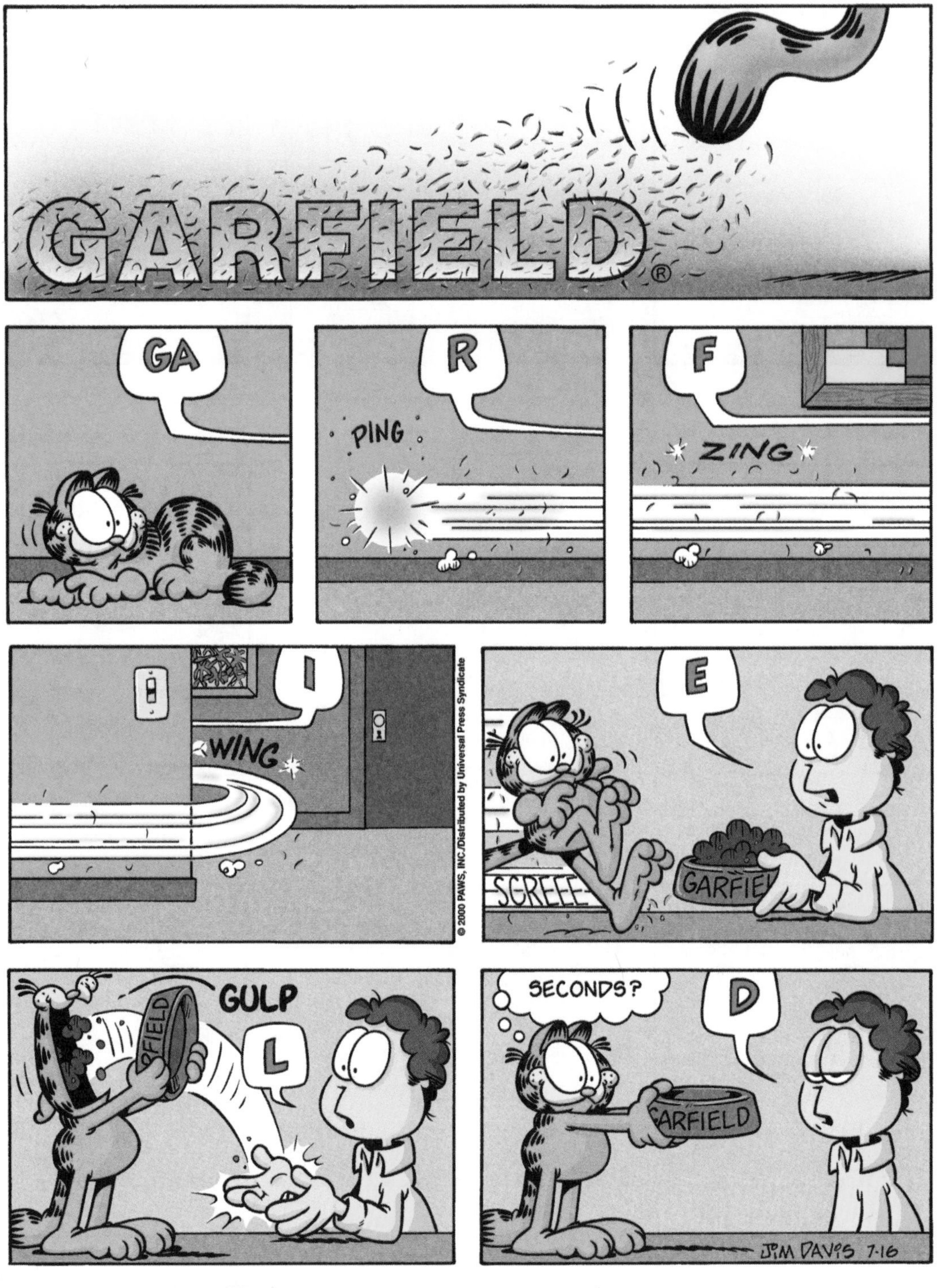
GARFIELD®
GA
R
PING
F
ZING
I
WING
© 2000 PAWS, INC./Distributed by Universal Press Syndicate
E
SCREEEE
GARFIEL
GULP
FIELD
L
SECONDS?
D
GARFIELD
JIM DAVIS 7-16

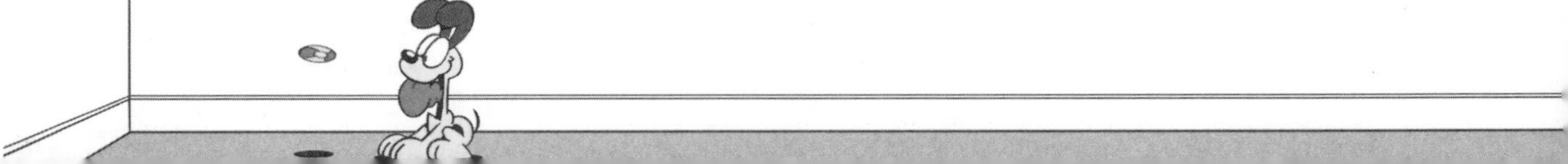

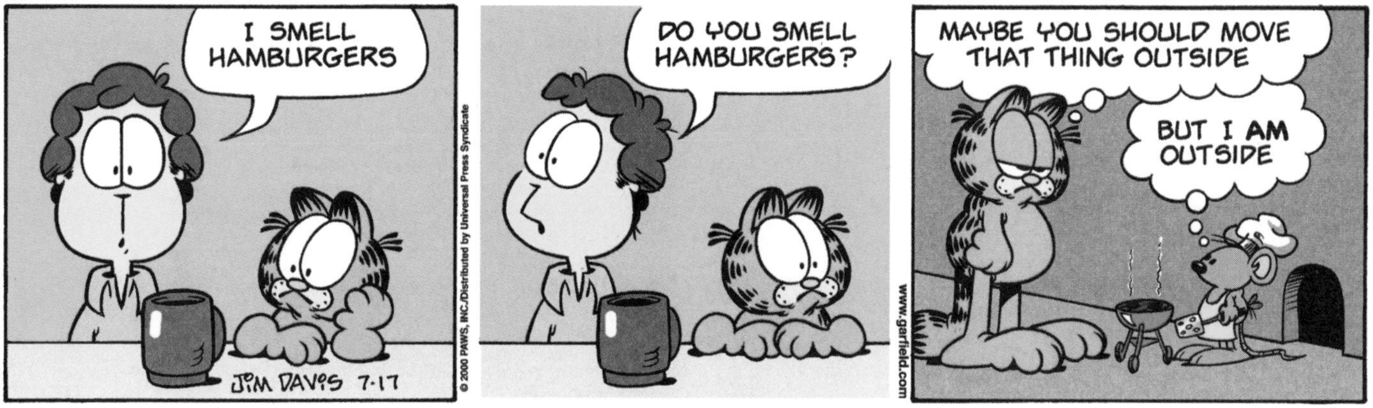
I SMELL HAMBURGERS
JIM DAVIS 7-17
© 2000 PAWS, INC./Distributed by Universal Press Syndicate
DO YOU SMELL HAMBURGERS?
www.garfield.com
MAYBE YOU SHOULD MOVE THAT THING OUTSIDE
BUT I AM OUTSIDE

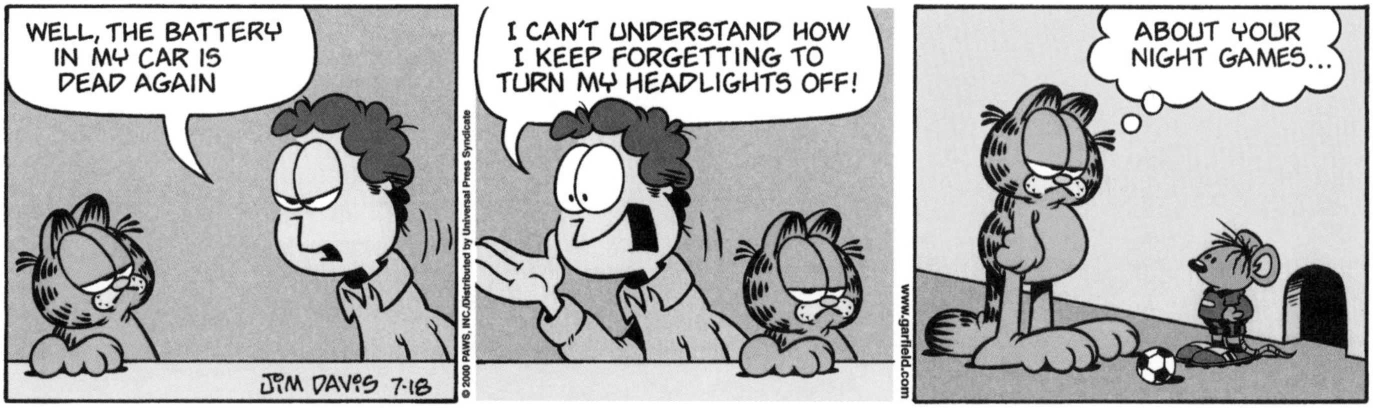
WELL, THE BATTERY IN MY CAR IS DEAD AGAIN
JIM DAVIS 7-18
© 2000 PAWS, INC./Distributed by Universal Press Syndicate
I CAN'T UNDERSTAND HOW I KEEP FORGETTING TO TURN MY HEADLIGHTS OFF!
www.garfield.com
ABOUT YOUR NIGHT GAMES...

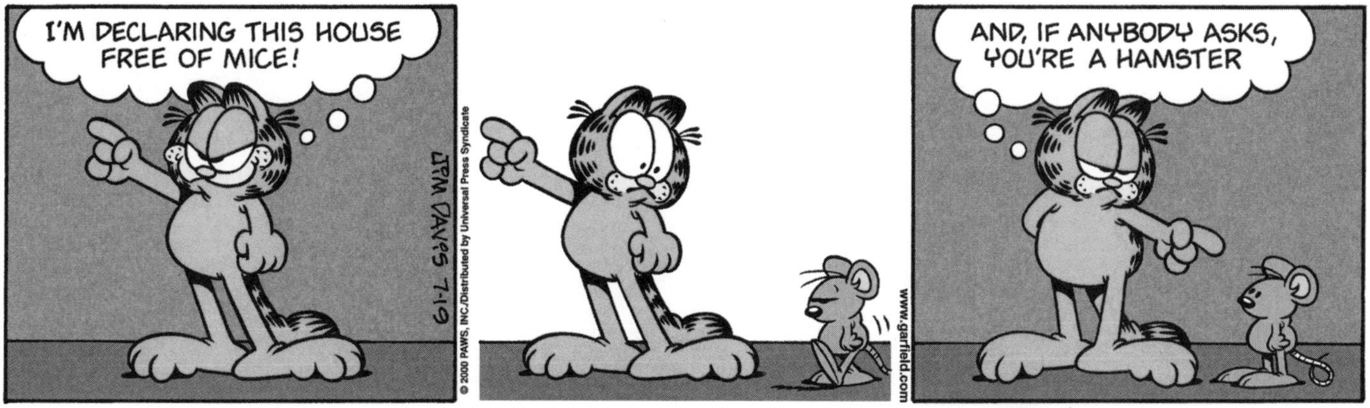
I'M DECLARING THIS HOUSE FREE OF MICE!
JIM DAVIS 7-19
© 2000 PAWS, INC./Distributed by Universal Press Syndicate
www.garfield.com
AND, IF ANYBODY ASKS, YOU'RE A HAMSTER

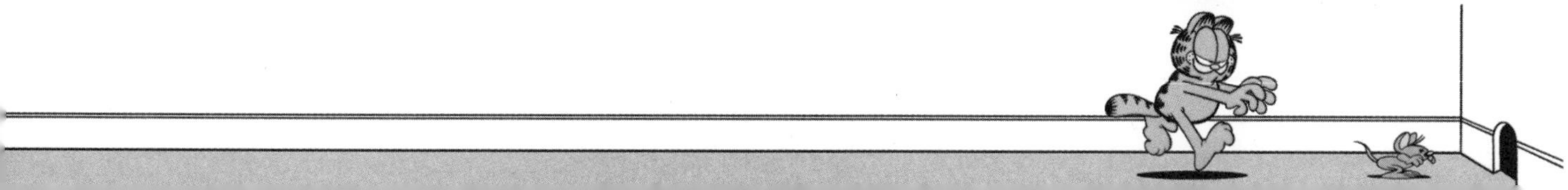

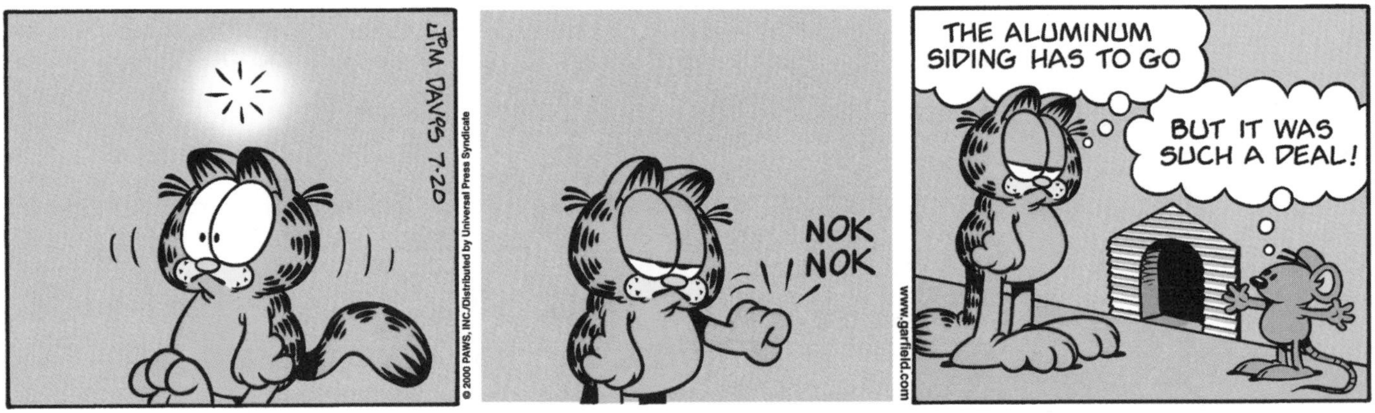
JIM DAVIS 7-20
© 2000 PAWS, INC./Distributed by Universal Press Syndicate
NOK
NOK
THE ALUMINUM SIDING HAS TO GO
BUT IT WAS SUCH A DEAL!
www.garfield.com

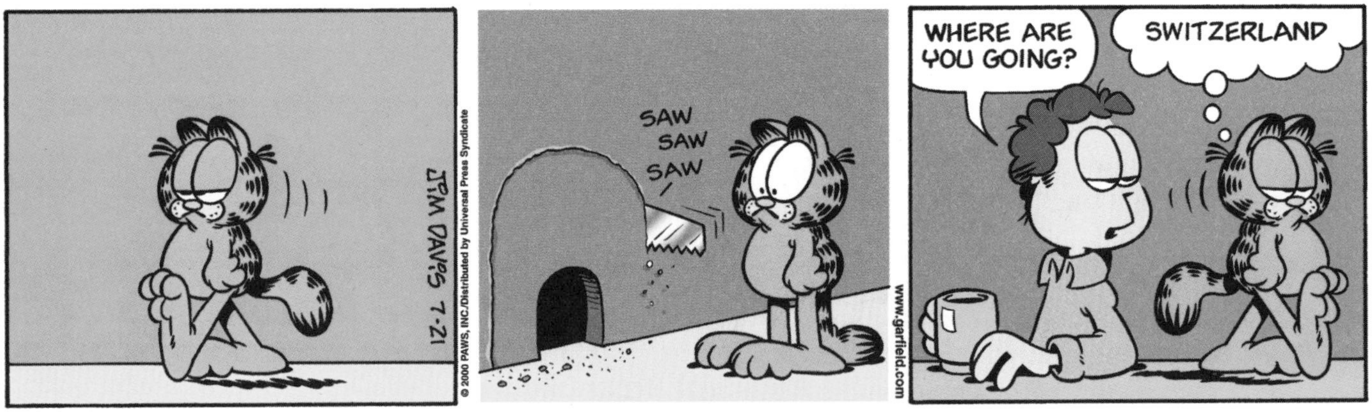
JIM DAVIS 7-21
© 2000 PAWS, INC./Distributed by Universal Press Syndicate
SAW
SAW
SAW
WHERE ARE YOU GOING?
SWITZERLAND
www.garfield.com

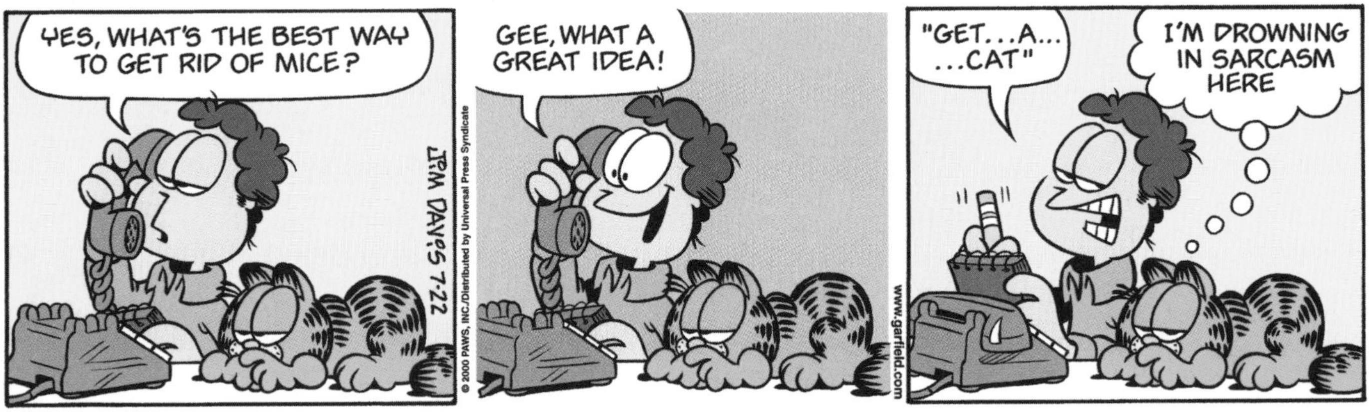
YES, WHAT'S THE BEST WAY TO GET RID OF MICE?
JIM DAVIS 7-22
© 2000 PAWS, INC./Distributed by Universal Press Syndicate
GEE, WHAT A GREAT IDEA!
"GET...A... ...CAT"
I'M DROWNING IN SARCASM HERE
www.garfield.com

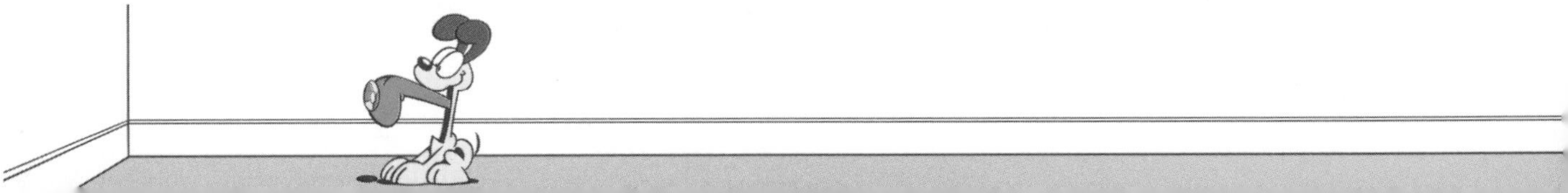

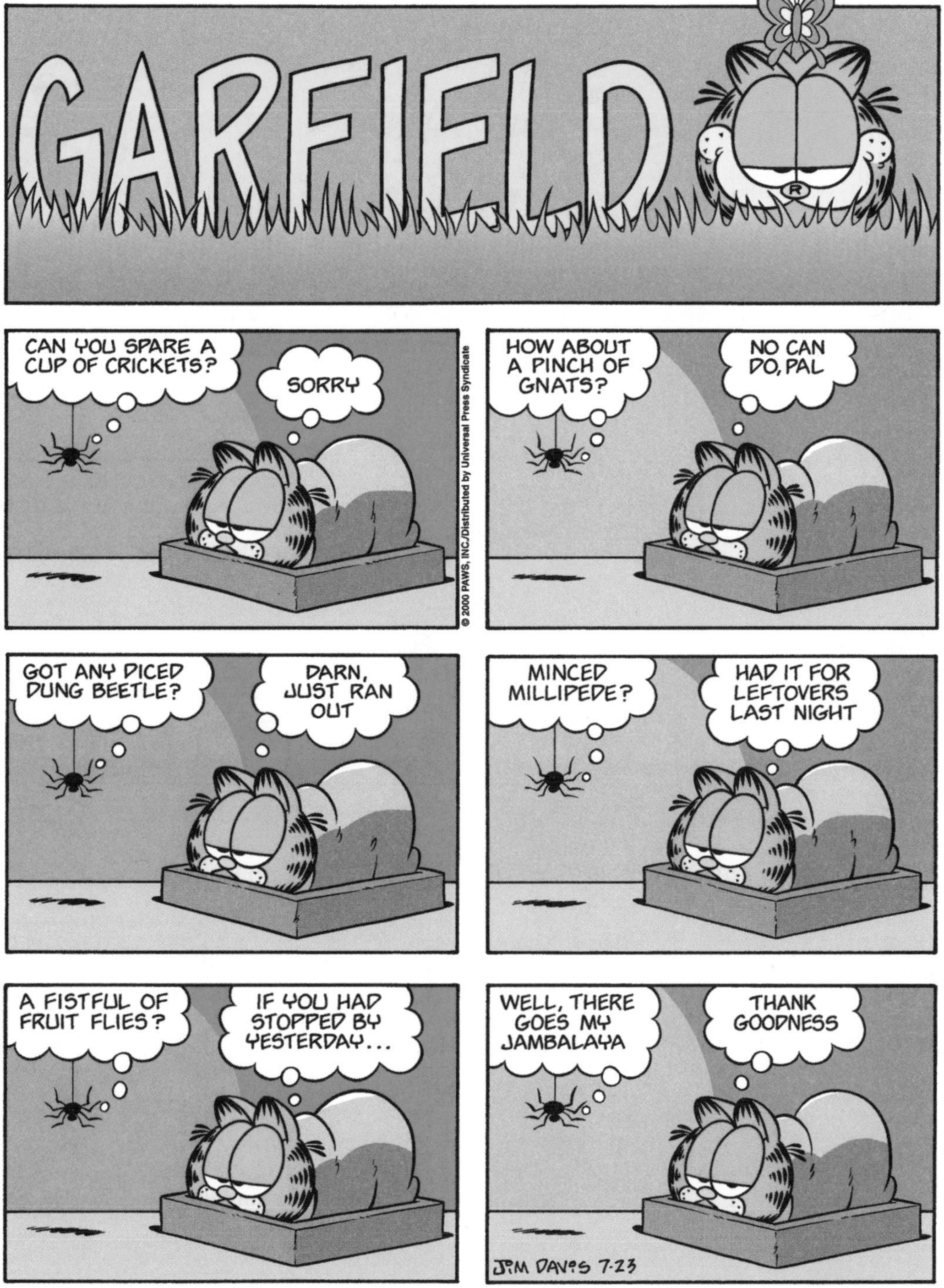
GARFIELD
CAN YOU SPARE A CUP OF CRICKETS?
SORRY
© 2000 PAWS, INC./Distributed by Universal Press Syndicate
HOW ABOUT A PINCH OF GNATS?
NO CAN DO, PAL
GOT ANY DICED DUNG BEETLE?
DARN, JUST RAN OUT
MINCED MILLIPEDE?
HAD IT FOR LEFTOVERS LAST NIGHT
A FISTFUL OF FRUIT FLIES?
IF YOU HAD STOPPED BY YESTERDAY...
WELL, THERE GOES MY JAMBALAYA
THANK GOODNESS
JIM DAVIS 7-23

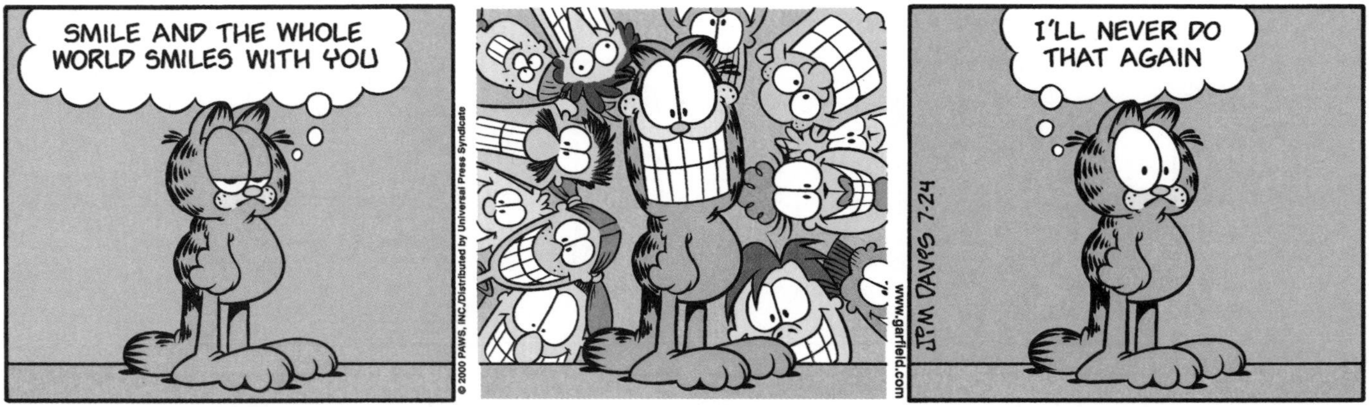

SMILE AND THE WHOLE WORLD SMILES WITH YOU
© 2000 PAWS, INC./Distributed by Universal Press Syndicate
www.garfield.com
JIM DAVIS 7-24
I'LL NEVER DO THAT AGAIN

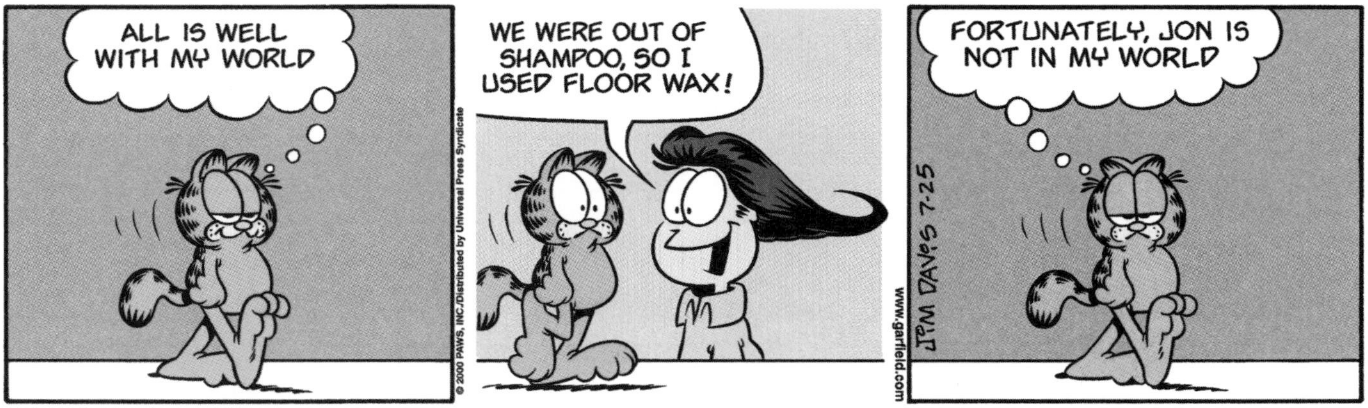

ALL IS WELL WITH MY WORLD
© 2000 PAWS, INC./Distributed by Universal Press Syndicate
WE WERE OUT OF SHAMPOO, SO I USED FLOOR WAX!
www.garfield.com
JIM DAVIS 7-25
FORTUNATELY, JON IS NOT IN MY WORLD

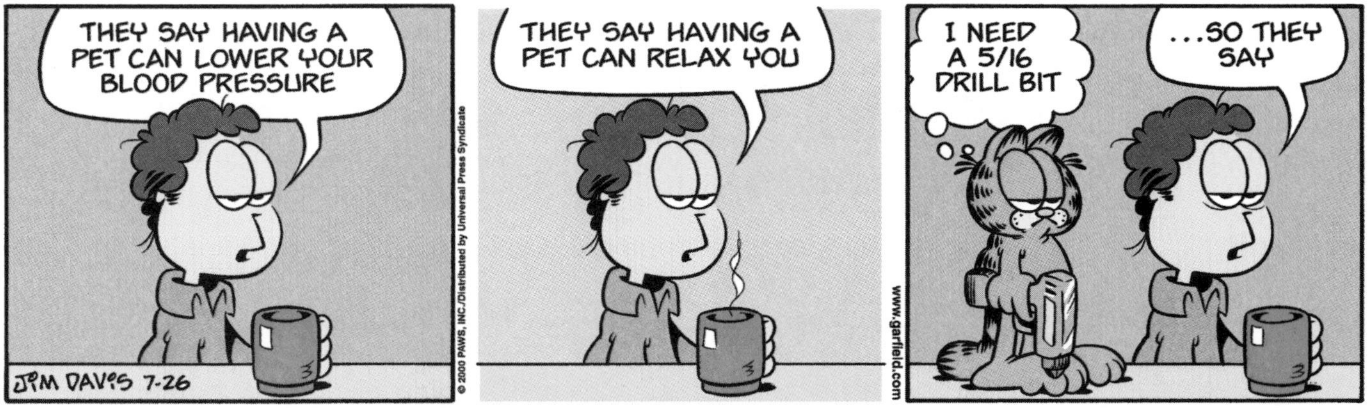

THEY SAY HAVING A PET CAN LOWER YOUR BLOOD PRESSURE
JIM DAVIS 7-26
© 2000 PAWS, INC./Distributed by Universal Press Syndicate
THEY SAY HAVING A PET CAN RELAX YOU
www.garfield.com
I NEED A 5/16 DRILL BIT
...SO THEY SAY

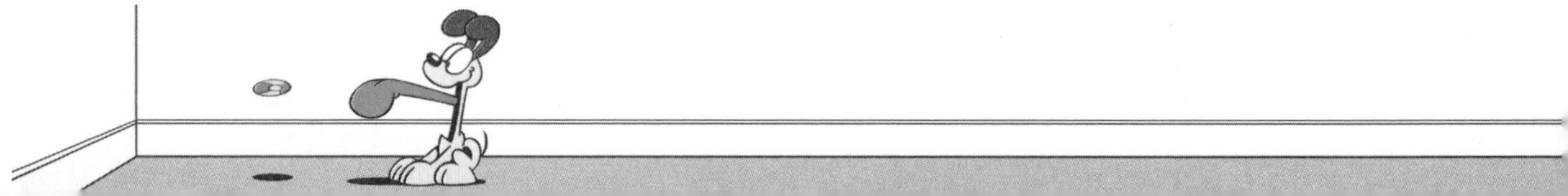

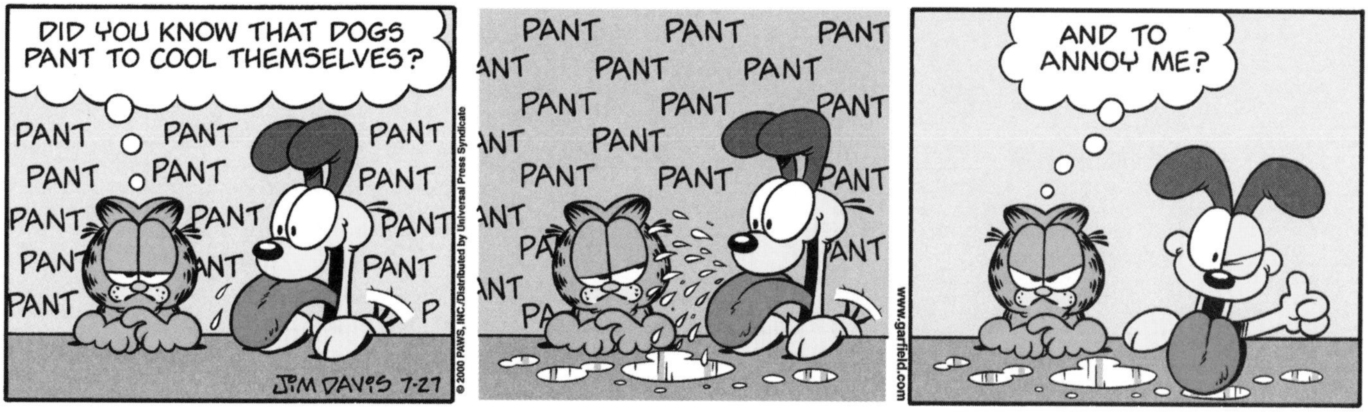
DID YOU KNOW THAT DOGS PANT TO COOL THEMSELVES?
PANT PANT PANT PANT PANT PANT PANT PANT PANT PANT PANT PANT
JIM DAVIS 7-27
© 2000 PAWS, INC./Distributed by Universal Press Syndicate
PANT PANT PANT PANT PANT PANT PANT PANT PANT PANT PANT
www.garfield.com
AND TO ANNOY ME?

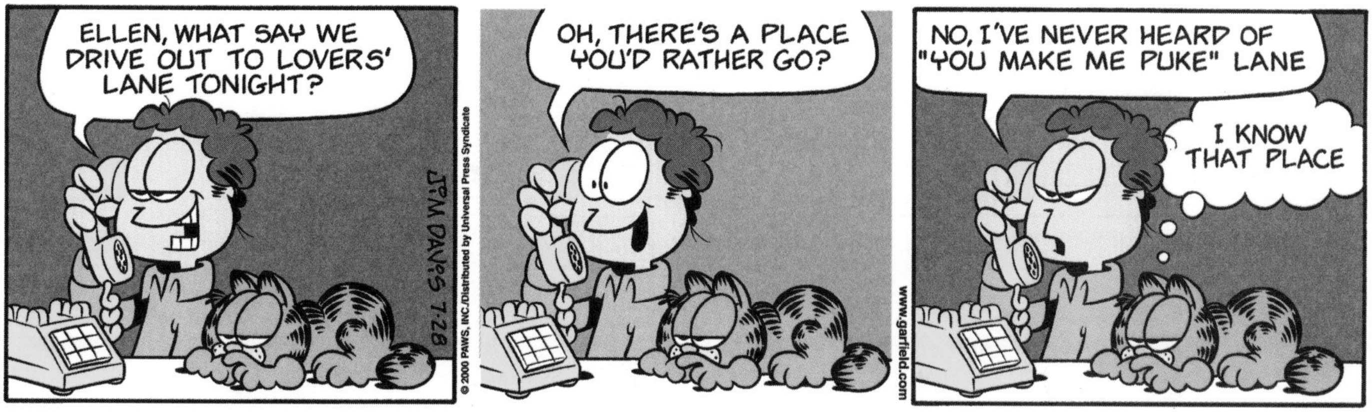
ELLEN, WHAT SAY WE DRIVE OUT TO LOVERS' LANE TONIGHT?
JIM DAVIS 7-28
© 2000 PAWS, INC./Distributed by Universal Press Syndicate
OH, THERE'S A PLACE YOU'D RATHER GO?
www.garfield.com
NO, I'VE NEVER HEARD OF "YOU MAKE ME PUKE" LANE
I KNOW THAT PLACE

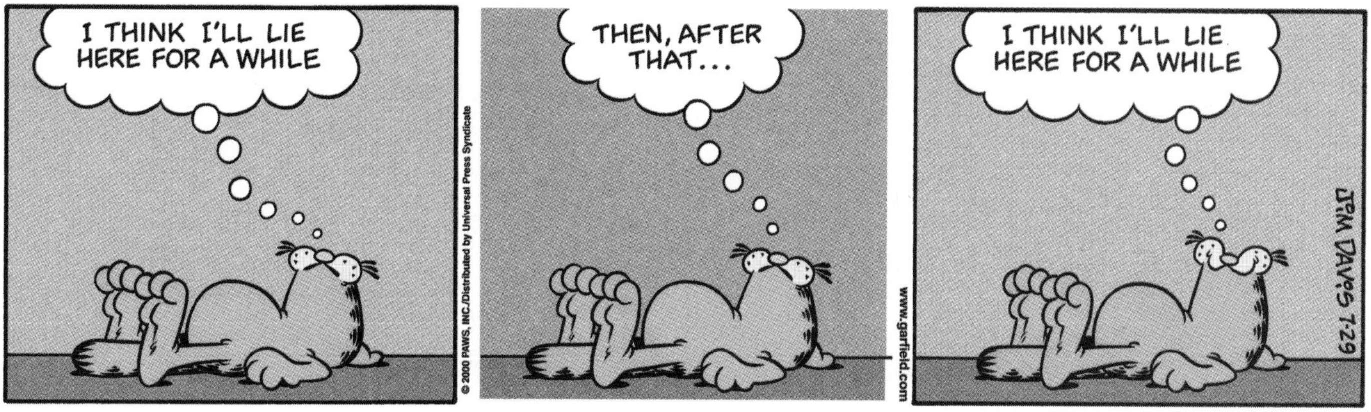
I THINK I'LL LIE HERE FOR A WHILE
© 2000 PAWS, INC./Distributed by Universal Press Syndicate
THEN, AFTER THAT...
www.garfield.com
I THINK I'LL LIE HERE FOR A WHILE
JIM DAVIS 7-29

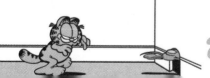

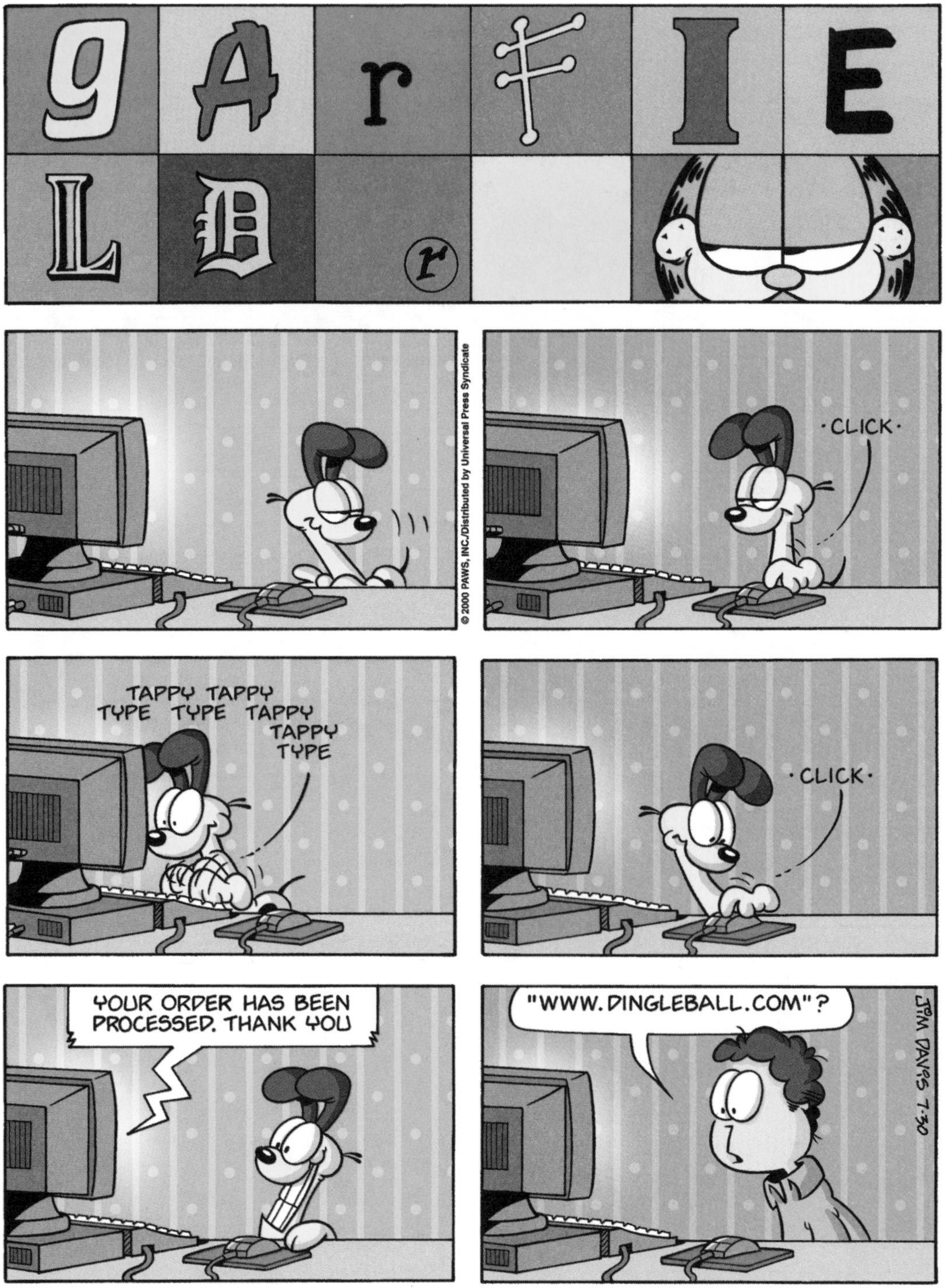
gArfIELD®
© 2000 PAWS, INC./Distributed by Universal Press Syndicate
·CLICK·
TAPPY TAPPY TYPE TYPE TAPPY TAPPY TYPE
·CLICK·
YOUR ORDER HAS BEEN PROCESSED. THANK YOU
"WWW.DINGLEBALL.COM"?
JIM DAVIS 7-30

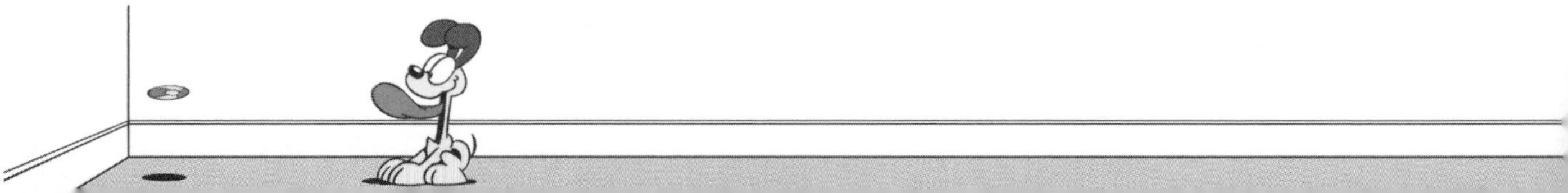

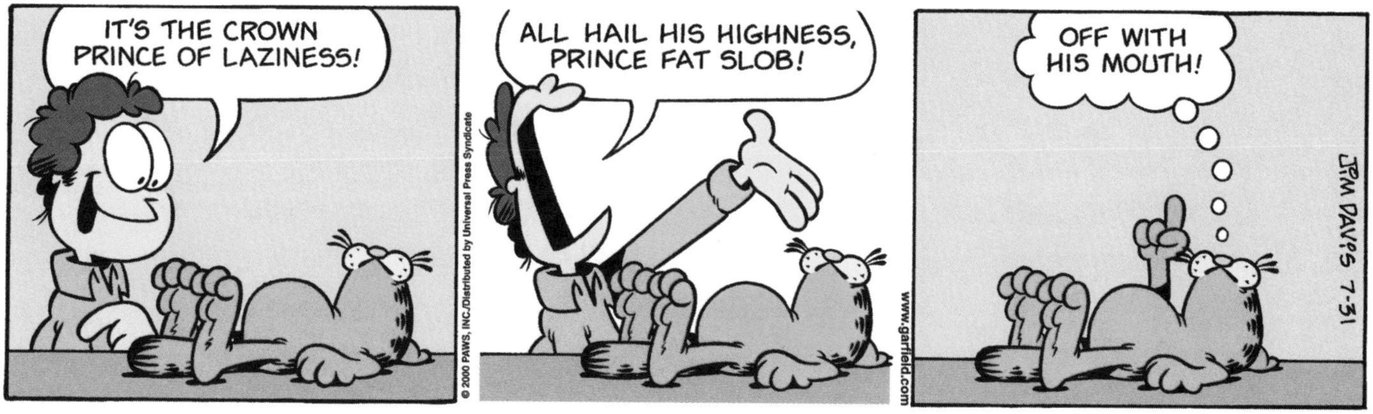
IT'S THE CROWN PRINCE OF LAZINESS!
ALL HAIL HIS HIGHNESS, PRINCE FAT SLOB!
OFF WITH HIS MOUTH!
© 2000 PAWS, INC./Distributed by Universal Press Syndicate
www.garfield.com
JIM DAVIS 7-31

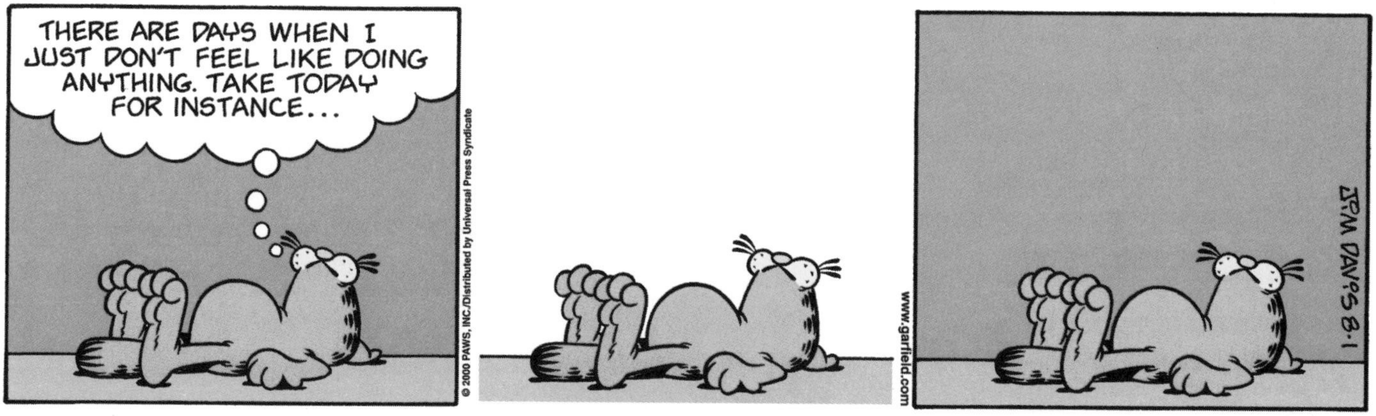
THERE ARE DAYS WHEN I JUST DON'T FEEL LIKE DOING ANYTHING. TAKE TODAY FOR INSTANCE...
© 2000 PAWS, INC./Distributed by Universal Press Syndicate
www.garfield.com
JIM DAVIS 8-1

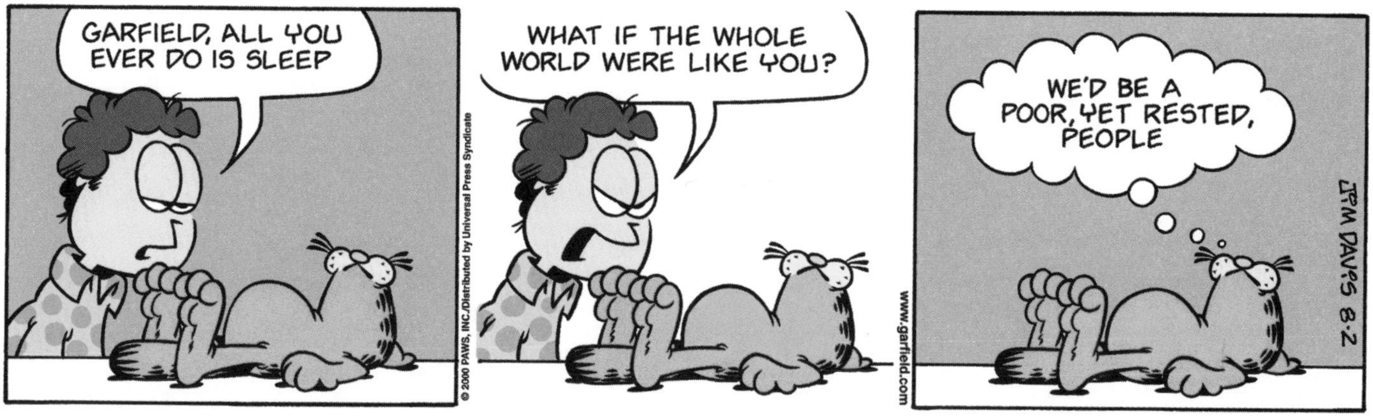
GARFIELD, ALL YOU EVER DO IS SLEEP
WHAT IF THE WHOLE WORLD WERE LIKE YOU?
WE'D BE A POOR, YET RESTED, PEOPLE
© 2000 PAWS, INC./Distributed by Universal Press Syndicate
www.garfield.com
JIM DAVIS 8-2

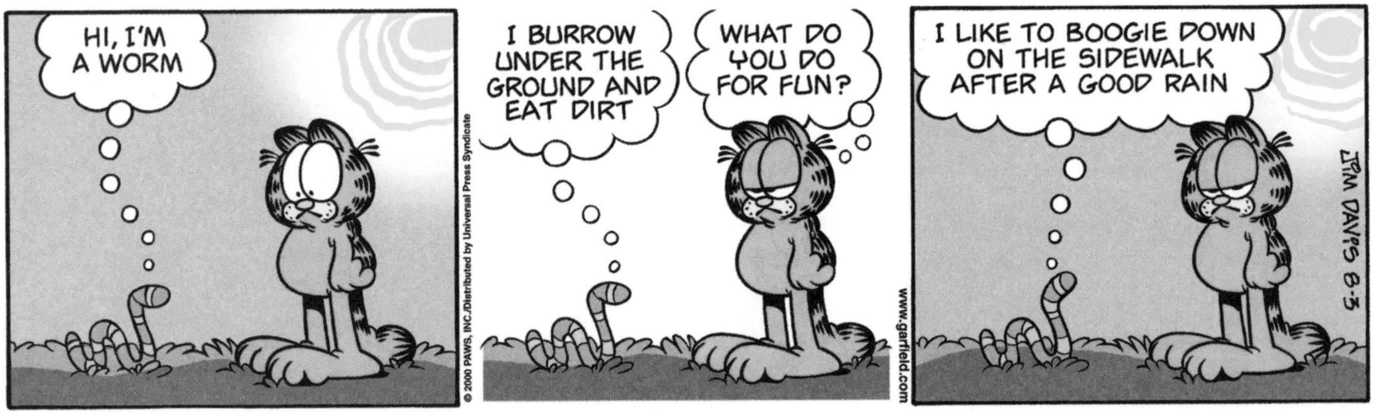

HI, I'M A WORM
I BURROW UNDER THE GROUND AND EAT DIRT
WHAT DO YOU DO FOR FUN?
I LIKE TO BOOGIE DOWN ON THE SIDEWALK AFTER A GOOD RAIN
© 2000 PAWS, INC./Distributed by Universal Press Syndicate
www.garfield.com
JIM DAVIS 8-3

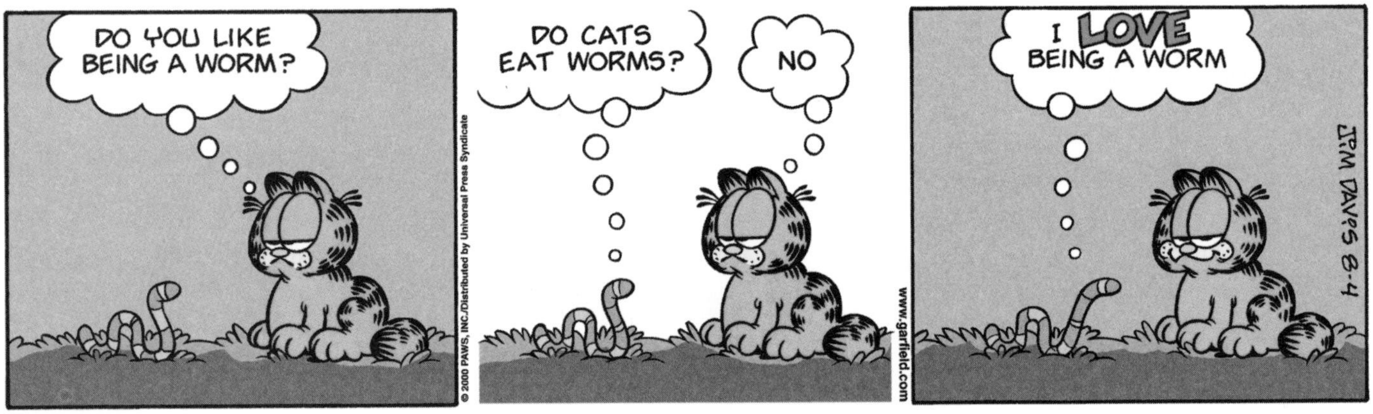

DO YOU LIKE BEING A WORM?
DO CATS EAT WORMS?
NO
I LOVE BEING A WORM
© 2000 PAWS, INC./Distributed by Universal Press Syndicate
www.garfield.com
JIM DAVIS 8-4

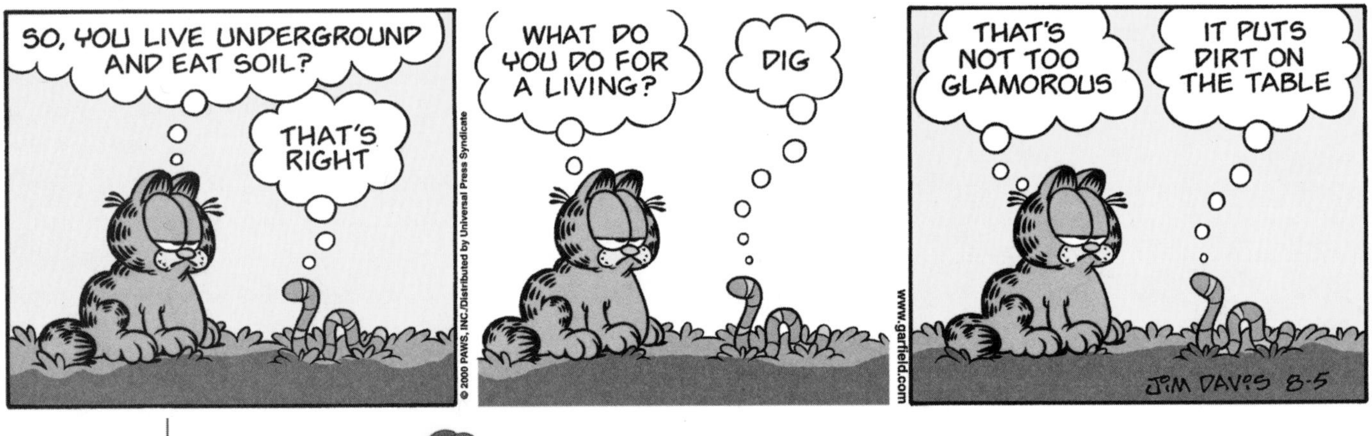

SO, YOU LIVE UNDERGROUND AND EAT SOIL?
THAT'S RIGHT
WHAT DO YOU DO FOR A LIVING?
DIG
THAT'S NOT TOO GLAMOROUS
IT PUTS DIRT ON THE TABLE
© 2000 PAWS, INC./Distributed by Universal Press Syndicate
www.garfield.com
JIM DAVIS 8-5

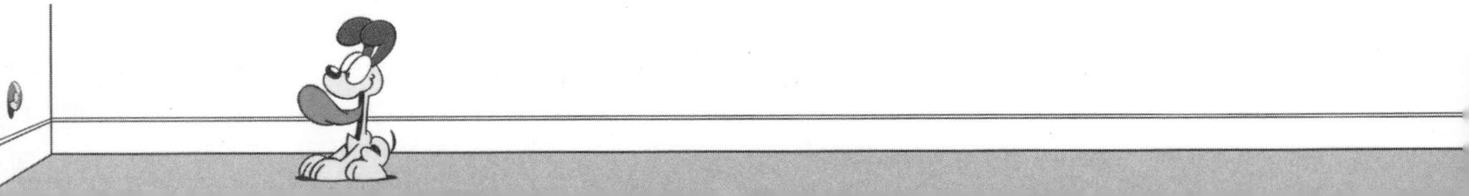

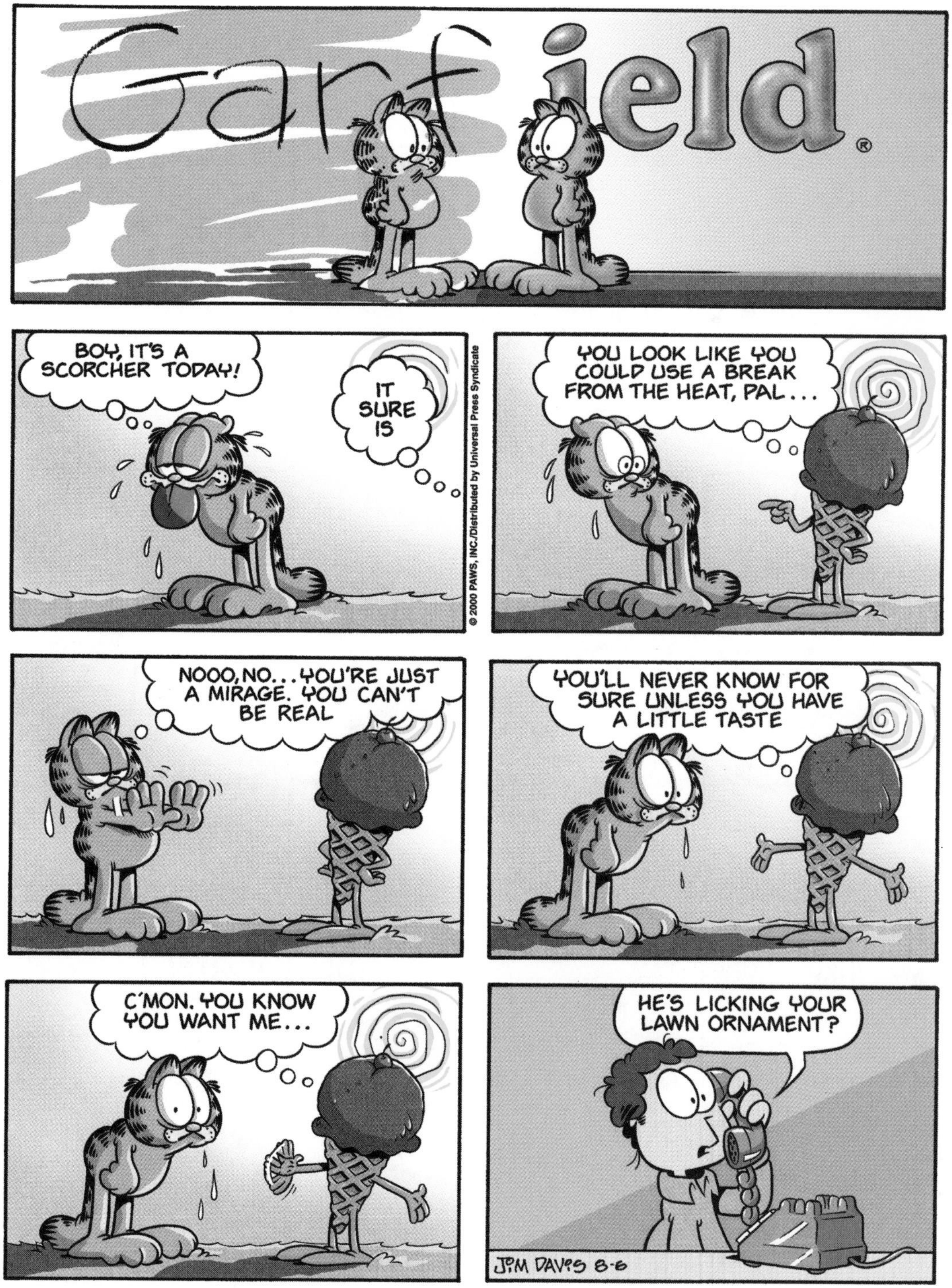

Garfield
BOY, IT'S A SCORCHER TODAY!
IT SURE IS
© 2000 PAWS, INC./Distributed by Universal Press Syndicate
YOU LOOK LIKE YOU COULD USE A BREAK FROM THE HEAT, PAL . . .
NOOO, NO . . . YOU'RE JUST A MIRAGE. YOU CAN'T BE REAL
YOU'LL NEVER KNOW FOR SURE UNLESS YOU HAVE A LITTLE TASTE
C'MON. YOU KNOW YOU WANT ME . . .
HE'S LICKING YOUR LAWN ORNAMENT?
JIM DAVIS 8-6

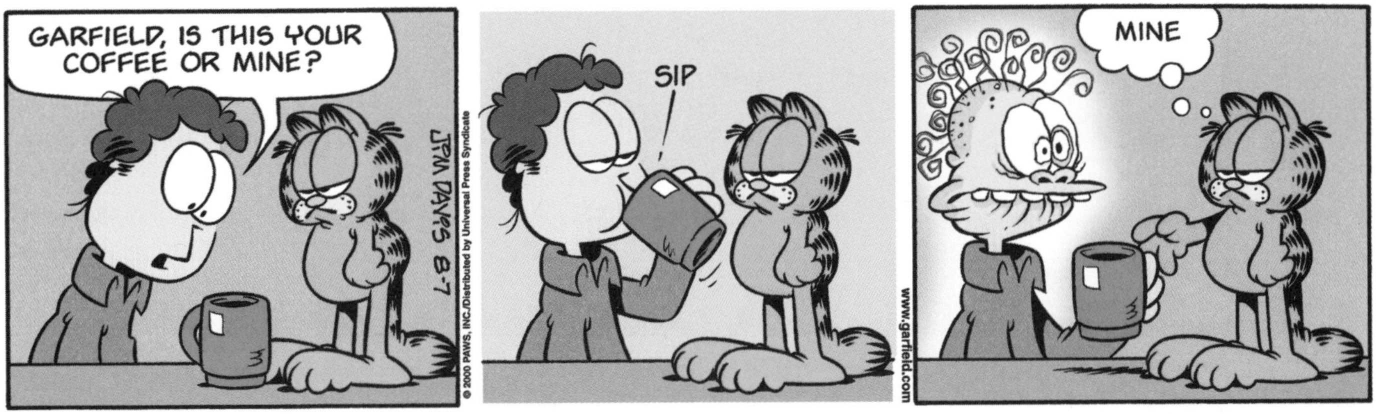
GARFIELD, IS THIS YOUR COFFEE OR MINE?
JIM DAVIS 8-7
© 2000 PAWS, INC./Distributed by Universal Press Syndicate
SIP
www.garfield.com
MINE

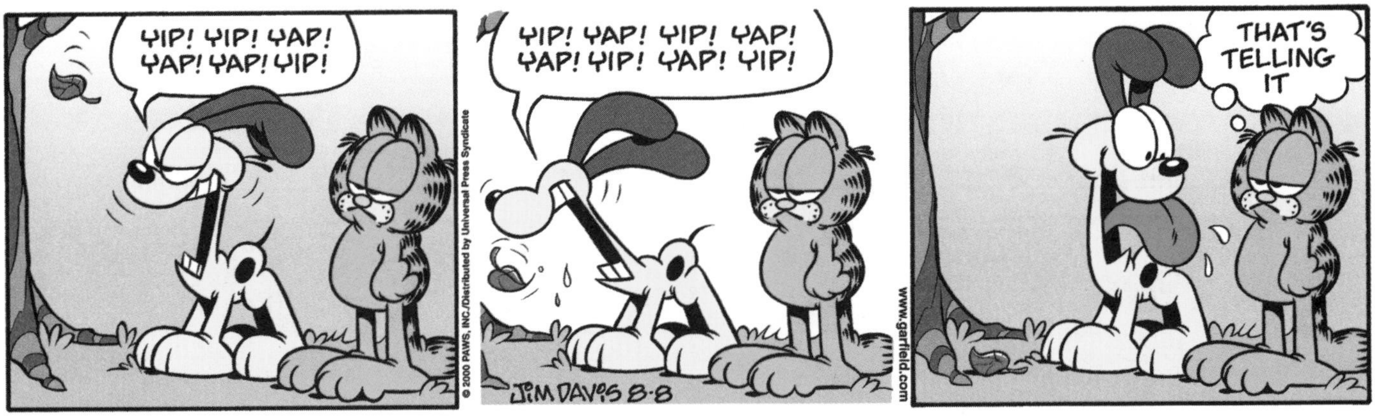
YIP! YIP! YAP! YAP! YAP! YIP!
© 2000 PAWS, INC./Distributed by Universal Press Syndicate
YIP! YAP! YIP! YAP! YAP! YIP! YAP! YIP!
JIM DAVIS 8-8
www.garfield.com
THAT'S TELLING IT

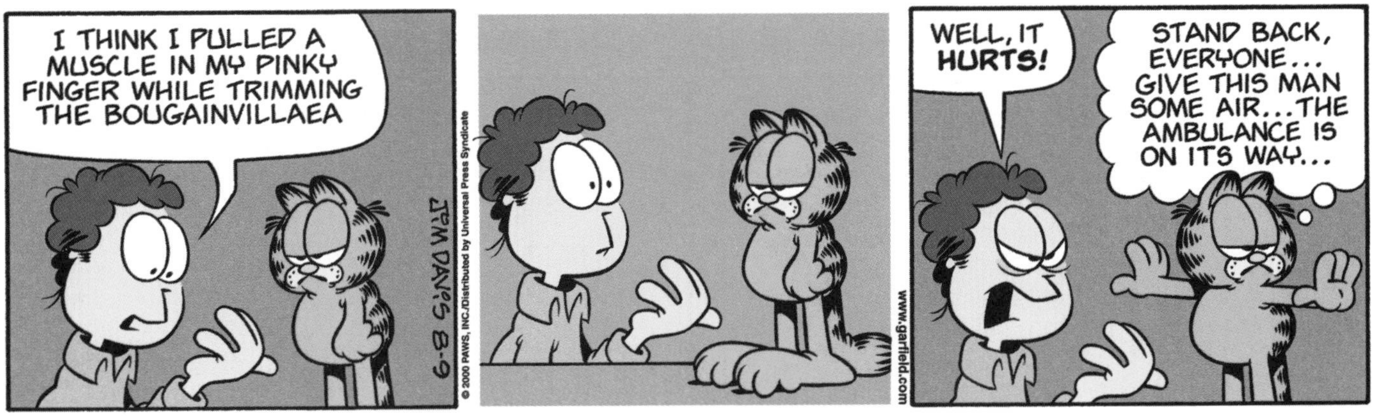
I THINK I PULLED A MUSCLE IN MY PINKY FINGER WHILE TRIMMING THE BOUGAINVILLAEA
JIM DAVIS 8-9
© 2000 PAWS, INC./Distributed by Universal Press Syndicate
www.garfield.com
WELL, IT **HURTS!**
STAND BACK, EVERYONE... GIVE THIS MAN SOME AIR...THE AMBULANCE IS ON ITS WAY...

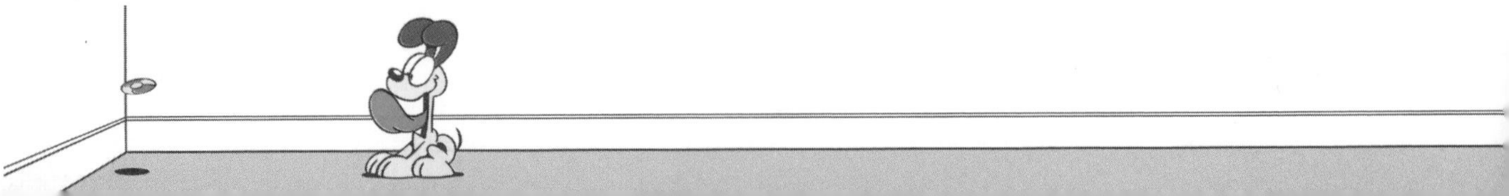

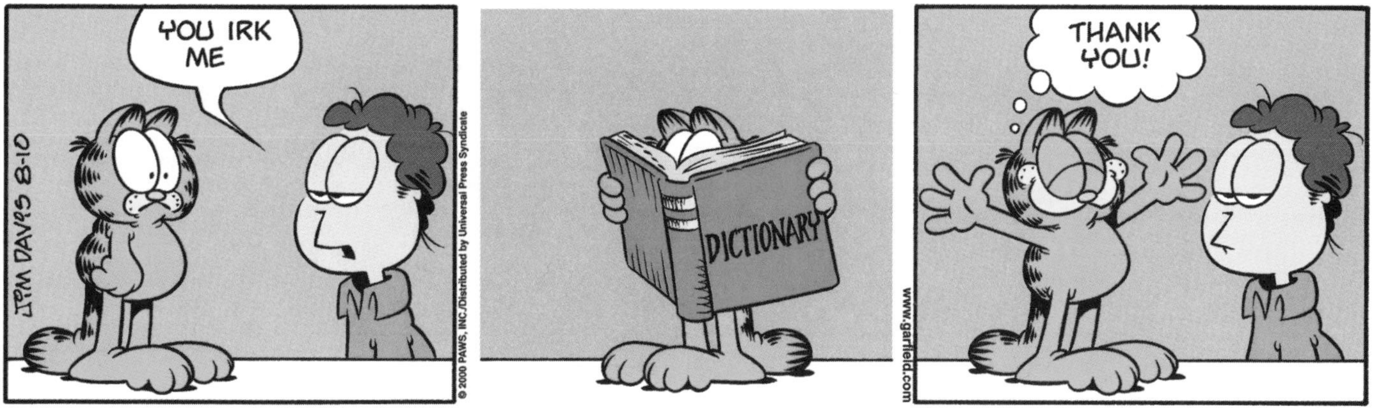
YOU IRK ME
JIM DAVIS 8-10
© 2000 PAWS, INC./Distributed by Universal Press Syndicate
DICTIONARY
www.garfield.com
THANK YOU!

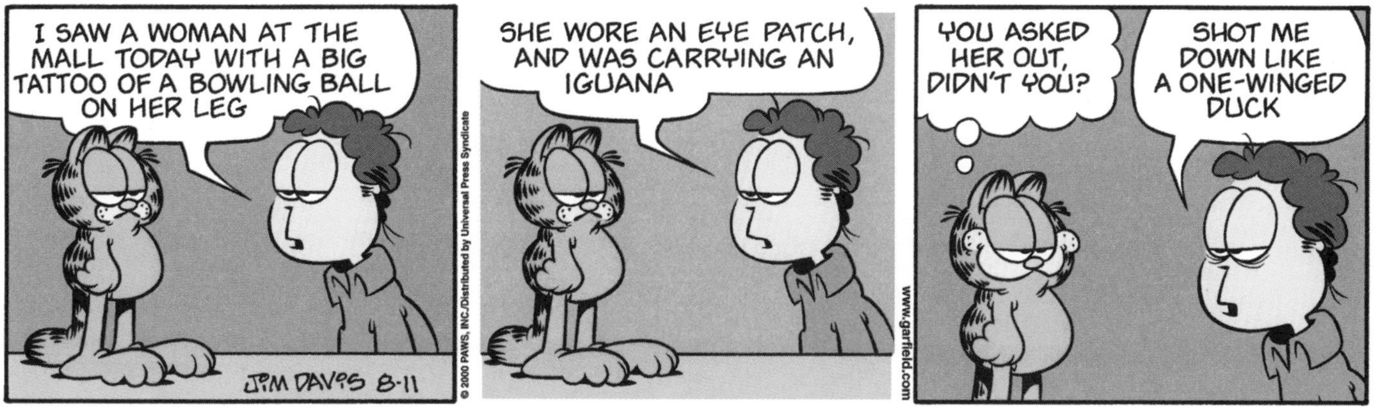
I SAW A WOMAN AT THE MALL TODAY WITH A BIG TATTOO OF A BOWLING BALL ON HER LEG
JIM DAVIS 8-11
© 2000 PAWS, INC./Distributed by Universal Press Syndicate
SHE WORE AN EYE PATCH, AND WAS CARRYING AN IGUANA
www.garfield.com
YOU ASKED HER OUT, DIDN'T YOU?
SHOT ME DOWN LIKE A ONE-WINGED DUCK

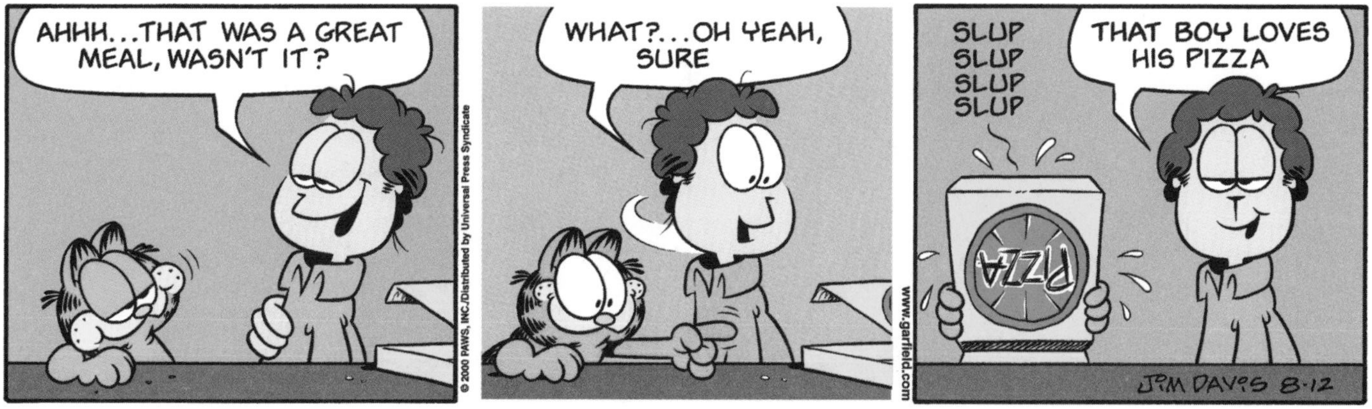
AHHH...THAT WAS A GREAT MEAL, WASN'T IT?
© 2000 PAWS, INC./Distributed by Universal Press Syndicate
WHAT?...OH YEAH, SURE
www.garfield.com
SLUP SLUP SLUP SLUP
PIZZA
THAT BOY LOVES HIS PIZZA
JIM DAVIS 8-12

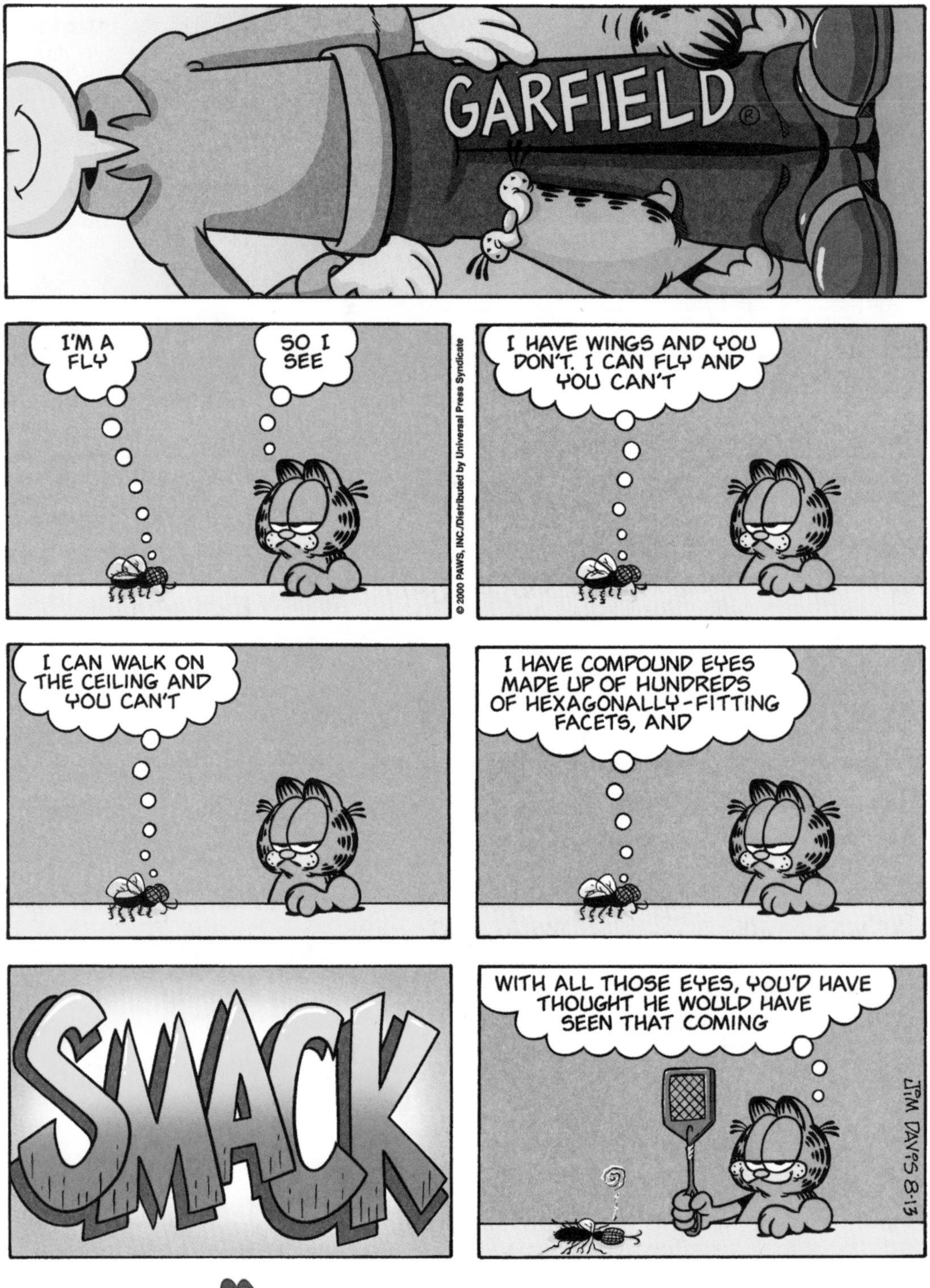
GARFIELD®
I'M A FLY
SO I SEE
© 2000 PAWS, INC./Distributed by Universal Press Syndicate
I HAVE WINGS AND YOU DON'T. I CAN FLY AND YOU CAN'T
I CAN WALK ON THE CEILING AND YOU CAN'T
I HAVE COMPOUND EYES MADE UP OF HUNDREDS OF HEXAGONALLY-FITTING FACETS, AND
SMACK
WITH ALL THOSE EYES, YOU'D HAVE THOUGHT HE WOULD HAVE SEEN THAT COMING
JIM DAVIS 8-13

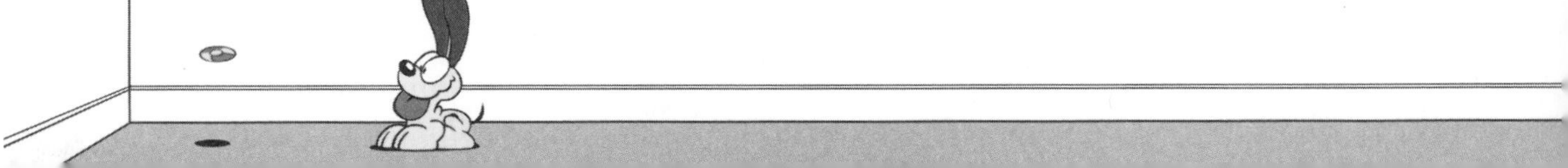

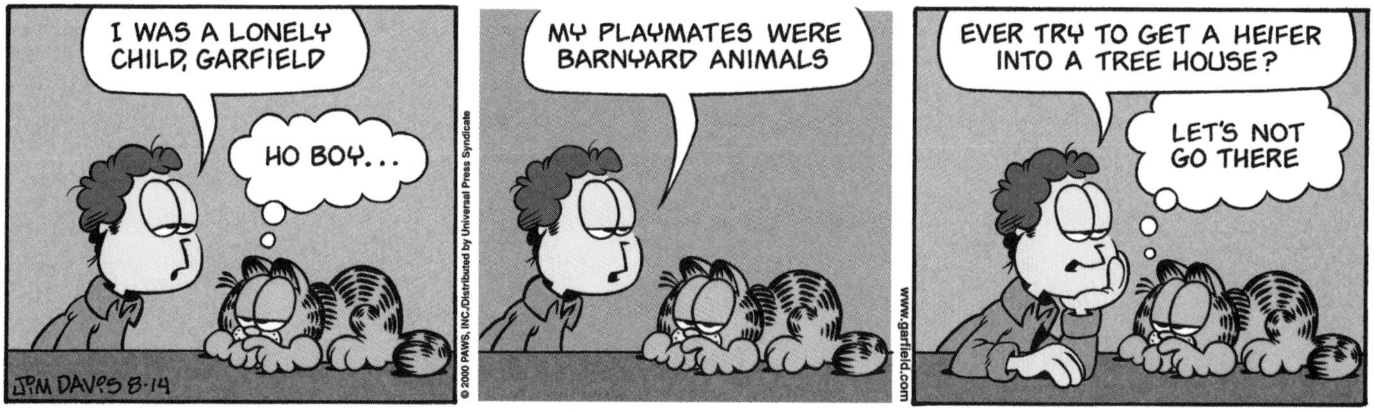
I WAS A LONELY CHILD, GARFIELD
HO BOY...
JIM DAVIS 8-14
© 2000 PAWS, INC./Distributed by Universal Press Syndicate
MY PLAYMATES WERE BARNYARD ANIMALS
www.garfield.com
EVER TRY TO GET A HEIFER INTO A TREE HOUSE?
LET'S NOT GO THERE

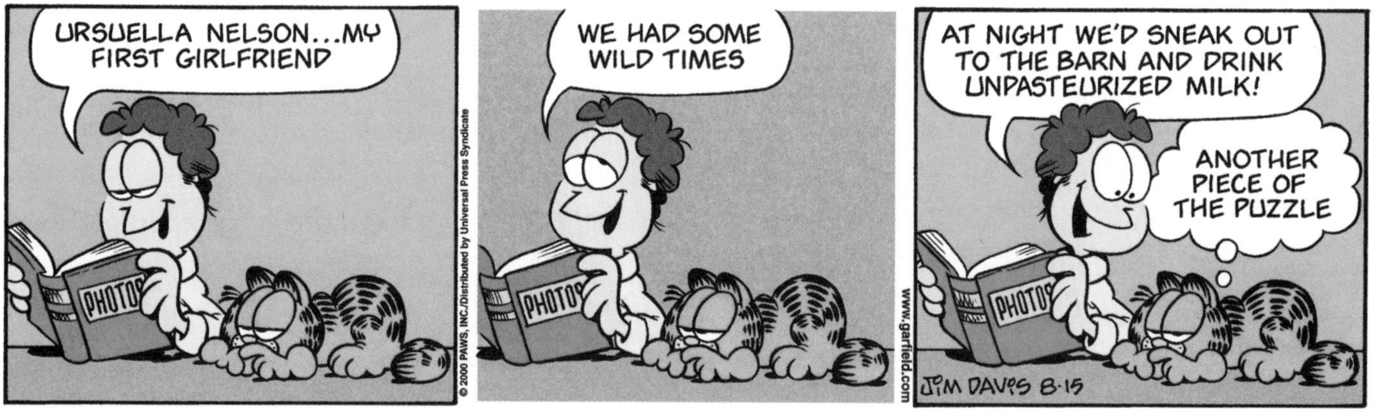
URSUELLA NELSON...MY FIRST GIRLFRIEND
PHOTOS
© 2000 PAWS, INC./Distributed by Universal Press Syndicate
WE HAD SOME WILD TIMES
www.garfield.com
AT NIGHT WE'D SNEAK OUT TO THE BARN AND DRINK UNPASTEURIZED MILK!
ANOTHER PIECE OF THE PUZZLE
JIM DAVIS 8-15

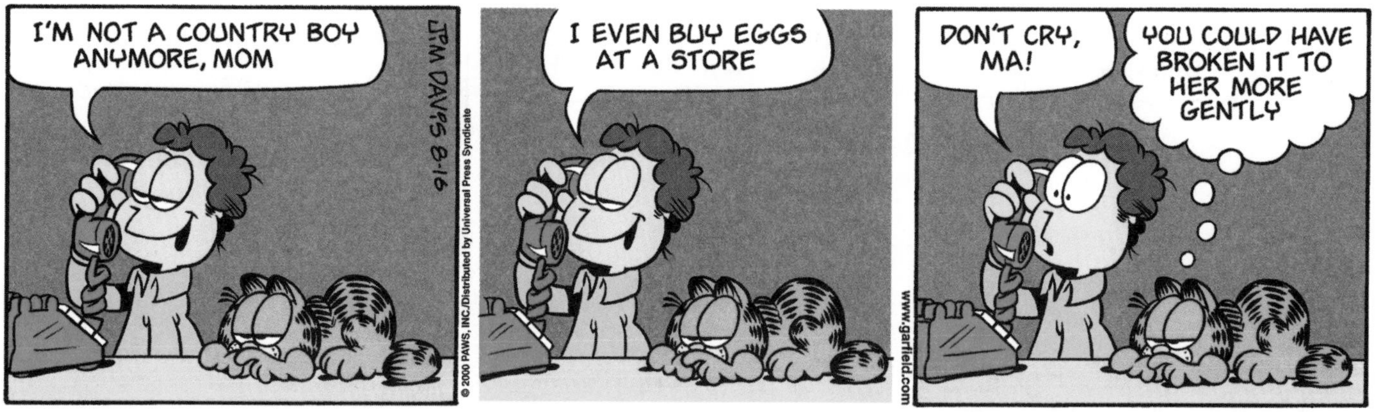
I'M NOT A COUNTRY BOY ANYMORE, MOM
JIM DAVIS 8-16
© 2000 PAWS, INC./Distributed by Universal Press Syndicate
I EVEN BUY EGGS AT A STORE
www.garfield.com
DON'T CRY, MA!
YOU COULD HAVE BROKEN IT TO HER MORE GENTLY

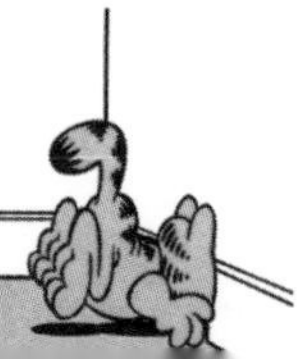

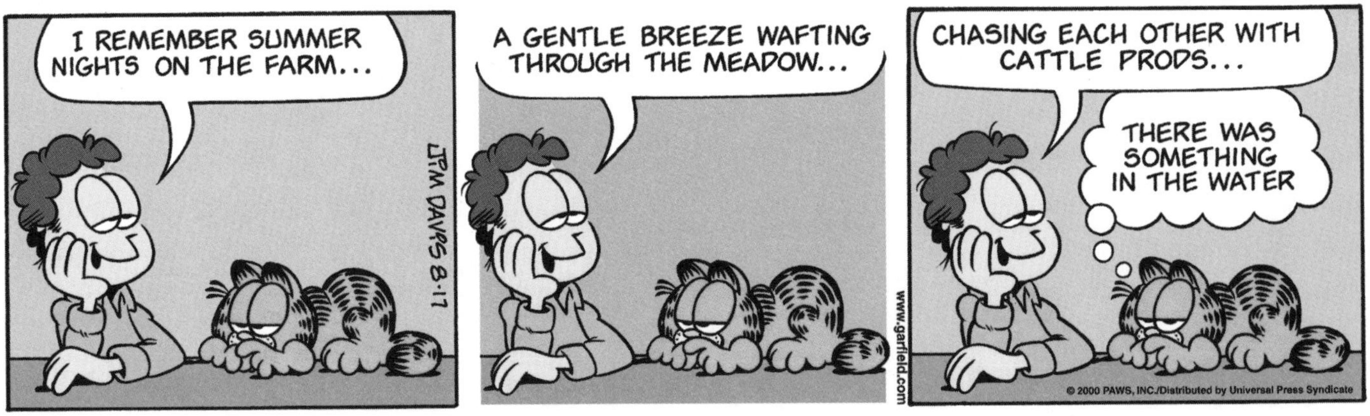
I REMEMBER SUMMER NIGHTS ON THE FARM...
JIM DAVIS 8-17
A GENTLE BREEZE WAFTING THROUGH THE MEADOW...
www.garfield.com
CHASING EACH OTHER WITH CATTLE PRODS...
THERE WAS SOMETHING IN THE WATER
© 2000 PAWS, INC./Distributed by Universal Press Syndicate

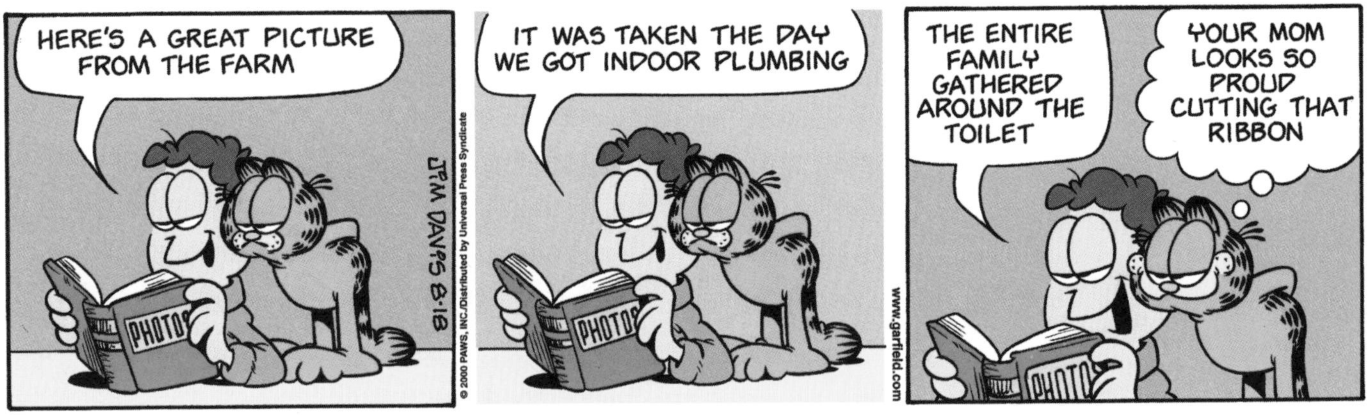
HERE'S A GREAT PICTURE FROM THE FARM
PHOTOS
JIM DAVIS 8-18
© 2000 PAWS, INC./Distributed by Universal Press Syndicate
IT WAS TAKEN THE DAY WE GOT INDOOR PLUMBING
www.garfield.com
THE ENTIRE FAMILY GATHERED AROUND THE TOILET
YOUR MOM LOOKS SO PROUD CUTTING THAT RIBBON

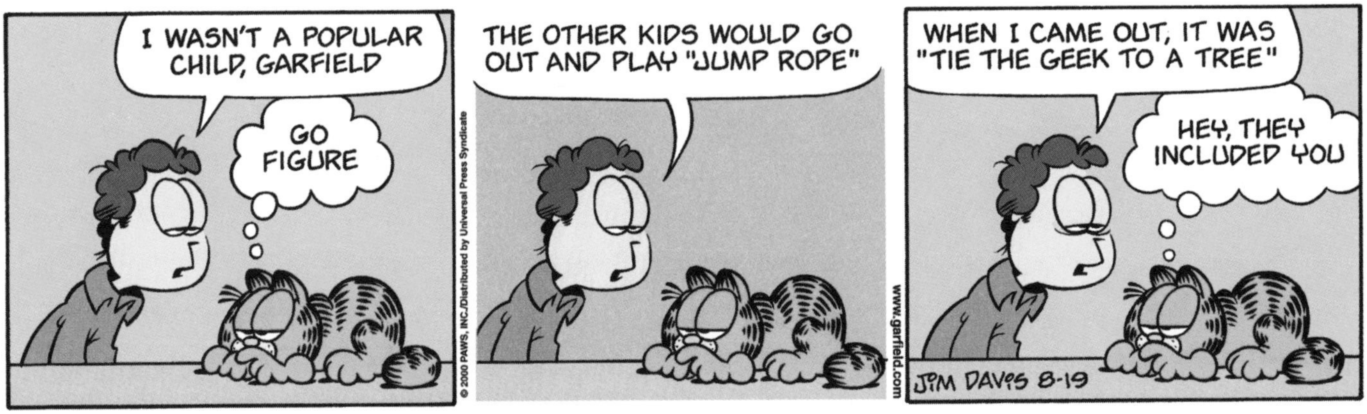
I WASN'T A POPULAR CHILD, GARFIELD
GO FIGURE
© 2000 PAWS, INC./Distributed by Universal Press Syndicate
THE OTHER KIDS WOULD GO OUT AND PLAY "JUMP ROPE"
www.garfield.com
WHEN I CAME OUT, IT WAS "TIE THE GEEK TO A TREE"
HEY, THEY INCLUDED YOU
JIM DAVIS 8-19

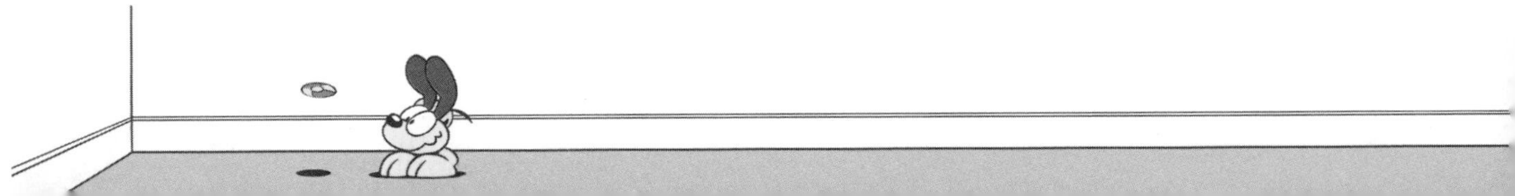

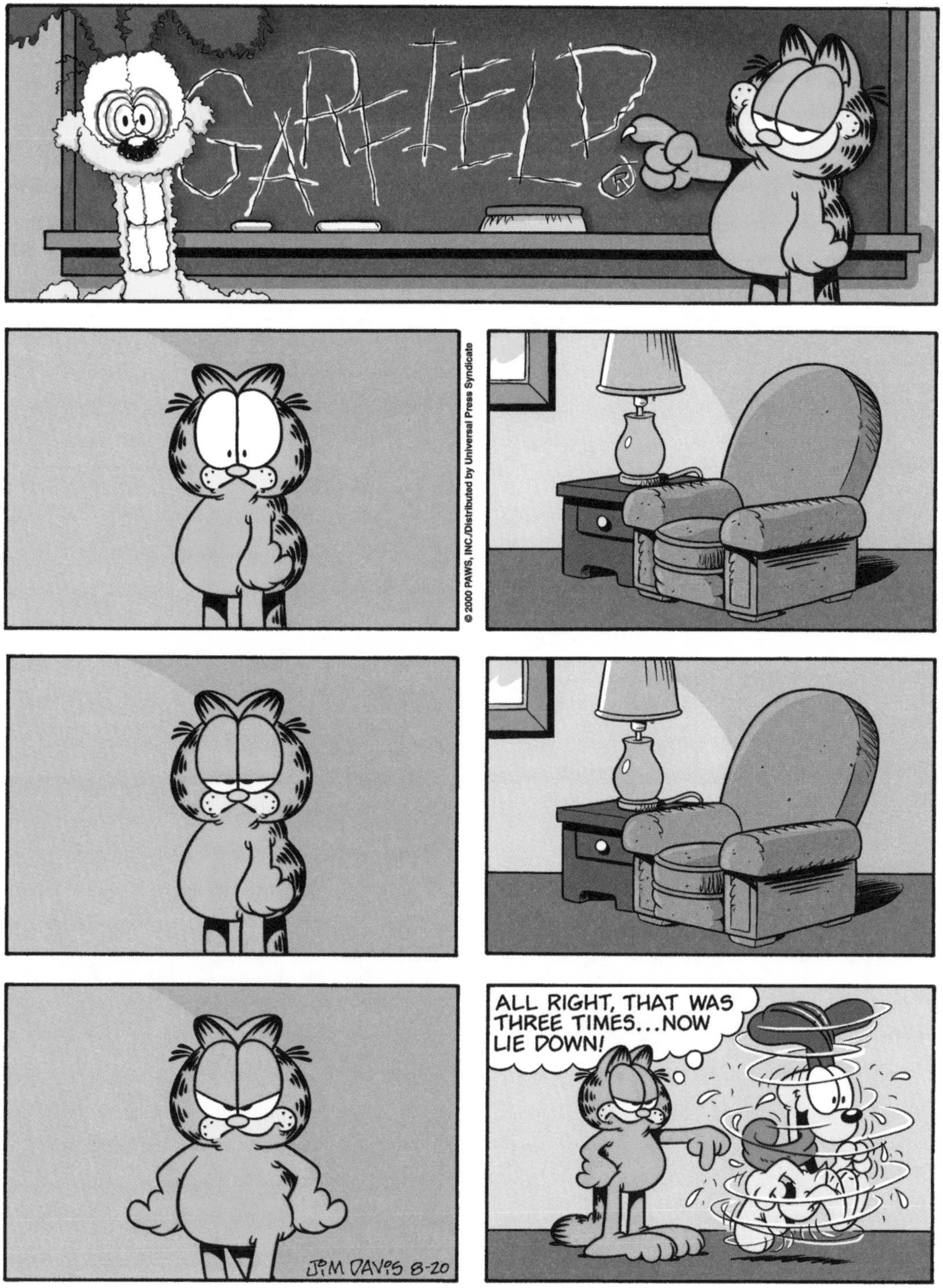
GARFIELD®
© 2000 PAWS, INC./Distributed by Universal Press Syndicate
JIM DAVIS 8-20
ALL RIGHT, THAT WAS THREE TIMES...NOW LIE DOWN!

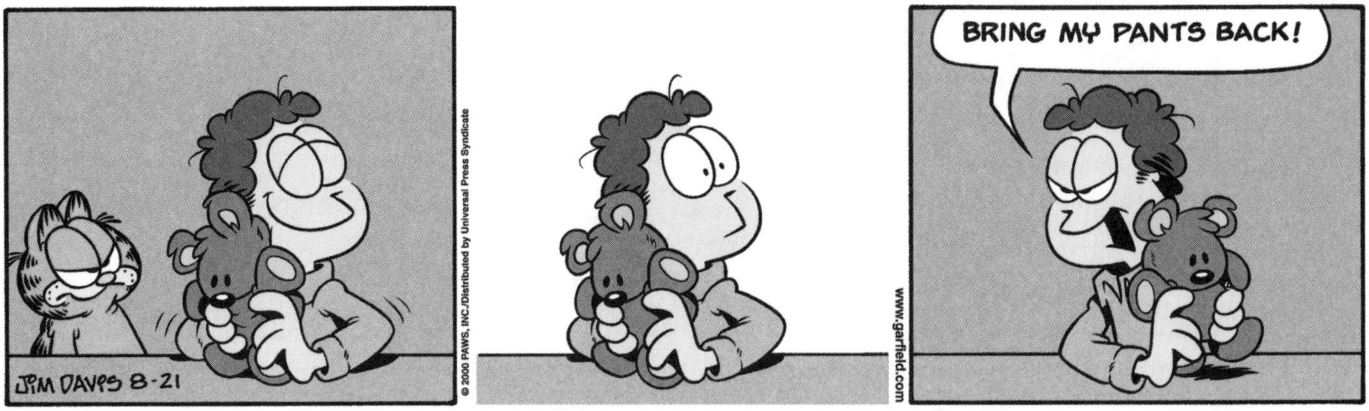
JIM DAVIS 8-21
© 2000 PAWS, INC./Distributed by Universal Press Syndicate
www.garfield.com
BRING MY PANTS BACK!

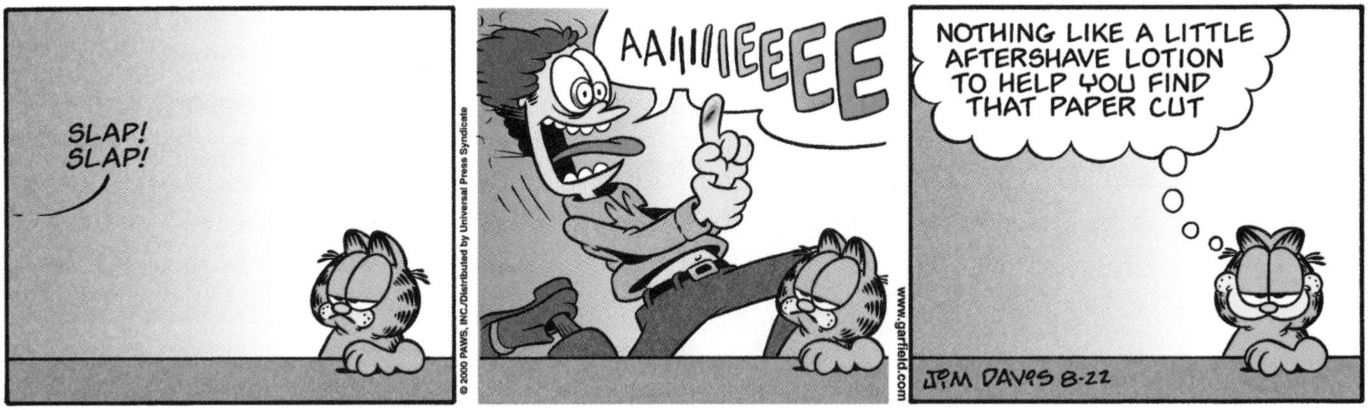
SLAP!
SLAP!
© 2000 PAWS, INC./Distributed by Universal Press Syndicate
AAIIIIIIEEEEE
www.garfield.com
NOTHING LIKE A LITTLE AFTERSHAVE LOTION TO HELP YOU FIND THAT PAPER CUT
JIM DAVIS 8-22

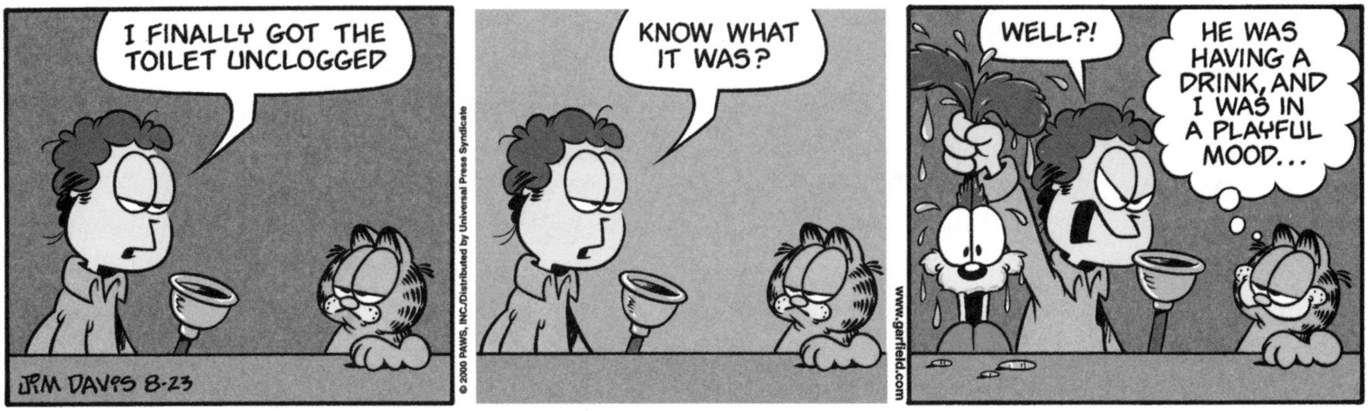
I FINALLY GOT THE TOILET UNCLOGGED
JIM DAVIS 8-23
© 2000 PAWS, INC./Distributed by Universal Press Syndicate
KNOW WHAT IT WAS?
www.garfield.com
WELL?!
HE WAS HAVING A DRINK, AND I WAS IN A PLAYFUL MOOD...

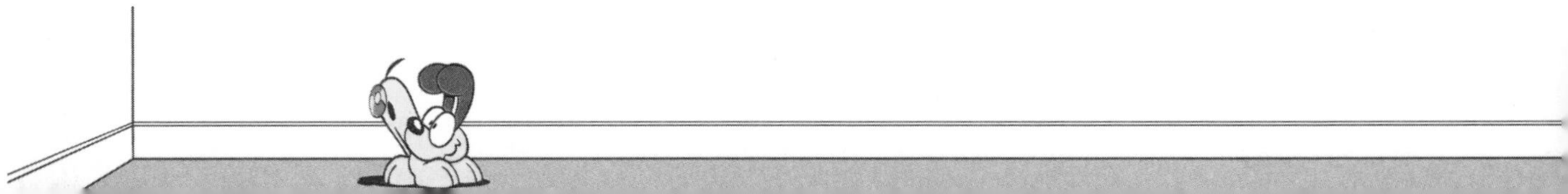

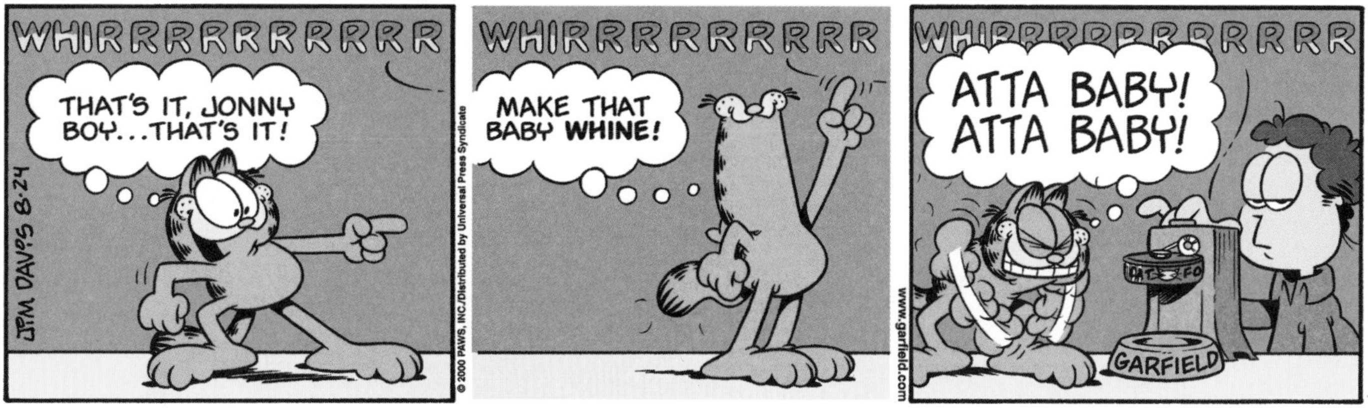
WHIRRRRRRRRRR
THAT'S IT, JONNY BOY...THAT'S IT!
JIM DAVIS 8-24
WHIRRRRRRRRRR
MAKE THAT BABY **WHINE!**
© 2000 PAWS, INC./Distributed by Universal Press Syndicate
WHIRRRRRRRRRRRRR
ATTA BABY! ATTA BABY!
GARFIELD
www.garfield.com

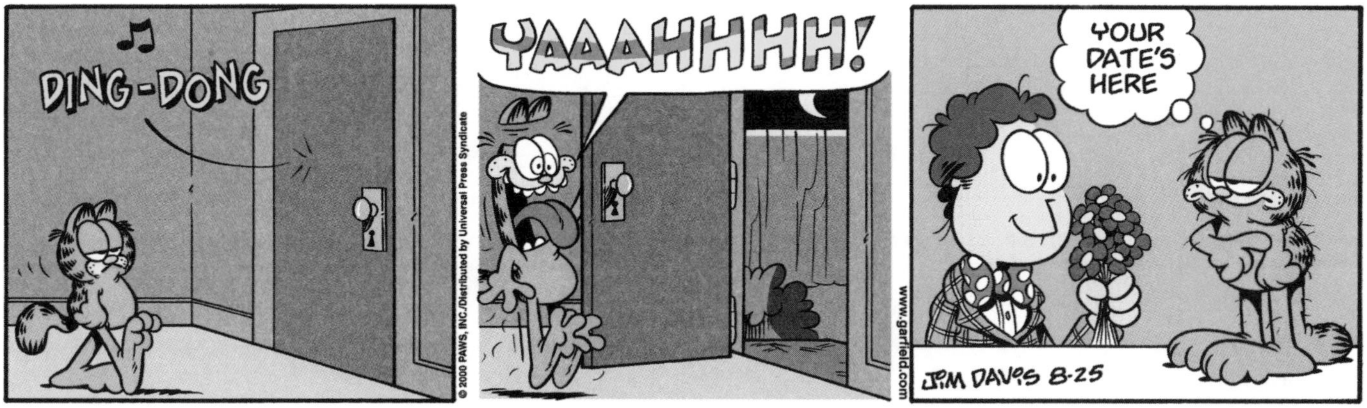
DING-DONG
© 2000 PAWS, INC./Distributed by Universal Press Syndicate
YAAAHHHH!
www.garfield.com
YOUR DATE'S HERE
JIM DAVIS 8-25

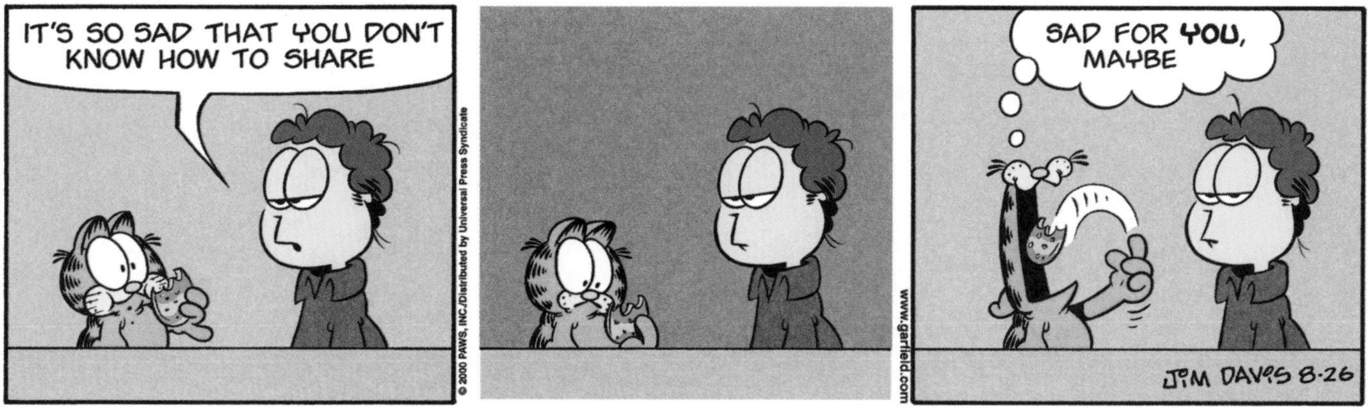
IT'S SO SAD THAT YOU DON'T KNOW HOW TO SHARE
© 2000 PAWS, INC./Distributed by Universal Press Syndicate
www.garfield.com
SAD FOR **YOU**, MAYBE
JIM DAVIS 8-26

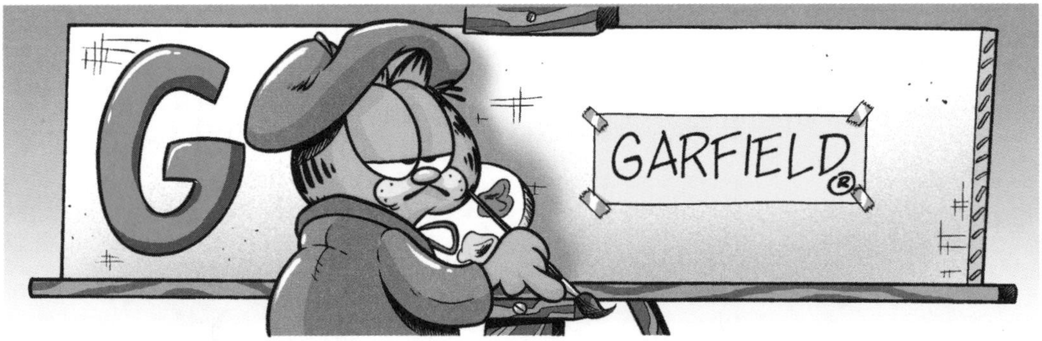
G
GARFIELD®

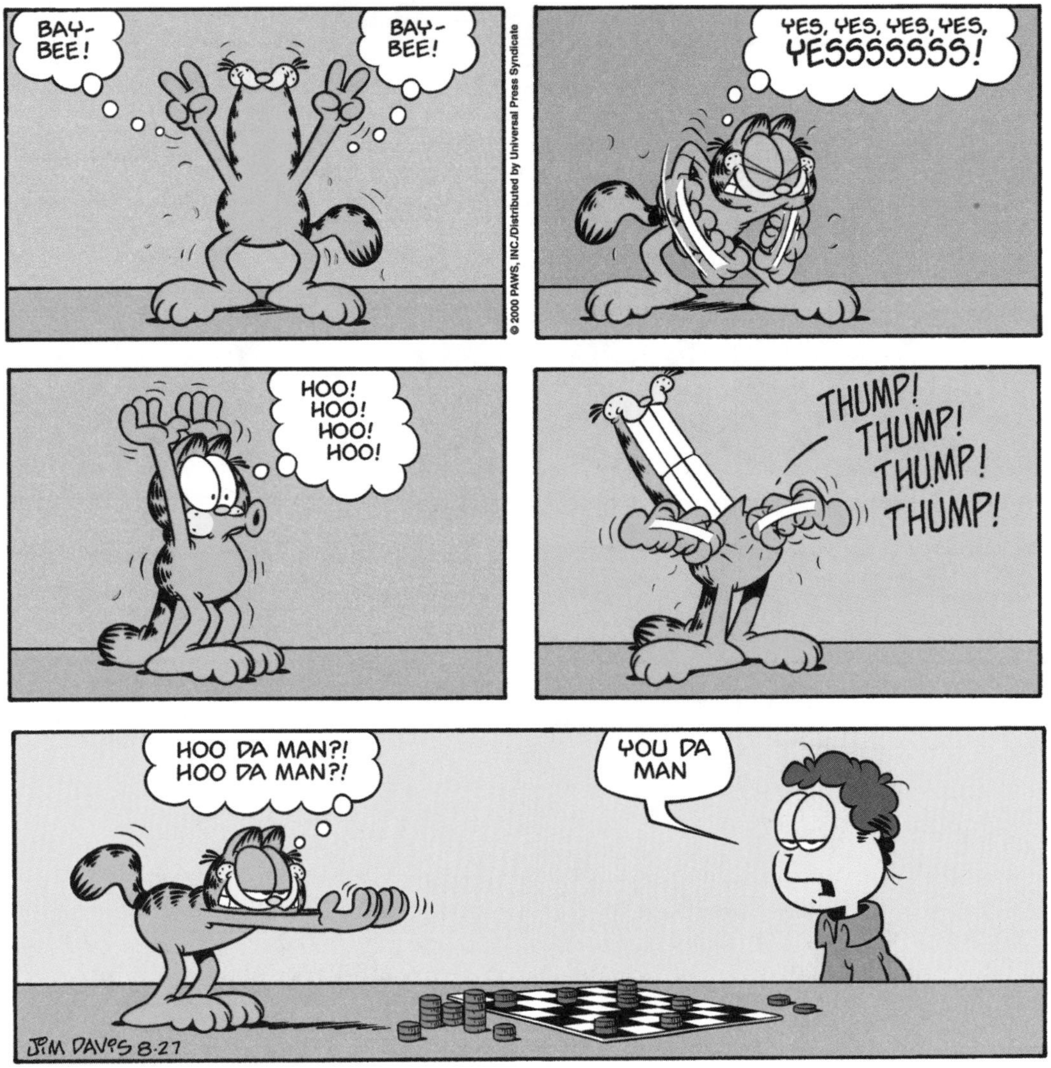
BAY-BEE!
BAY-BEE!
YES, YES, YES, YES, YESSSSSSSS!
HOO! HOO! HOO! HOO!
THUMP! THUMP! THUMP! THUMP!
HOO DA MAN?! HOO DA MAN?!
YOU DA MAN
JIM DAVIS 8-27

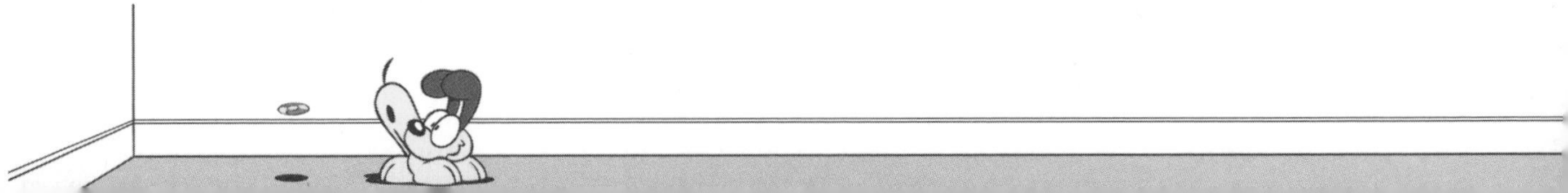

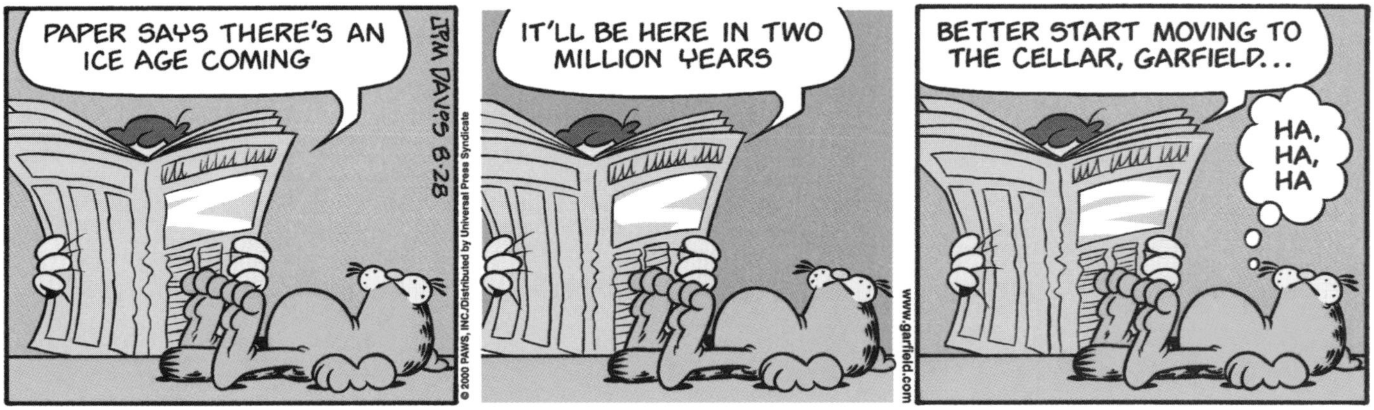
PAPER SAYS THERE'S AN ICE AGE COMING
JIM DAVIS 8-28
© 2000 PAWS, INC./Distributed by Universal Press Syndicate
IT'LL BE HERE IN TWO MILLION YEARS
www.garfield.com
BETTER START MOVING TO THE CELLAR, GARFIELD...
HA, HA, HA

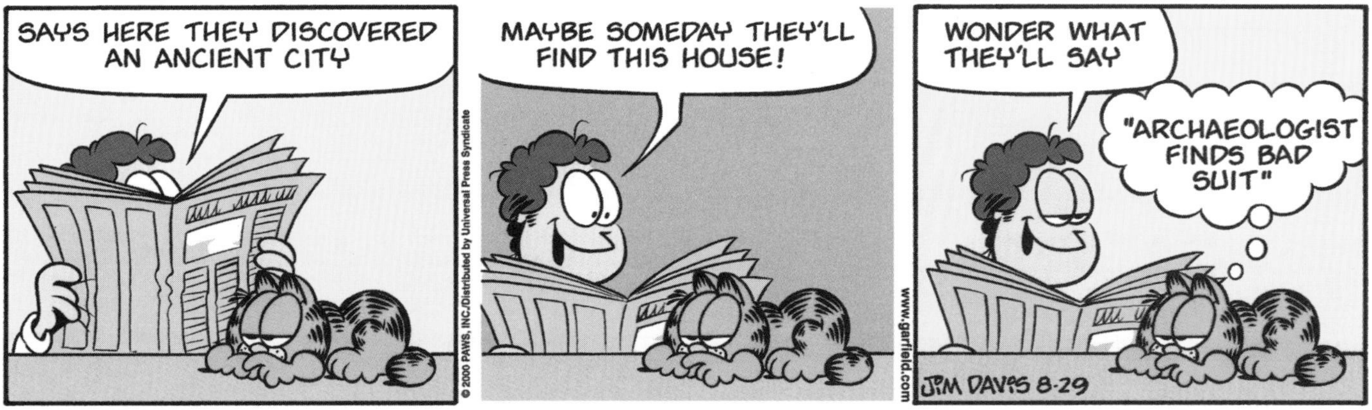
SAYS HERE THEY DISCOVERED AN ANCIENT CITY
© 2000 PAWS, INC./Distributed by Universal Press Syndicate
MAYBE SOMEDAY THEY'LL FIND THIS HOUSE!
www.garfield.com
WONDER WHAT THEY'LL SAY
"ARCHAEOLOGIST FINDS BAD SUIT"
JIM DAVIS 8-29

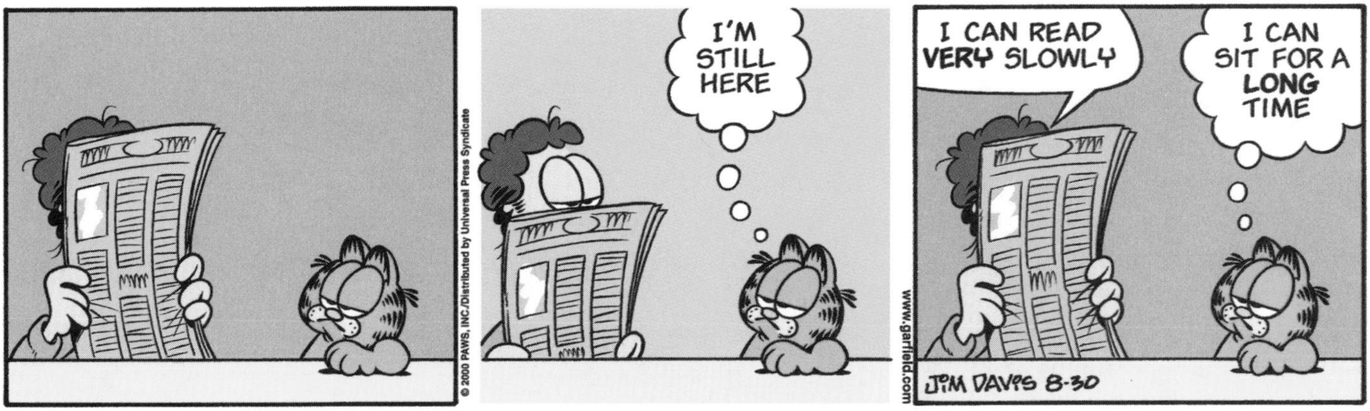
© 2000 PAWS, INC./Distributed by Universal Press Syndicate
I'M STILL HERE
www.garfield.com
I CAN READ **VERY** SLOWLY
I CAN SIT FOR A **LONG** TIME
JIM DAVIS 8-30

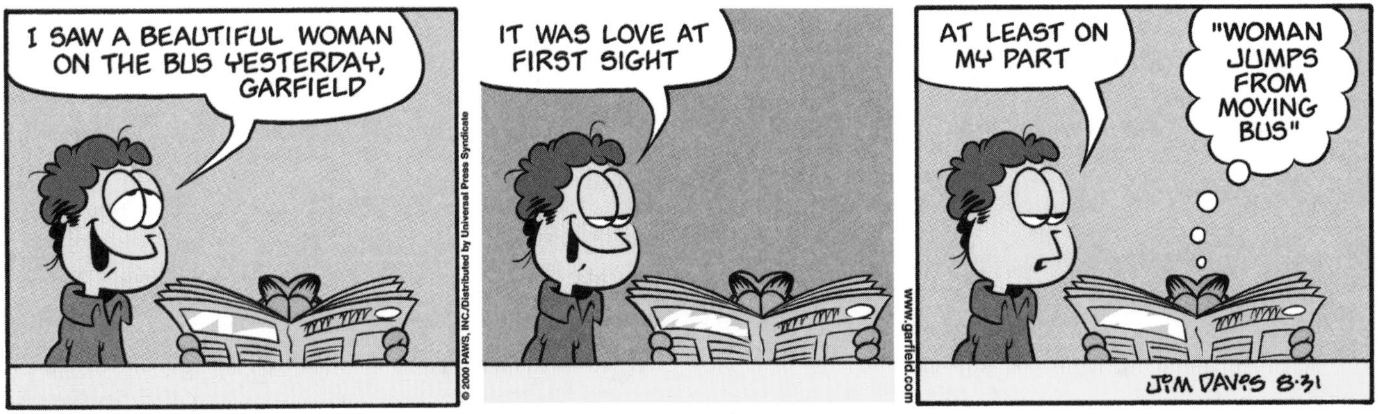
I SAW A BEAUTIFUL WOMAN ON THE BUS YESTERDAY, GARFIELD
© 2000 PAWS, INC/Distributed by Universal Press Syndicate
IT WAS LOVE AT FIRST SIGHT
www.garfield.com
AT LEAST ON MY PART
"WOMAN JUMPS FROM MOVING BUS"
JIM DAVIS 8-31

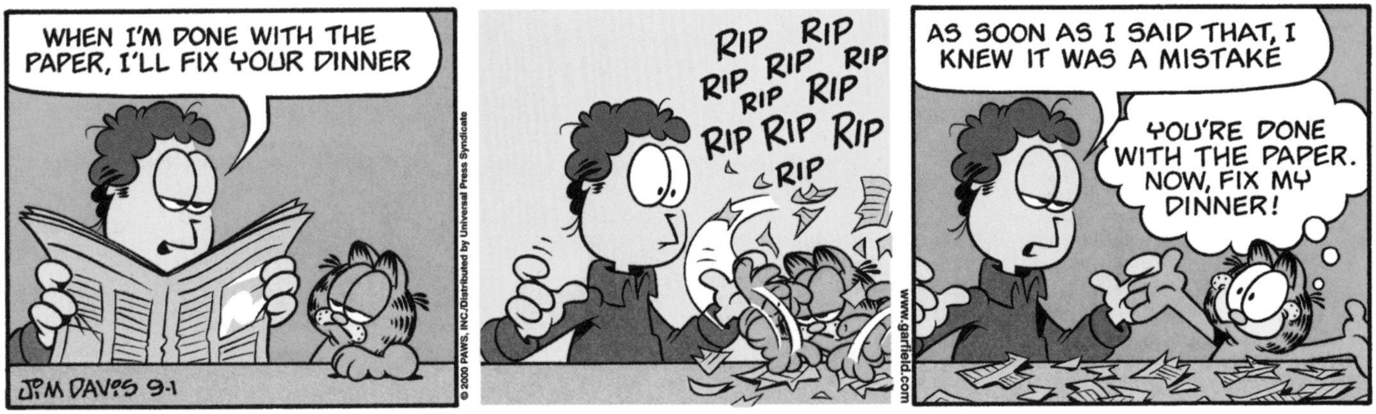
WHEN I'M DONE WITH THE PAPER, I'LL FIX YOUR DINNER
JIM DAVIS 9-1
© 2000 PAWS, INC/Distributed by Universal Press Syndicate
RIP RIP RIP RIP RIP RIP RIP RIP RIP RIP RIP
www.garfield.com
AS SOON AS I SAID THAT, I KNEW IT WAS A MISTAKE
YOU'RE DONE WITH THE PAPER. NOW, FIX MY DINNER!

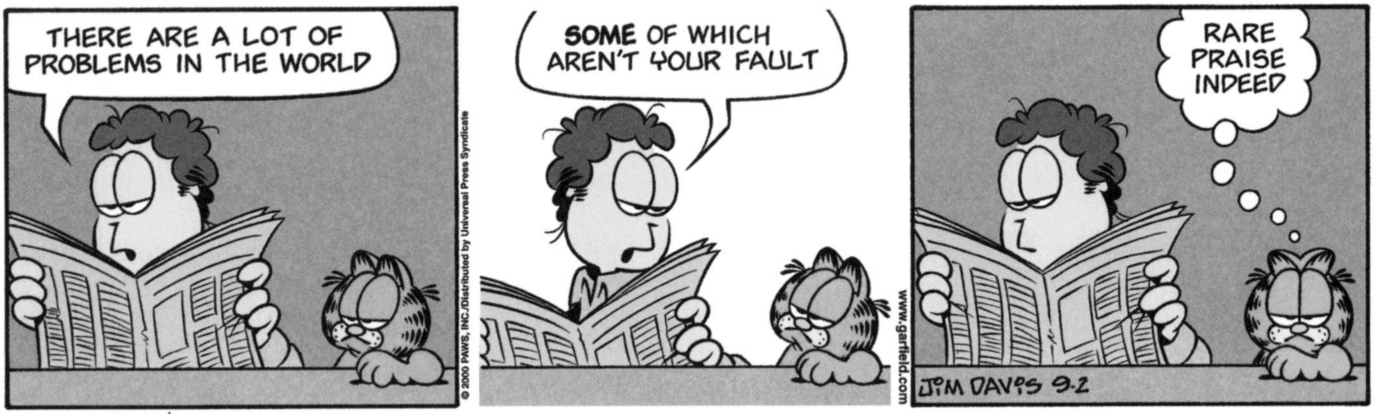
THERE ARE A LOT OF PROBLEMS IN THE WORLD
© 2000 PAWS, INC/Distributed by Universal Press Syndicate
SOME OF WHICH AREN'T YOUR FAULT
www.garfield.com
RARE PRAISE INDEED
JIM DAVIS 9-2

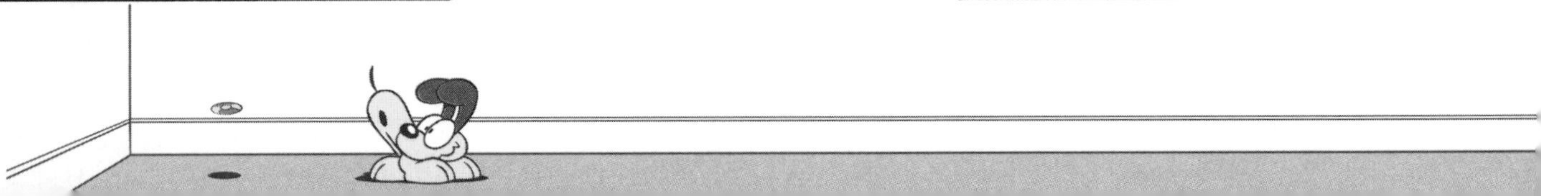

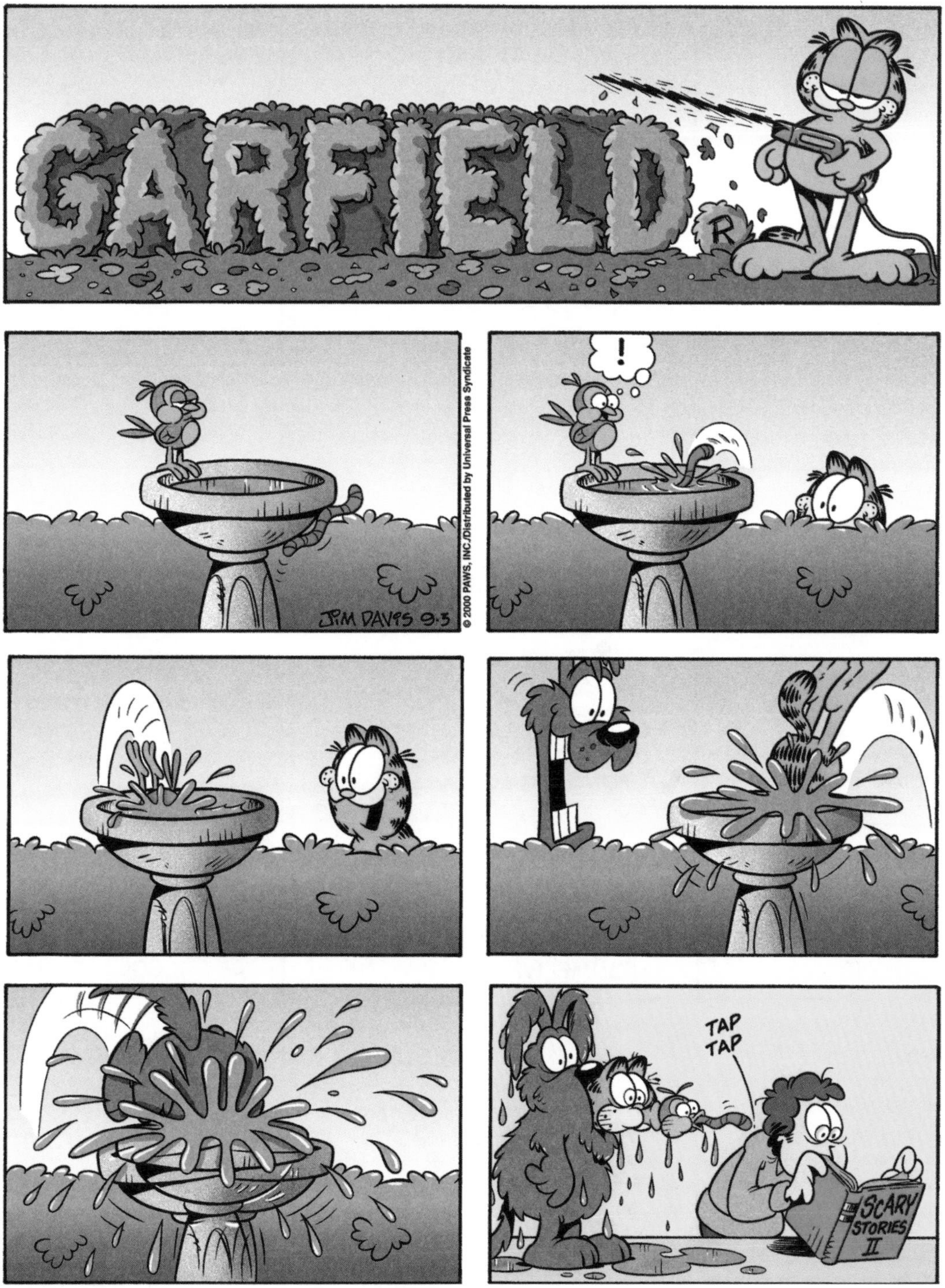
GARFIELD ®
© 2000 PAWS, INC./Distributed by Universal Press Syndicate
JIM DAVIS 9-3
!
TAP
TAP
SCARY STORIES II

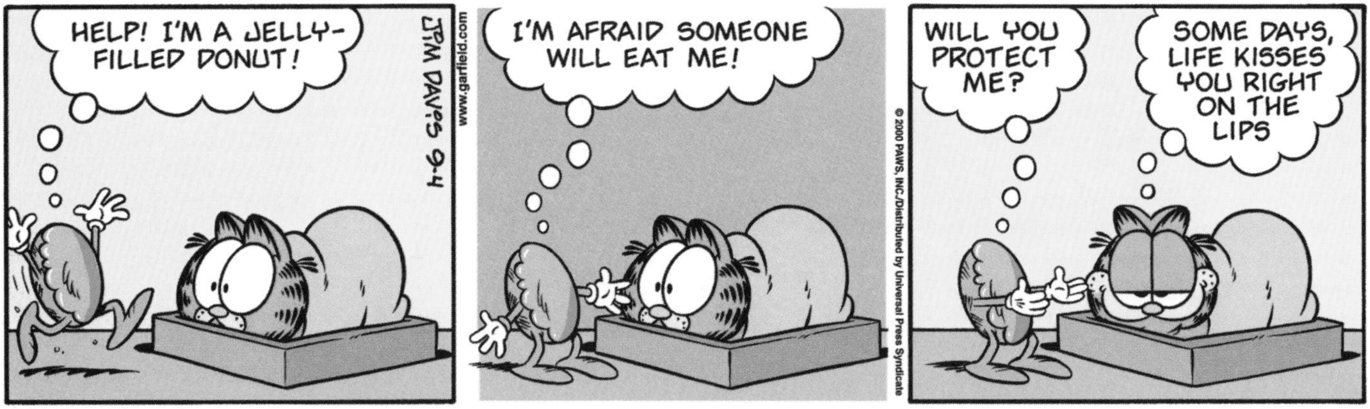
HELP! I'M A JELLY-FILLED DONUT!
JIM DAVIS 9-4
www.garfield.com
I'M AFRAID SOMEONE WILL EAT ME!
© 2000 PAWS, INC./Distributed by Universal Press Syndicate
WILL YOU PROTECT ME?
SOME DAYS, LIFE KISSES YOU RIGHT ON THE LIPS

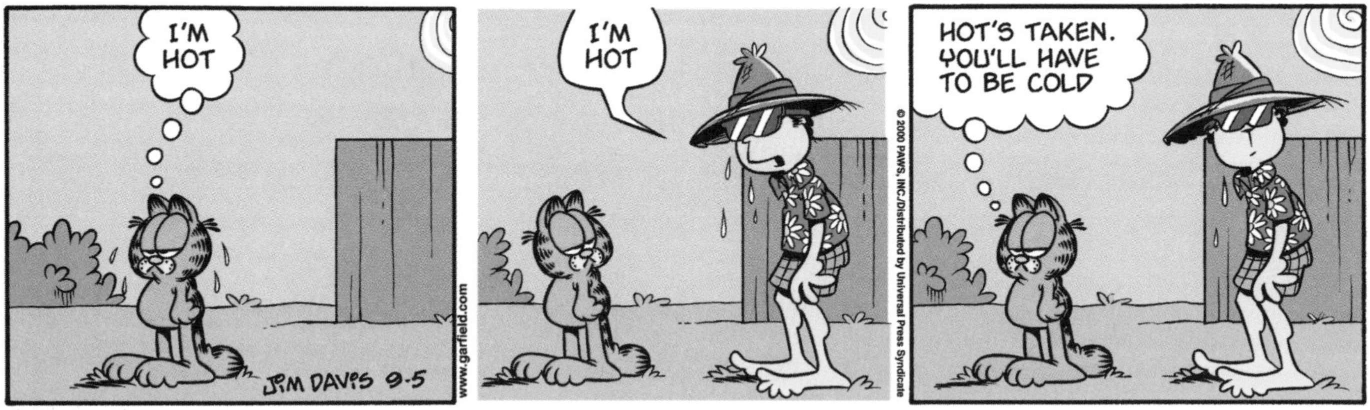
I'M HOT
JIM DAVIS 9-5
www.garfield.com
I'M HOT
© 2000 PAWS, INC./Distributed by Universal Press Syndicate
HOT'S TAKEN. YOU'LL HAVE TO BE COLD

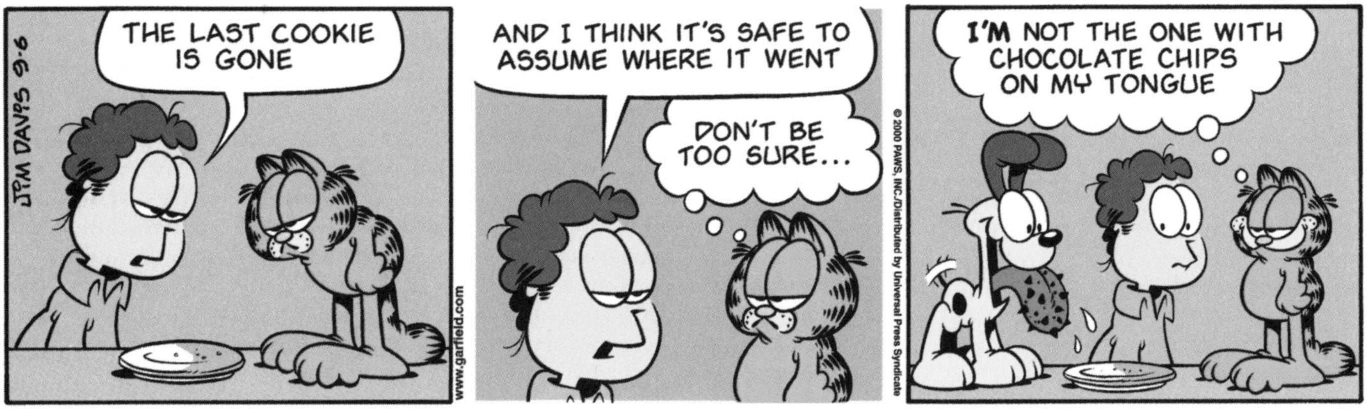
JIM DAVIS 9-6
THE LAST COOKIE IS GONE
www.garfield.com
AND I THINK IT'S SAFE TO ASSUME WHERE IT WENT
DON'T BE TOO SURE...
© 2000 PAWS, INC./Distributed by Universal Press Syndicate
I'M NOT THE ONE WITH CHOCOLATE CHIPS ON MY TONGUE

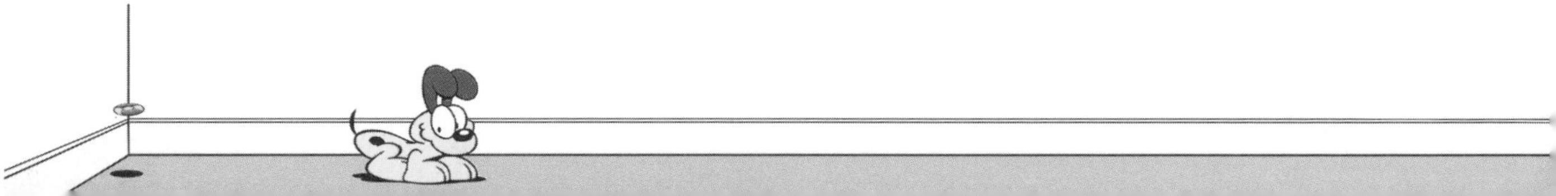

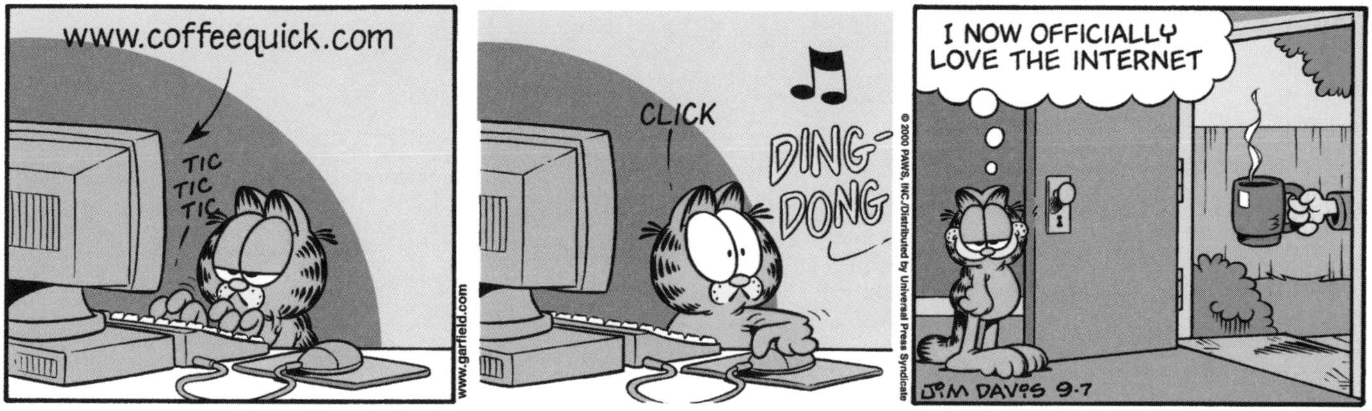
www.coffeequick.com
TIC TIC TIC
www.garfield.com
CLICK
DING-DONG
© 2000 PAWS, INC./Distributed by Universal Press Syndicate
I NOW OFFICIALLY LOVE THE INTERNET
JIM DAVIS 9-7

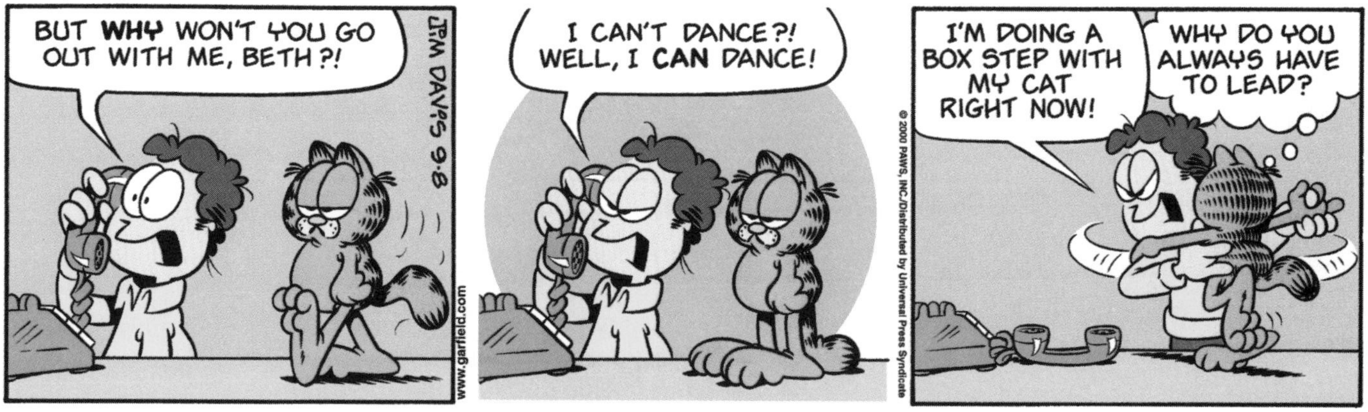
BUT **WHY** WON'T YOU GO OUT WITH ME, BETH?!
JIM DAVIS 9-8
www.garfield.com
I CAN'T DANCE?! WELL, I **CAN** DANCE!
© 2000 PAWS, INC./Distributed by Universal Press Syndicate
I'M DOING A BOX STEP WITH MY CAT RIGHT NOW!
WHY DO YOU ALWAYS HAVE TO LEAD?

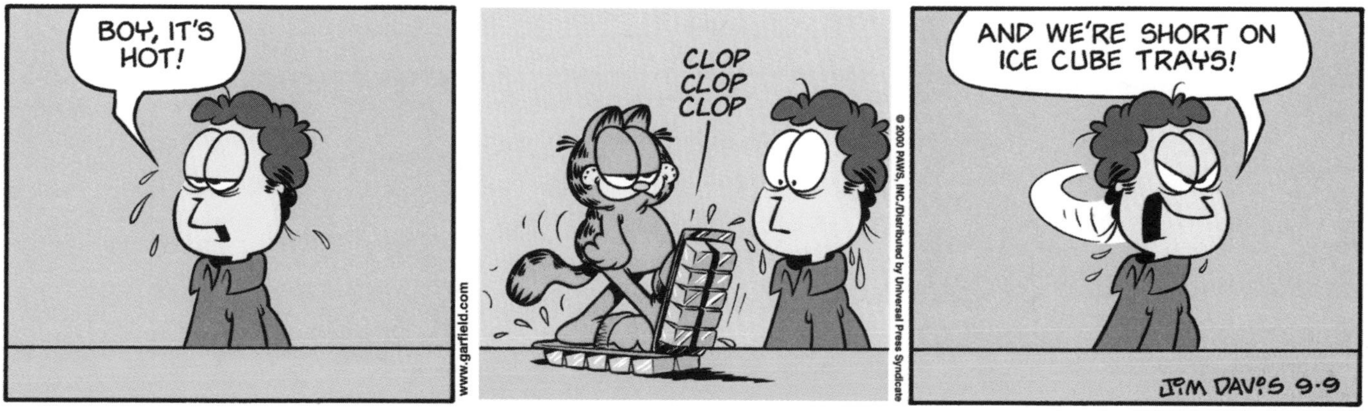
BOY, IT'S HOT!
www.garfield.com
CLOP CLOP CLOP
© 2000 PAWS, INC./Distributed by Universal Press Syndicate
AND WE'RE SHORT ON ICE CUBE TRAYS!
JIM DAVIS 9-9

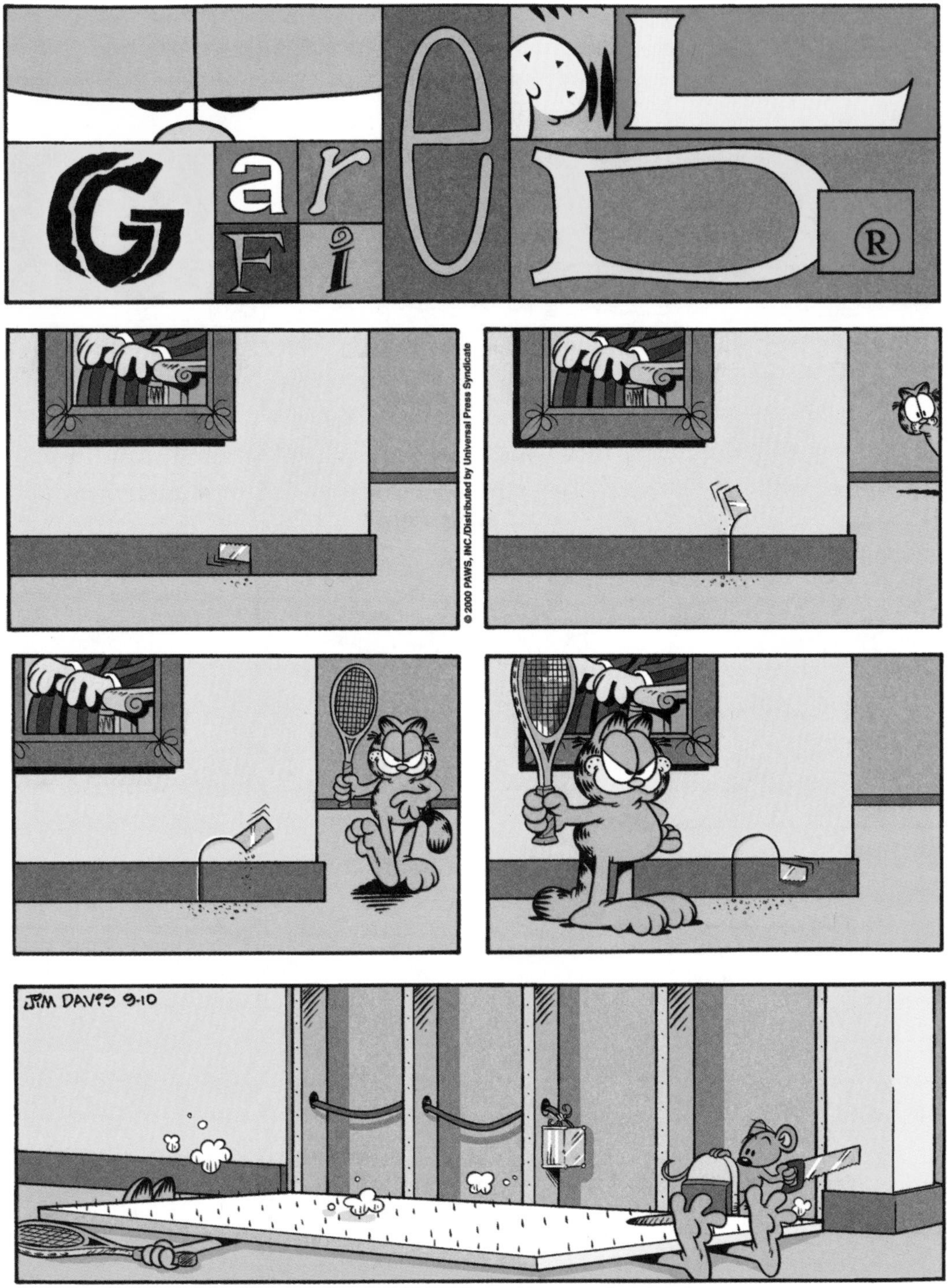
GarFiELD®
© 2000 PAWS, INC./Distributed by Universal Press Syndicate
JIM DAVIS 9-10

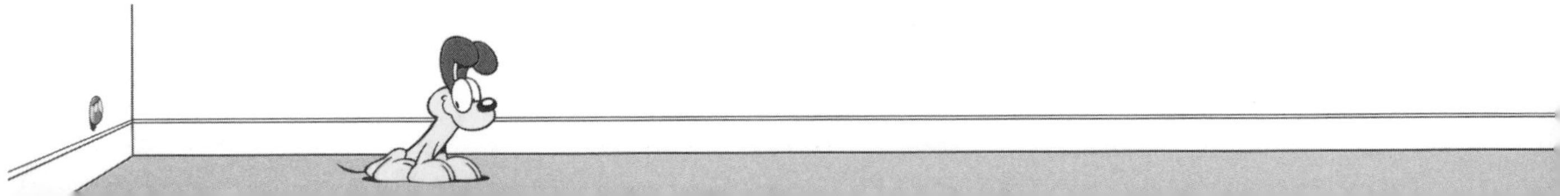

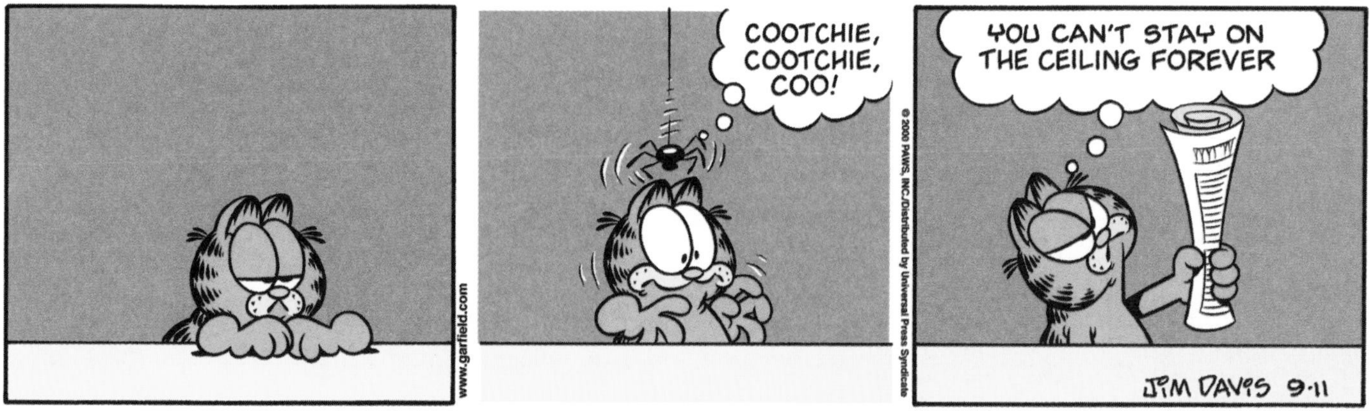
www.garfield.com
COOTCHIE, COOTCHIE, COO!
© 2000 PAWS, INC./Distributed by Universal Press Syndicate
YOU CAN'T STAY ON THE CEILING FOREVER
JIM DAVIS 9-11

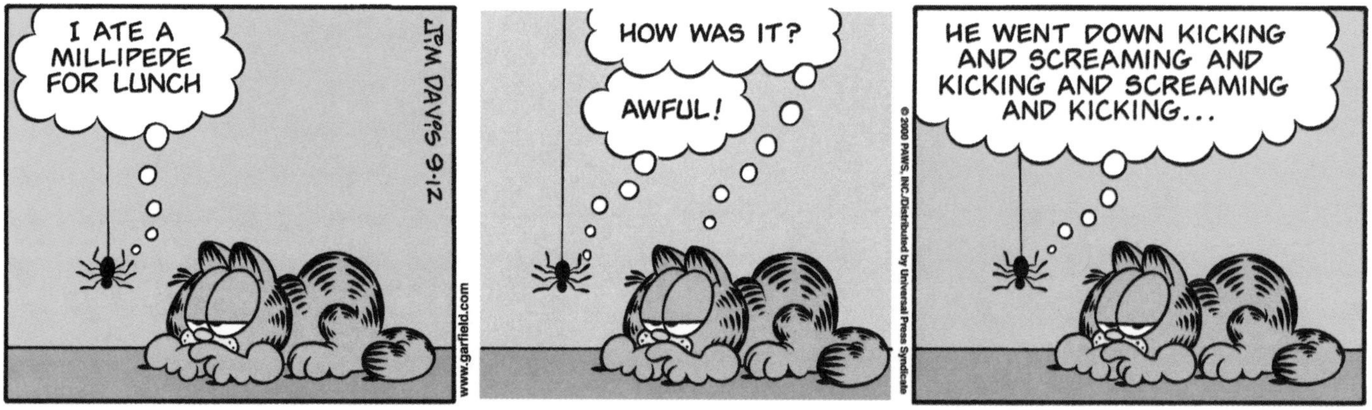
I ATE A MILLIPEDE FOR LUNCH
JIM DAVIS 9-12
www.garfield.com
HOW WAS IT?
AWFUL!
© 2000 PAWS, INC./Distributed by Universal Press Syndicate
HE WENT DOWN KICKING AND SCREAMING AND KICKING AND SCREAMING AND KICKING...

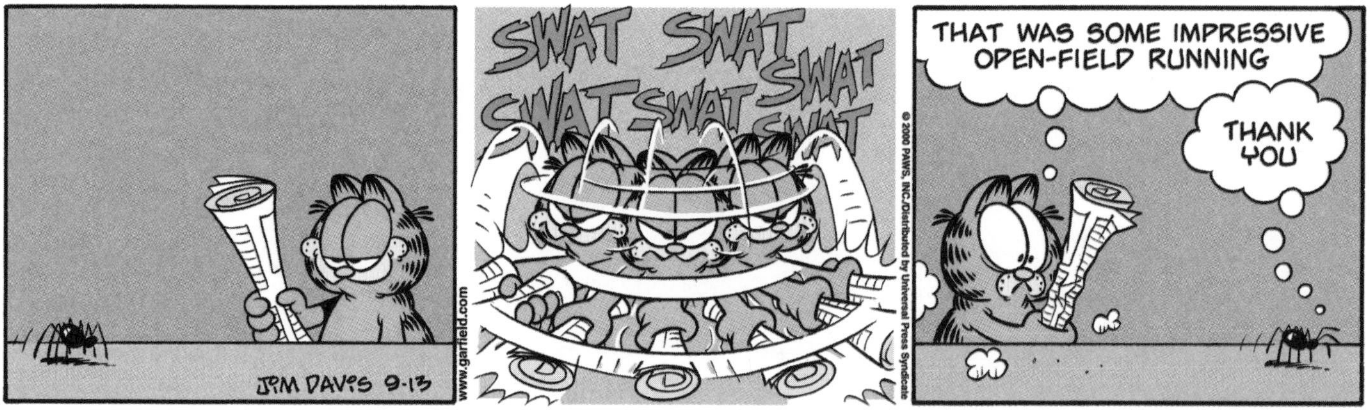
JIM DAVIS 9-13
www.garfield.com
SWAT SWAT SWAT SWAT SWAT SWAT SWAT
© 2000 PAWS, INC./Distributed by Universal Press Syndicate
THAT WAS SOME IMPRESSIVE OPEN-FIELD RUNNING
THANK YOU

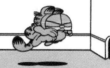

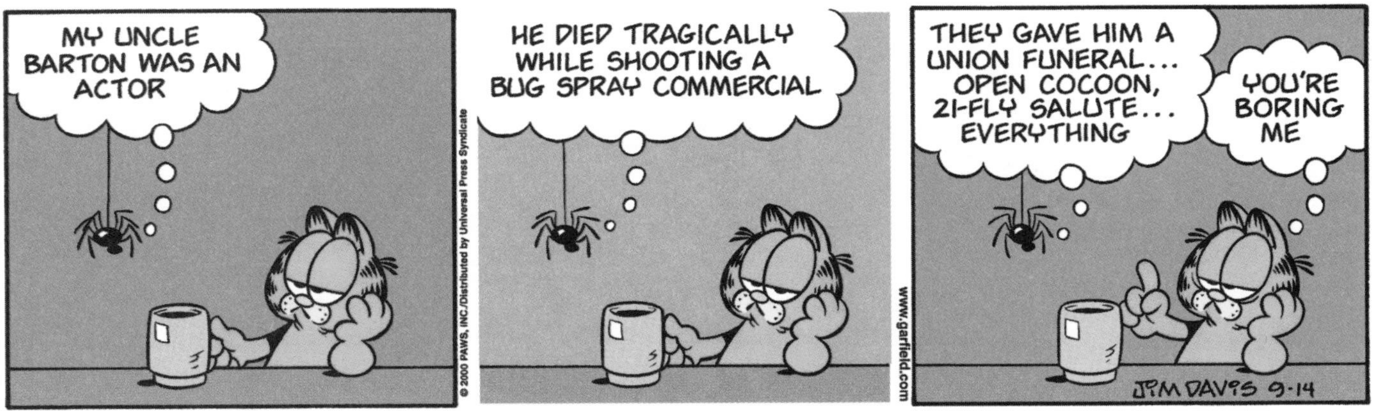
MY UNCLE BARTON WAS AN ACTOR
© 2000 PAWS, INC./Distributed by Universal Press Syndicate
HE DIED TRAGICALLY WHILE SHOOTING A BUG SPRAY COMMERCIAL
www.garfield.com
THEY GAVE HIM A UNION FUNERAL... OPEN COCOON, 21-FLY SALUTE... EVERYTHING
YOU'RE BORING ME
JIM DAVIS 9-14

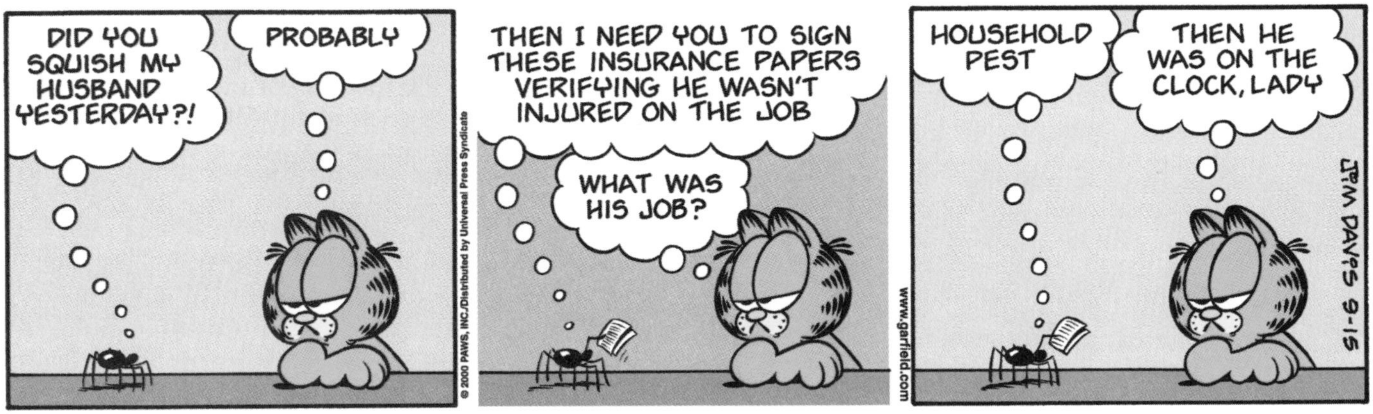
DID YOU SQUISH MY HUSBAND YESTERDAY?!
PROBABLY
© 2000 PAWS, INC./Distributed by Universal Press Syndicate
THEN I NEED YOU TO SIGN THESE INSURANCE PAPERS VERIFYING HE WASN'T INJURED ON THE JOB
WHAT WAS HIS JOB?
www.garfield.com
HOUSEHOLD PEST
THEN HE WAS ON THE CLOCK, LADY
JIM DAVIS 9-15

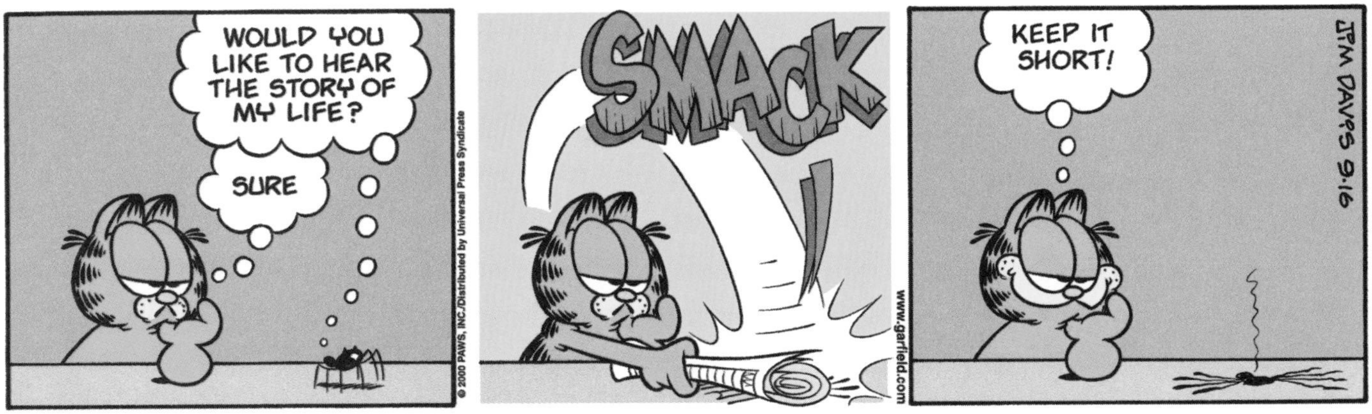
WOULD YOU LIKE TO HEAR THE STORY OF MY LIFE?
SURE
© 2000 PAWS, INC./Distributed by Universal Press Syndicate
SMACK
www.garfield.com
KEEP IT SHORT!
JIM DAVIS 9-16

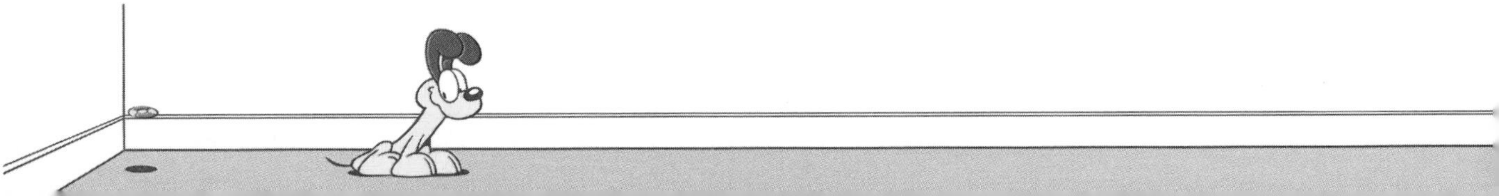

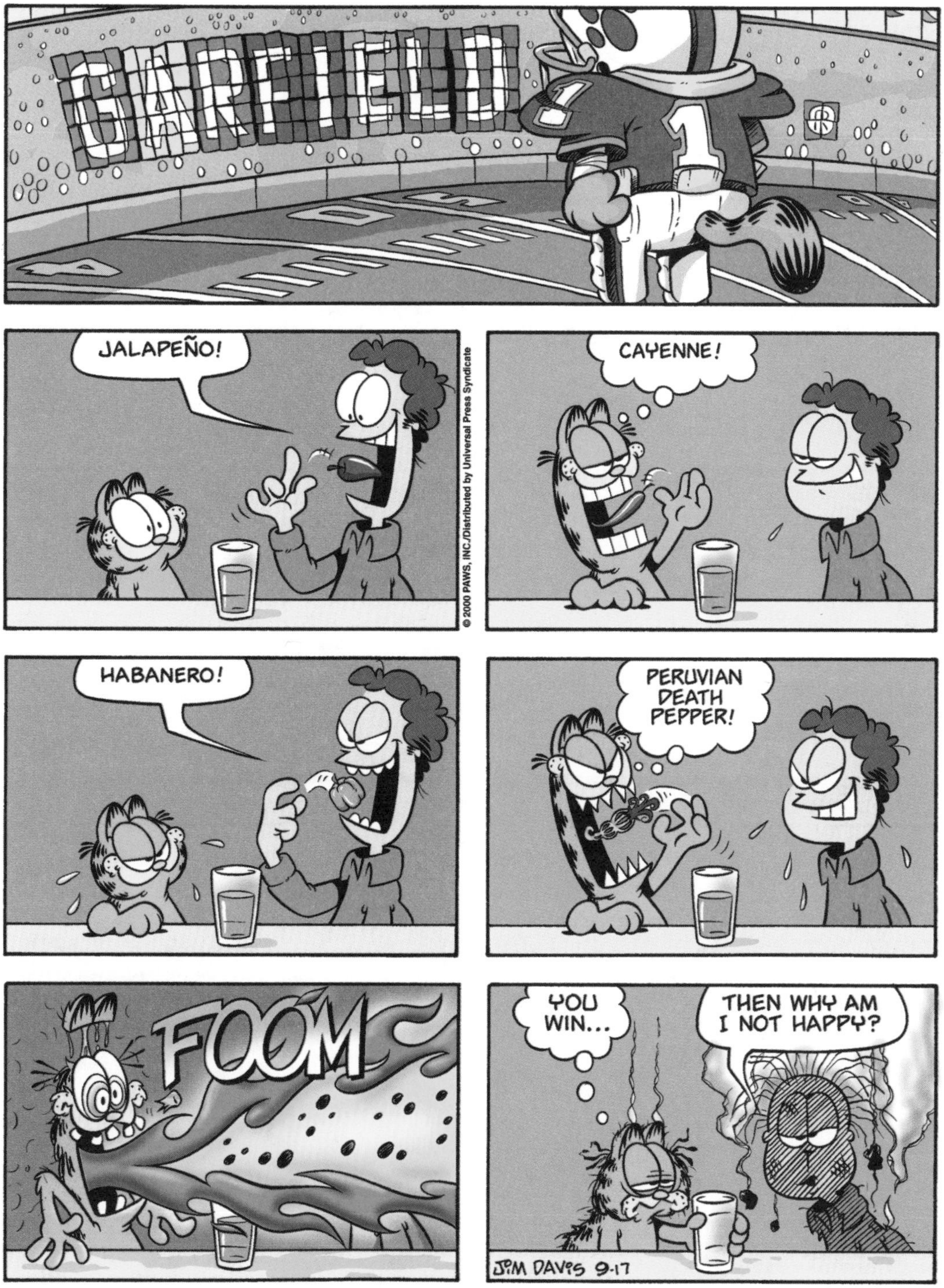
GARFIELD
JALAPEÑO!
CAYENNE!
HABANERO!
PERUVIAN DEATH PEPPER!
FOOM
YOU WIN...
THEN WHY AM I NOT HAPPY?
JIM DAVIS 9-17
© 2000 PAWS, INC./Distributed by Universal Press Syndicate

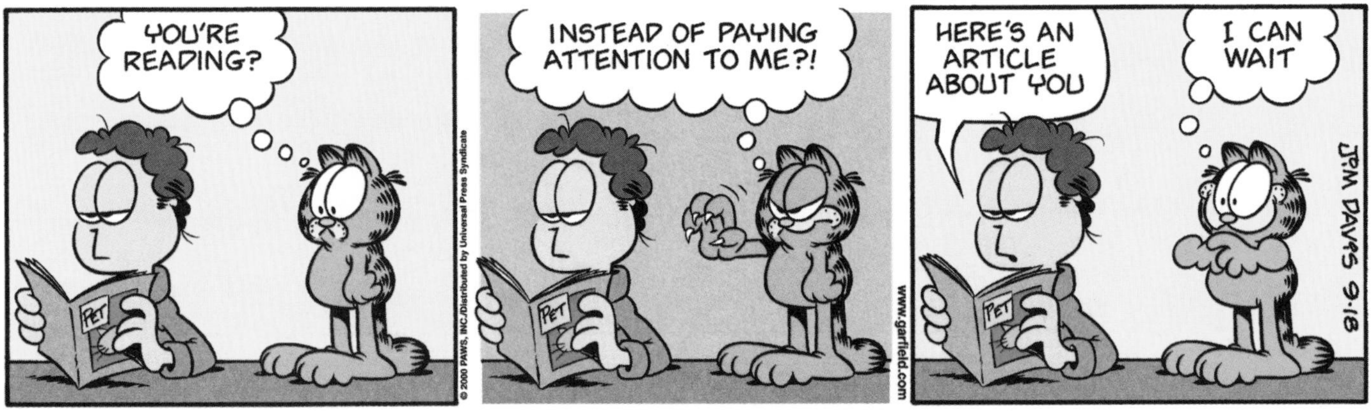
YOU'RE READING?
© 2000 PAWS, INC./Distributed by Universal Press Syndicate
INSTEAD OF PAYING ATTENTION TO ME?!
www.garfield.com
HERE'S AN ARTICLE ABOUT YOU
I CAN WAIT
JIM DAVIS 9·18

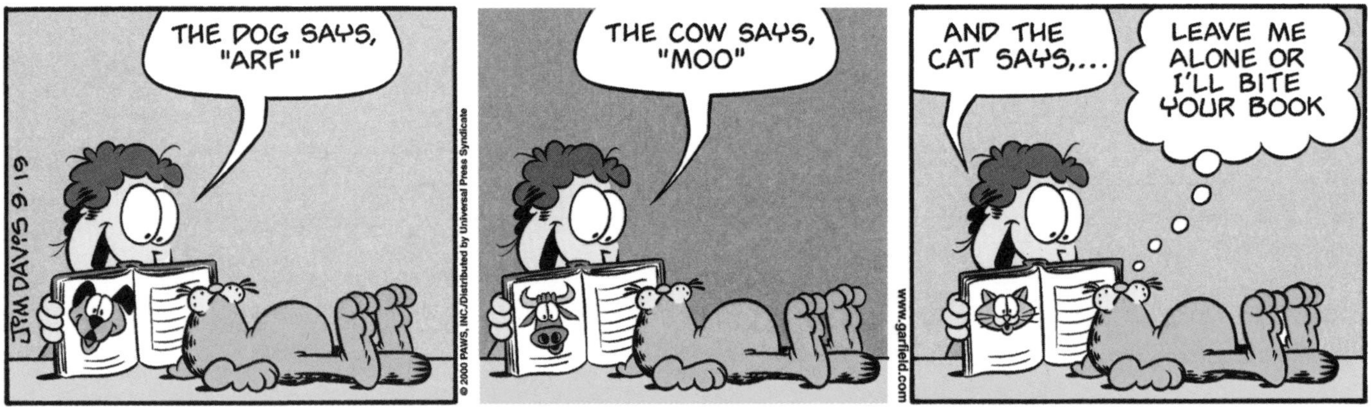
JIM DAVIS 9·19
THE DOG SAYS, "ARF"
© 2000 PAWS, INC./Distributed by Universal Press Syndicate
THE COW SAYS, "MOO"
www.garfield.com
AND THE CAT SAYS,...
LEAVE ME ALONE OR I'LL BITE YOUR BOOK

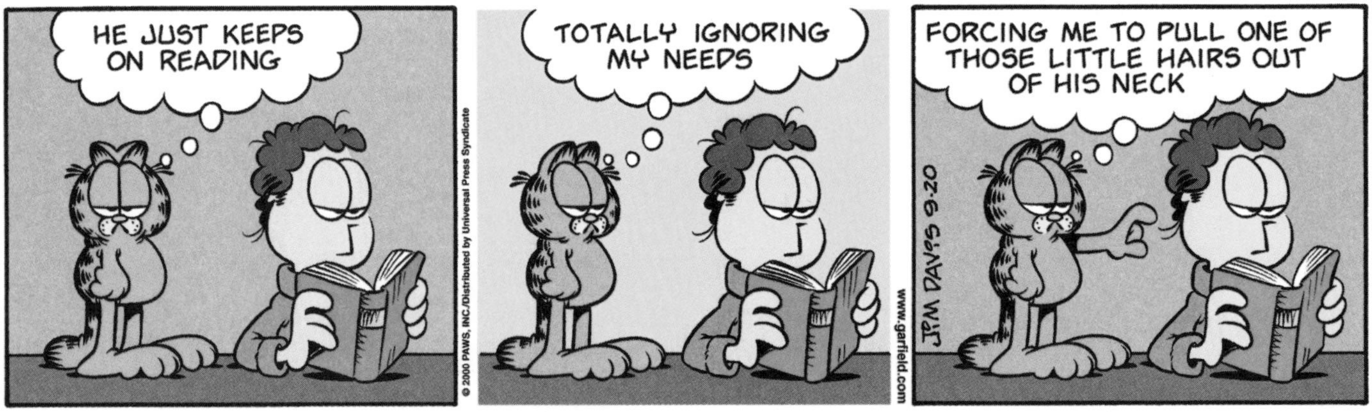
HE JUST KEEPS ON READING
© 2000 PAWS, INC./Distributed by Universal Press Syndicate
TOTALLY IGNORING MY NEEDS
www.garfield.com
FORCING ME TO PULL ONE OF THOSE LITTLE HAIRS OUT OF HIS NECK
JIM DAVIS 9·20

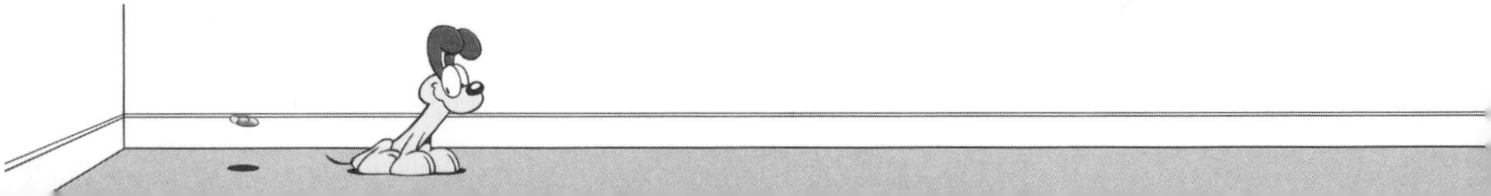

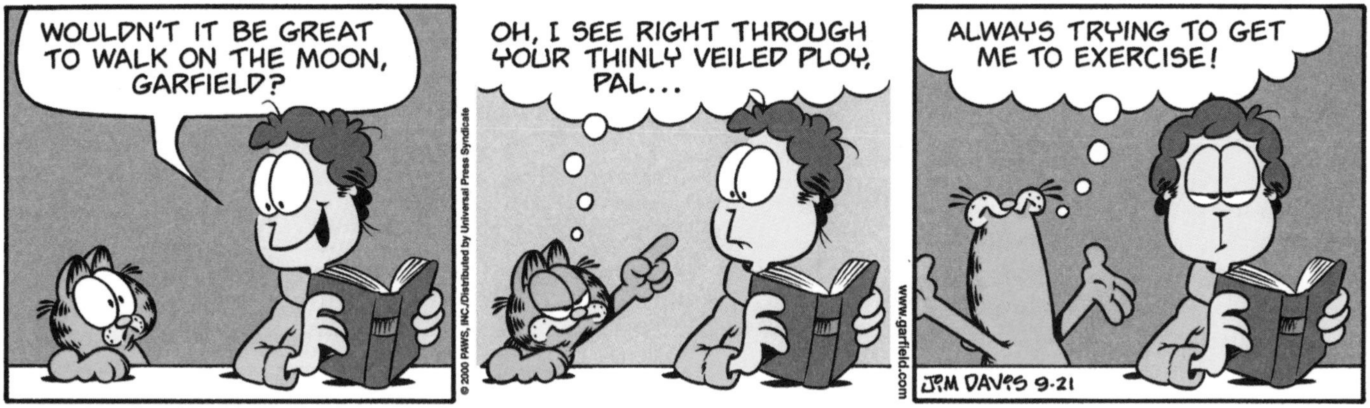
WOULDN'T IT BE GREAT TO WALK ON THE MOON, GARFIELD?
OH, I SEE RIGHT THROUGH YOUR THINLY VEILED PLOY, PAL...
ALWAYS TRYING TO GET ME TO EXERCISE!
JIM DAVIS 9-21
© 2000 PAWS, INC./Distributed by Universal Press Syndicate
www.garfield.com

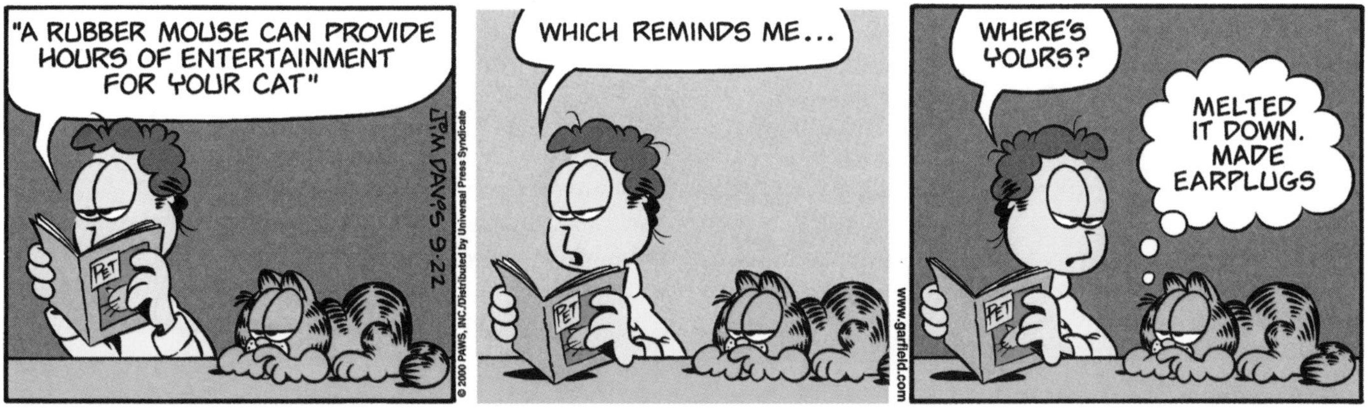
"A RUBBER MOUSE CAN PROVIDE HOURS OF ENTERTAINMENT FOR YOUR CAT"
JIM DAVIS 9-22
WHICH REMINDS ME...
WHERE'S YOURS?
MELTED IT DOWN. MADE EARPLUGS
PET
© 2000 PAWS, INC./Distributed by Universal Press Syndicate
www.garfield.com

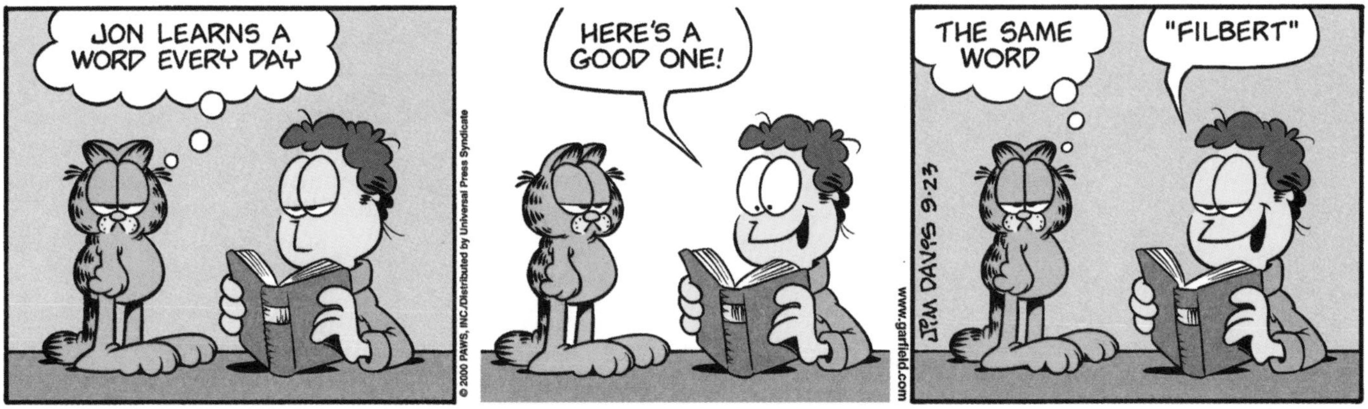
JON LEARNS A WORD EVERY DAY
HERE'S A GOOD ONE!
THE SAME WORD
"FILBERT"
JIM DAVIS 9-23
© 2000 PAWS, INC./Distributed by Universal Press Syndicate
www.garfield.com

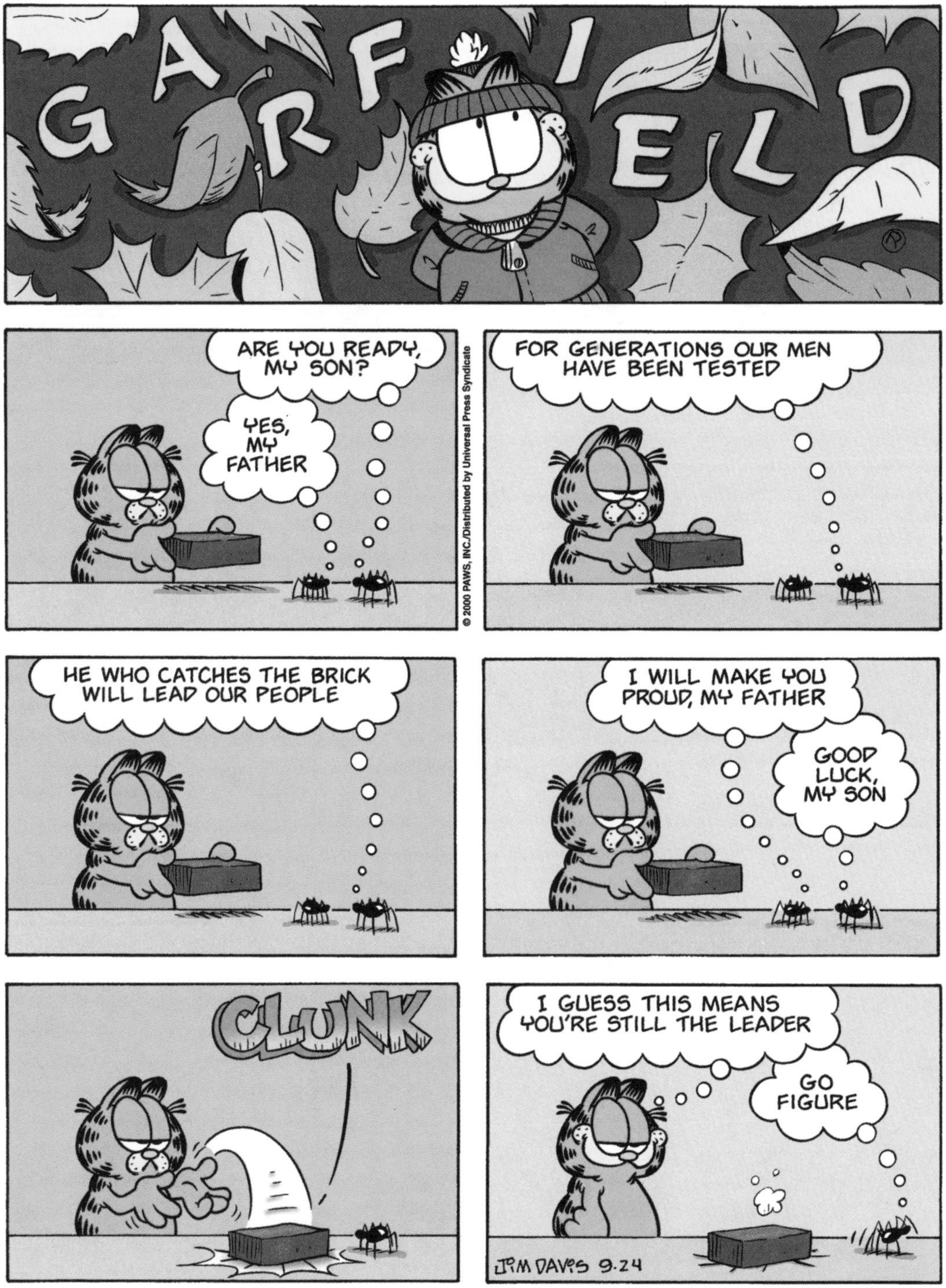
GARFIELD®
© 2000 PAWS, INC./Distributed by Universal Press Syndicate
ARE YOU READY, MY SON?
YES, MY FATHER
FOR GENERATIONS OUR MEN HAVE BEEN TESTED
HE WHO CATCHES THE BRICK WILL LEAD OUR PEOPLE
I WILL MAKE YOU PROUD, MY FATHER
GOOD LUCK, MY SON
CLUNK
I GUESS THIS MEANS YOU'RE STILL THE LEADER
GO FIGURE
JIM DAVIS 9.24

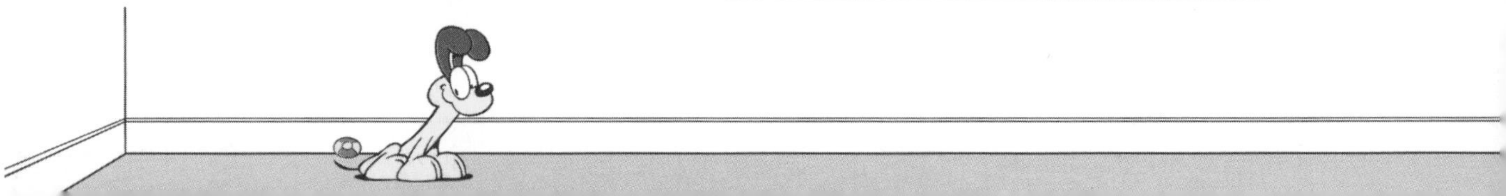

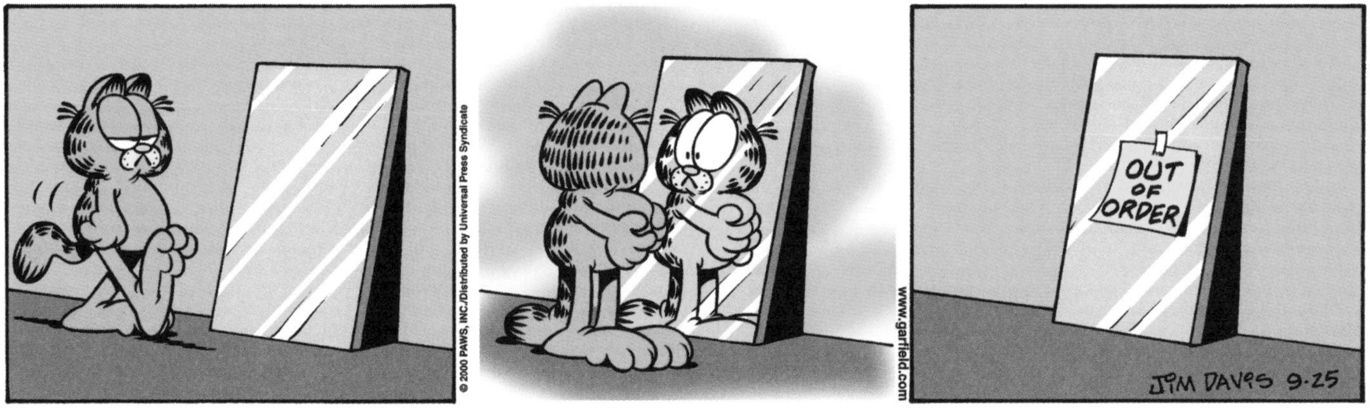
© 2000 PAWS, INC./Distributed by Universal Press Syndicate
www.garfield.com
OUT OF ORDER
JIM DAVIS 9-25

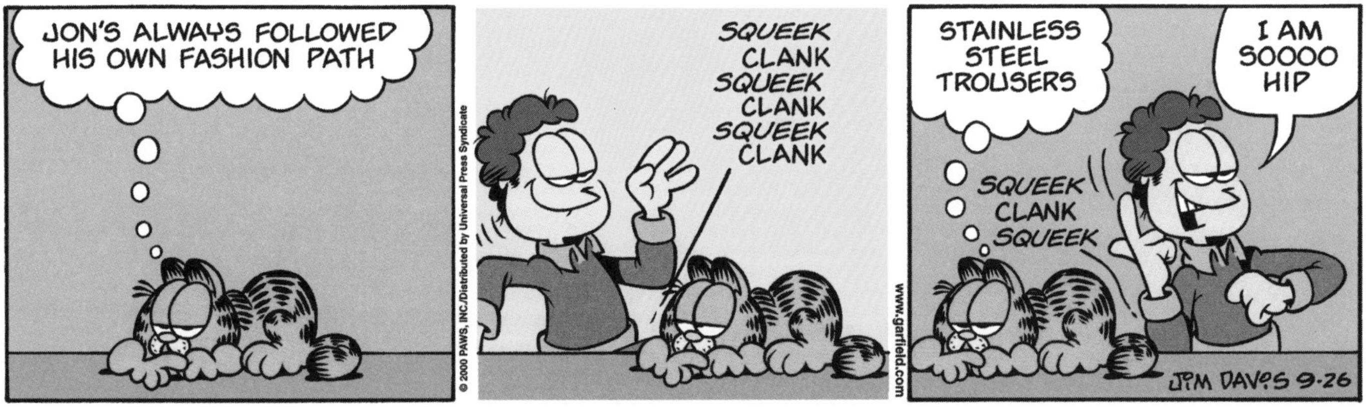
JON'S ALWAYS FOLLOWED HIS OWN FASHION PATH
© 2000 PAWS, INC./Distributed by Universal Press Syndicate
SQUEEK CLANK SQUEEK CLANK SQUEEK CLANK
www.garfield.com
STAINLESS STEEL TROUSERS
I AM SOOOO HIP
SQUEEK CLANK SQUEEK
JIM DAVIS 9-26

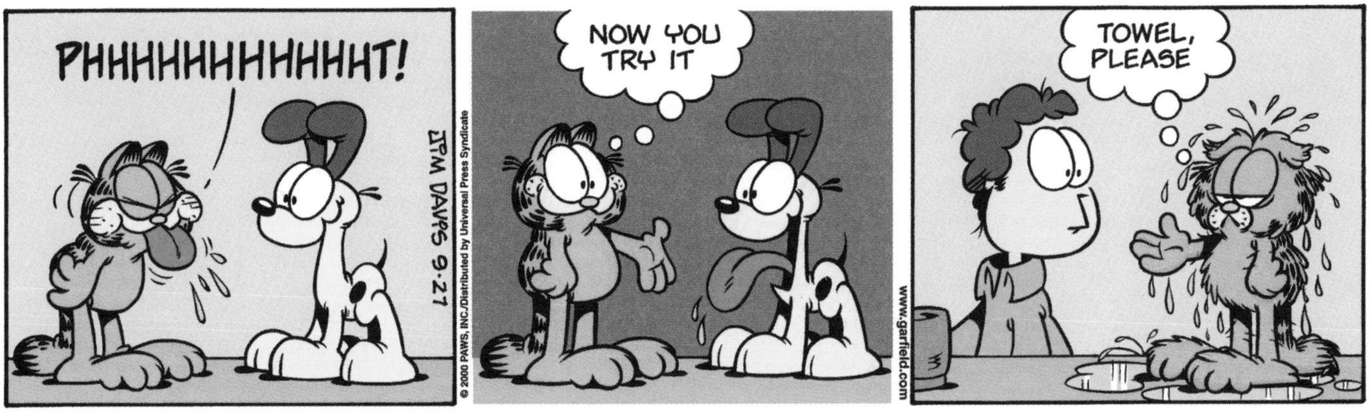
PHHHHHHHHHHHT!
JIM DAVIS 9-27
© 2000 PAWS, INC./Distributed by Universal Press Syndicate
NOW YOU TRY IT
www.garfield.com
TOWEL, PLEASE

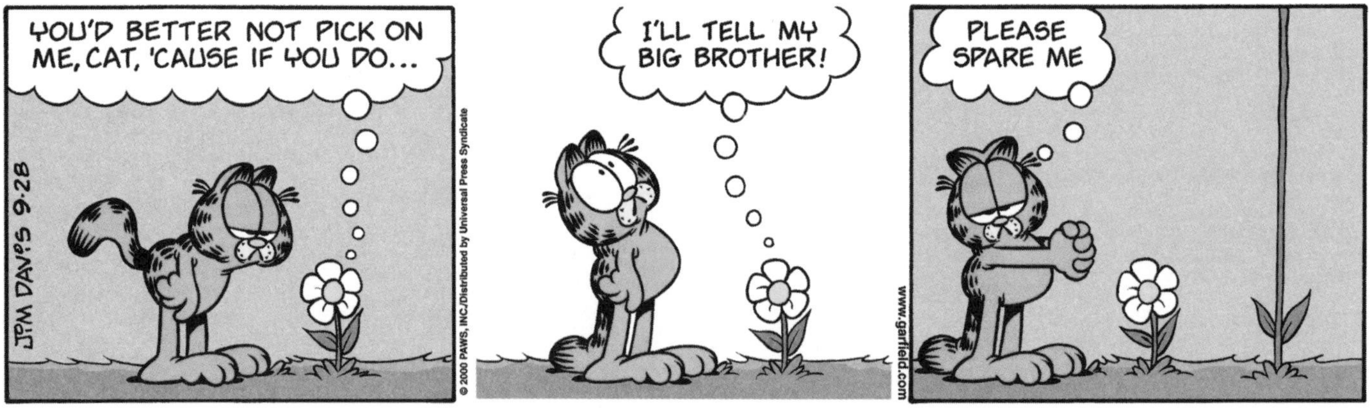
YOU'D BETTER NOT PICK ON ME, CAT, 'CAUSE IF YOU DO...
JIM DAVIS 9·28
© 2000 PAWS, INC./Distributed by Universal Press Syndicate
I'LL TELL MY BIG BROTHER!
www.garfield.com
PLEASE SPARE ME

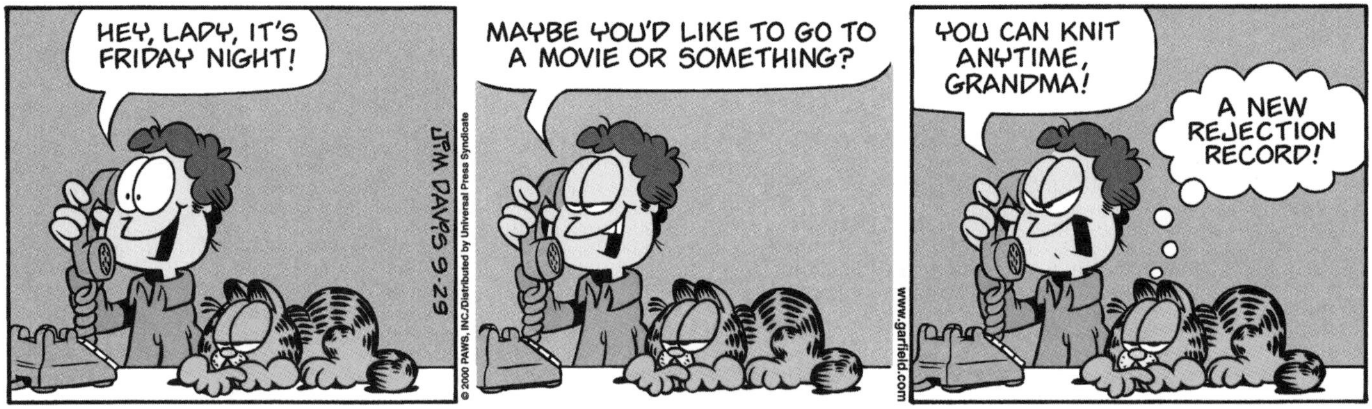
HEY, LADY, IT'S FRIDAY NIGHT!
JIM DAVIS 9·29
© 2000 PAWS, INC./Distributed by Universal Press Syndicate
MAYBE YOU'D LIKE TO GO TO A MOVIE OR SOMETHING?
www.garfield.com
YOU CAN KNIT ANYTIME, GRANDMA!
A NEW REJECTION RECORD!

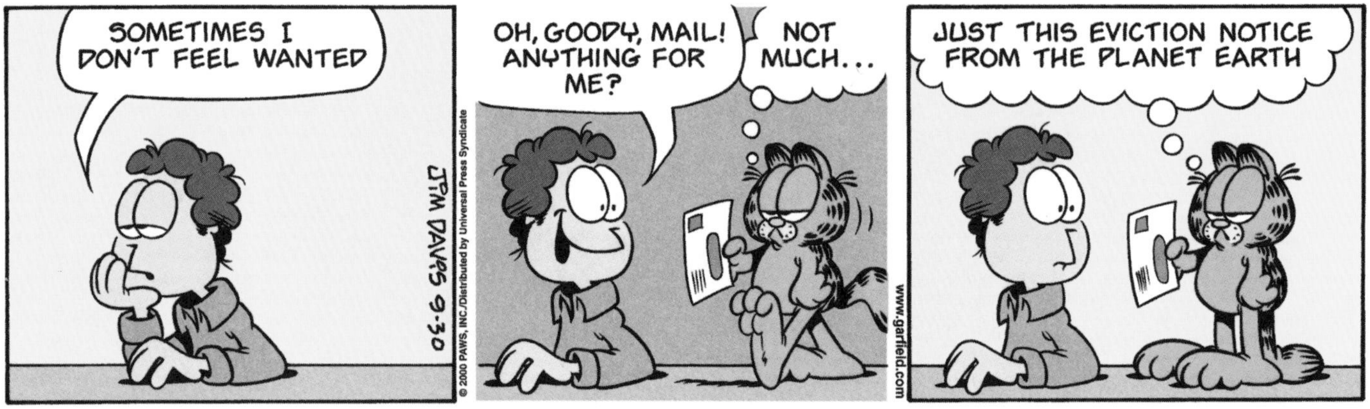
SOMETIMES I DON'T FEEL WANTED
JIM DAVIS 9·30
© 2000 PAWS, INC./Distributed by Universal Press Syndicate
OH, GOODY, MAIL! ANYTHING FOR ME?
NOT MUCH...
www.garfield.com
JUST THIS EVICTION NOTICE FROM THE PLANET EARTH

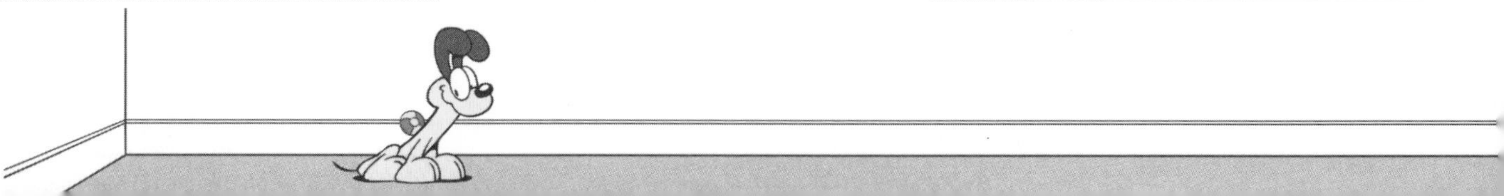

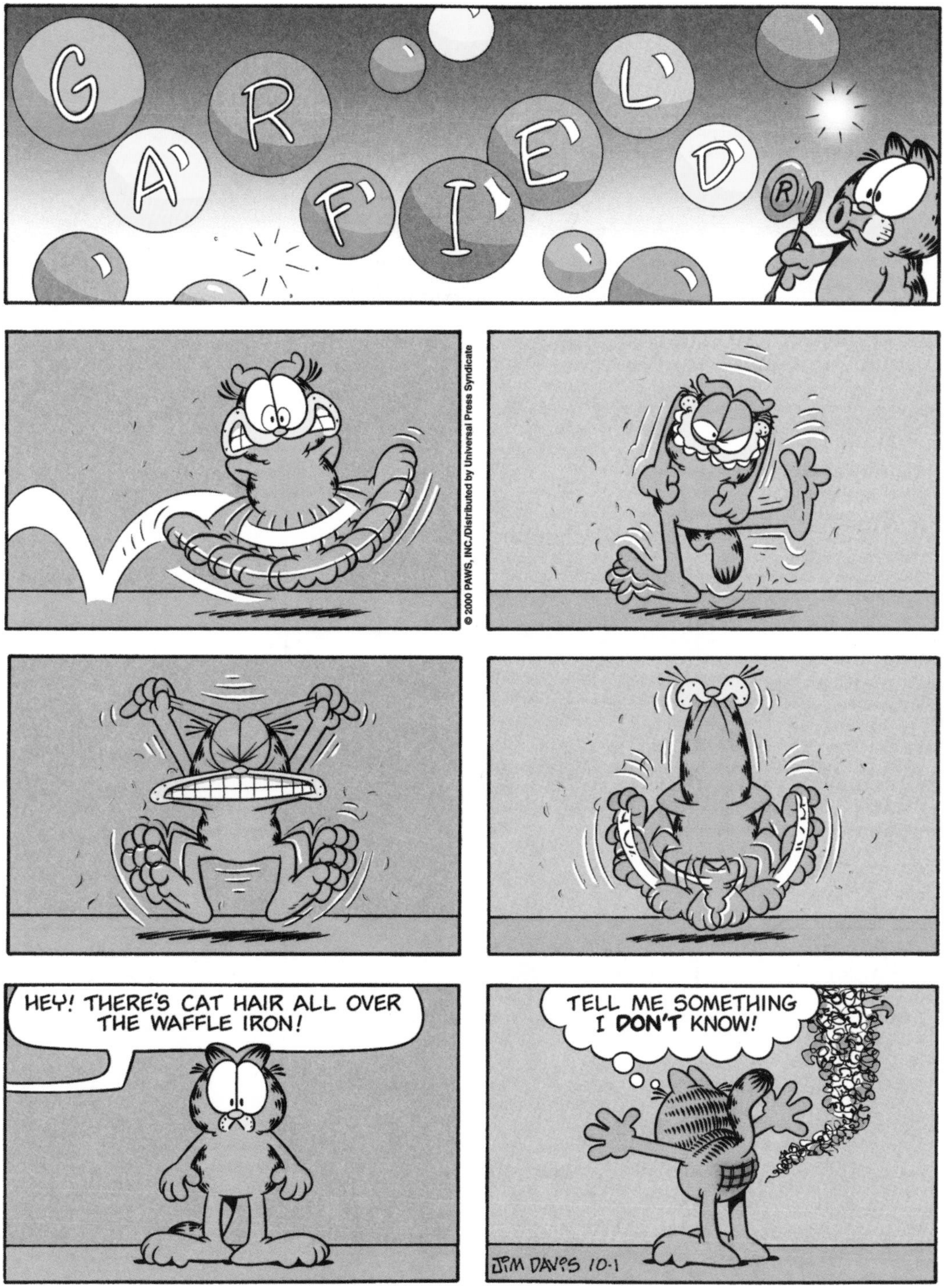
GARFIELD
© 2000 PAWS, INC./Distributed by Universal Press Syndicate
HEY! THERE'S CAT HAIR ALL OVER THE WAFFLE IRON!
TELL ME SOMETHING I **DON'T** KNOW!
JIM DAVIS 10-1

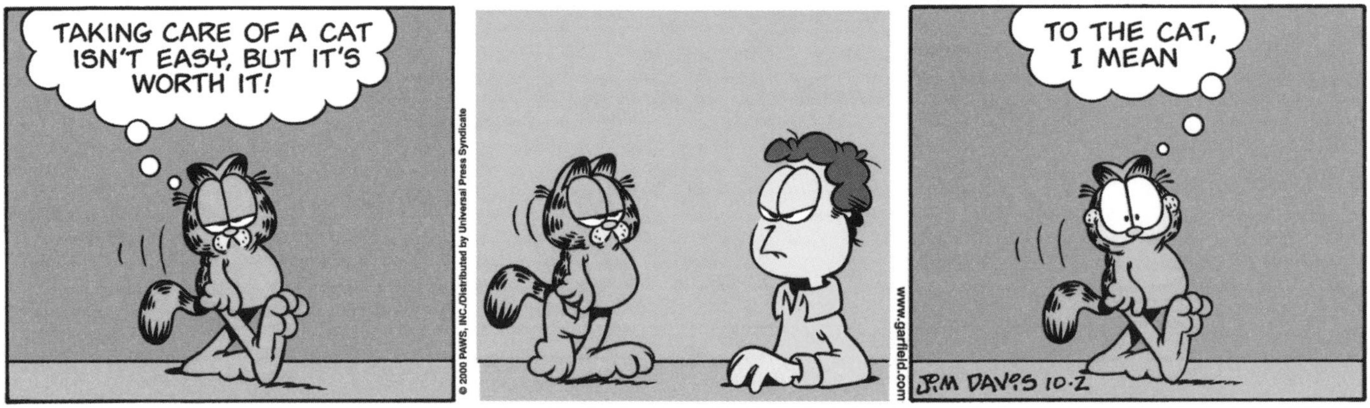
TAKING CARE OF A CAT ISN'T EASY, BUT IT'S WORTH IT!
© 2000 PAWS, INC./Distributed by Universal Press Syndicate
www.garfield.com
TO THE CAT, I MEAN
JIM DAVIS 10-2

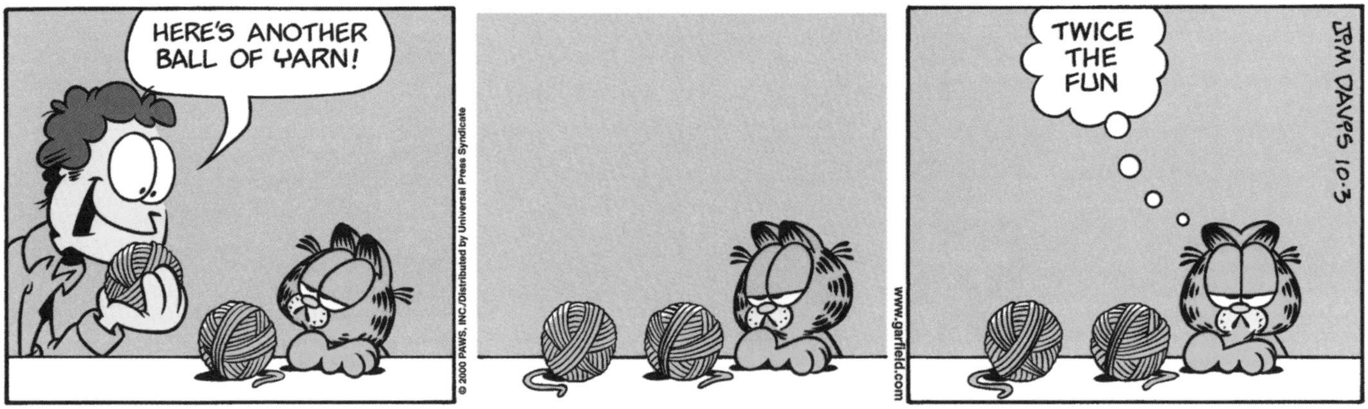
HERE'S ANOTHER BALL OF YARN!
© 2000 PAWS, INC./Distributed by Universal Press Syndicate
www.garfield.com
TWICE THE FUN
JIM DAVIS 10-3

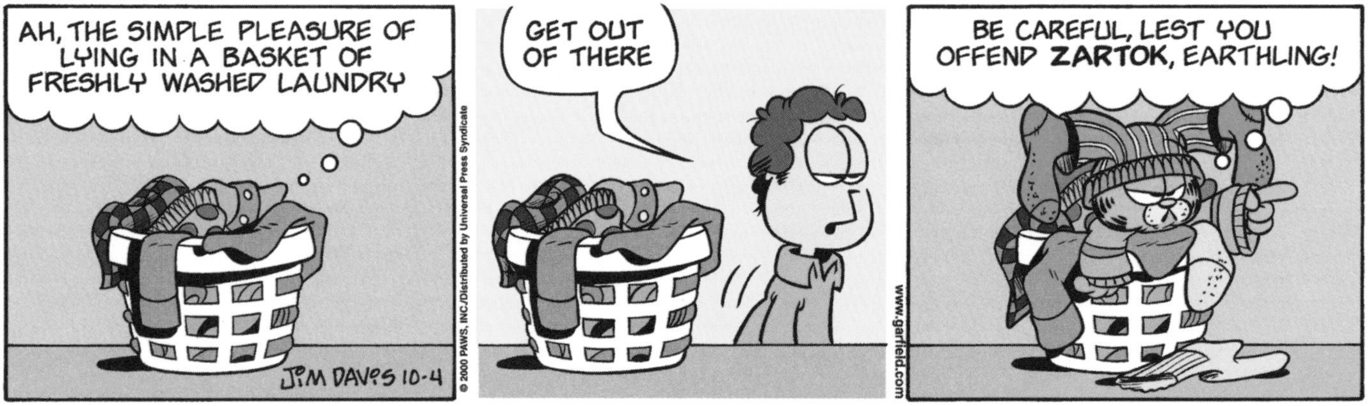
AH, THE SIMPLE PLEASURE OF LYING IN A BASKET OF FRESHLY WASHED LAUNDRY
JIM DAVIS 10-4
© 2000 PAWS, INC./Distributed by Universal Press Syndicate
GET OUT OF THERE
www.garfield.com
BE CAREFUL, LEST YOU OFFEND **ZARTOK**, EARTHLING!

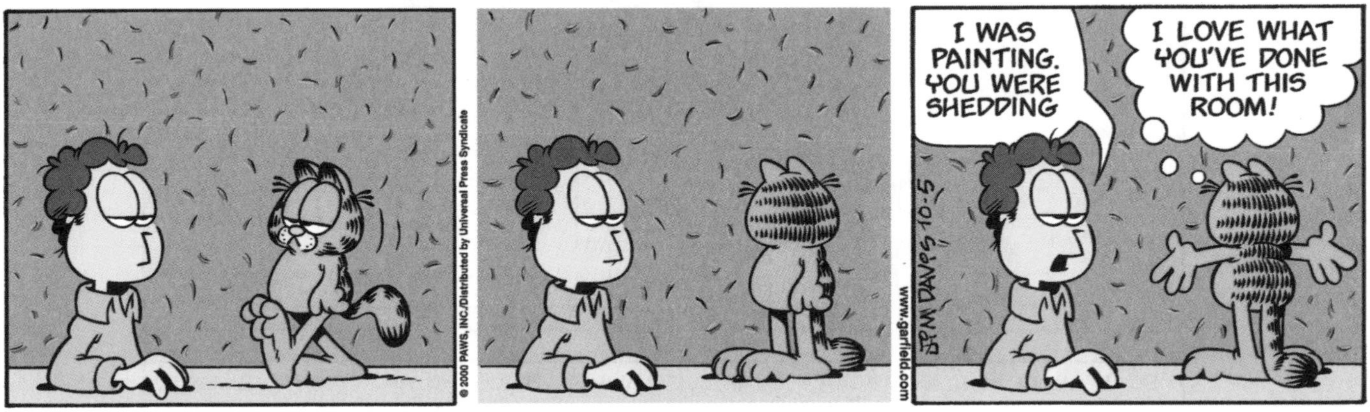
© 2000 PAWS, INC./Distributed by Universal Press Syndicate
I WAS PAINTING. YOU WERE SHEDDING
I LOVE WHAT YOU'VE DONE WITH THIS ROOM!
JIM DAVIS 10-5
www.garfield.com

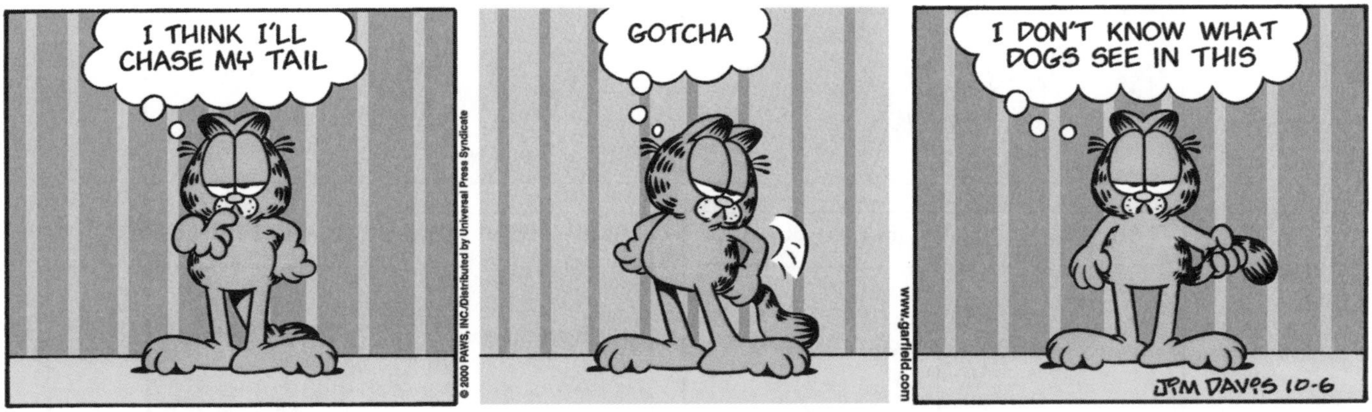
I THINK I'LL CHASE MY TAIL
© 2000 PAWS, INC./Distributed by Universal Press Syndicate
GOTCHA
www.garfield.com
I DON'T KNOW WHAT DOGS SEE IN THIS
JIM DAVIS 10-6

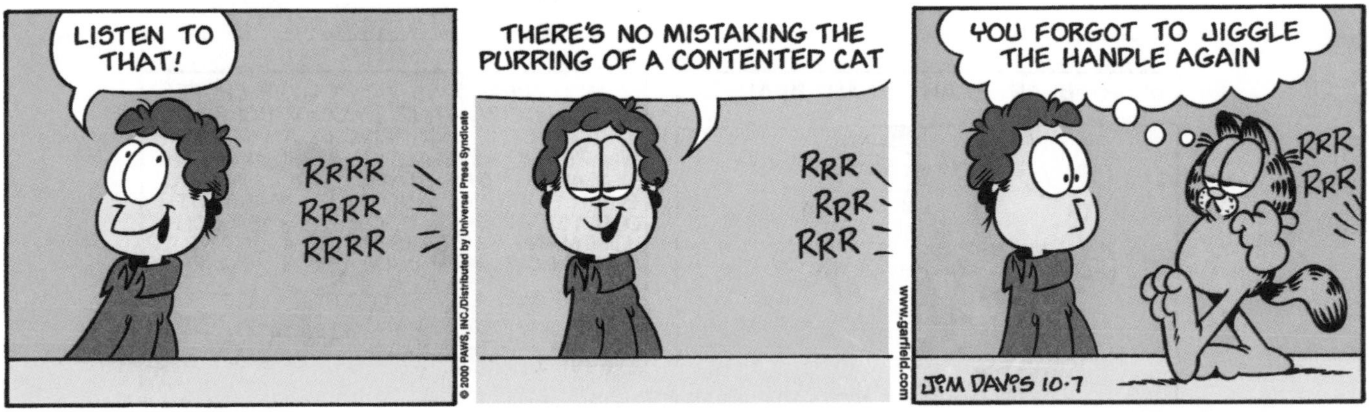
LISTEN TO THAT!
RRRR RRRR RRRR
© 2000 PAWS, INC./Distributed by Universal Press Syndicate
THERE'S NO MISTAKING THE PURRING OF A CONTENTED CAT
RRR RRR RRR
www.garfield.com
YOU FORGOT TO JIGGLE THE HANDLE AGAIN
RRR RRR
JIM DAVIS 10-7

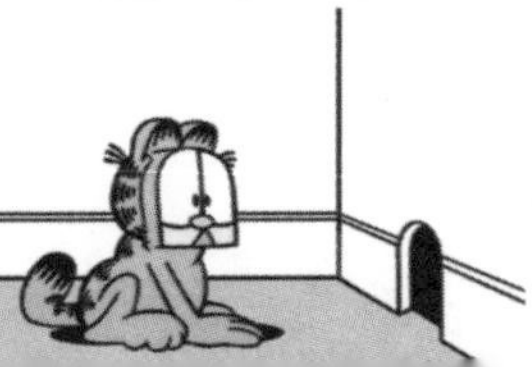

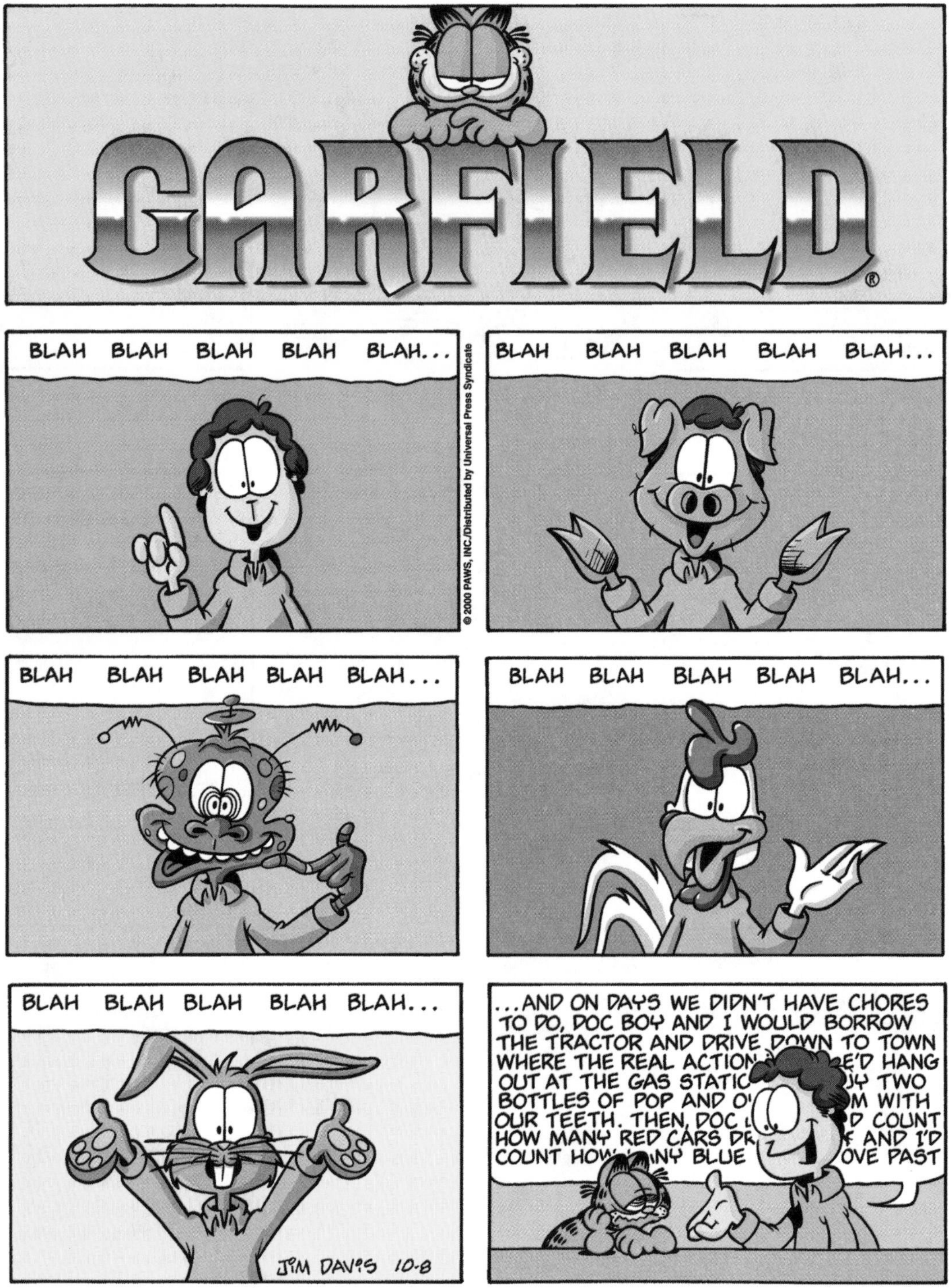
GARFIELD®
BLAH BLAH BLAH BLAH BLAH...
© 2000 PAWS, INC./Distributed by Universal Press Syndicate
BLAH BLAH BLAH BLAH BLAH...
BLAH BLAH BLAH BLAH BLAH...
BLAH BLAH BLAH BLAH BLAH...
BLAH BLAH BLAH BLAH BLAH...
JIM DAVIS 10-8
...AND ON DAYS WE DIDN'T HAVE CHORES TO DO, DOC BOY AND I WOULD BORROW THE TRACTOR AND DRIVE DOWN TO TOWN WHERE THE REAL ACTION ... E'D HANG OUT AT THE GAS STATIC ... Y TWO BOTTLES OF POP AND O ... M WITH OUR TEETH. THEN, DOC ... D COUNT HOW MANY RED CARS DR ... AND I'D COUNT HOW ... NY BLUE ... OVE PAST

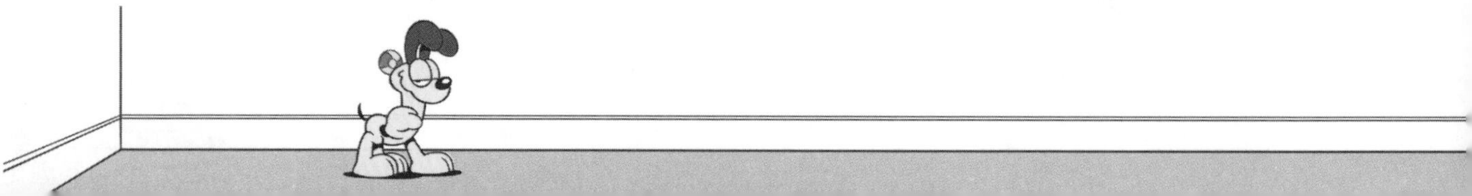

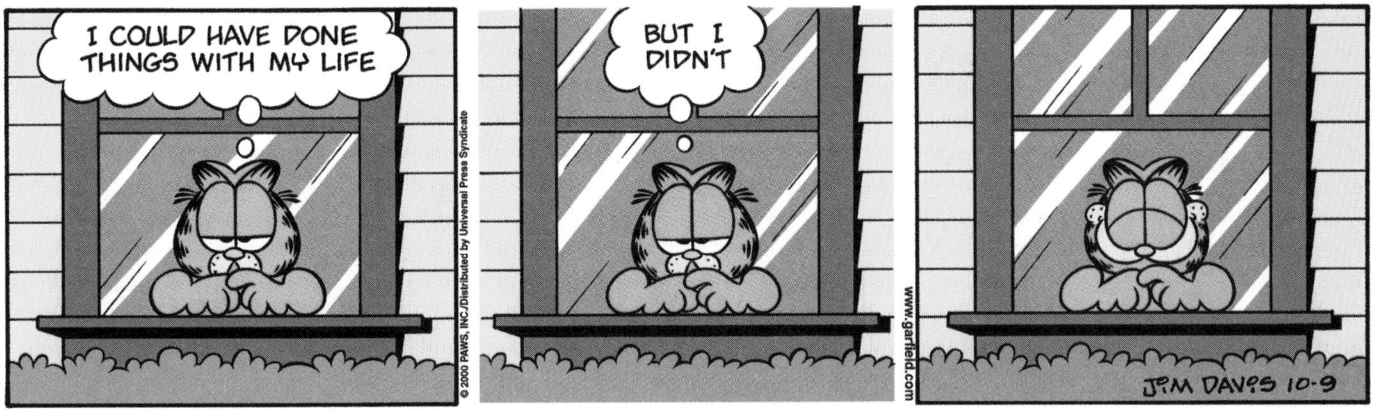
I COULD HAVE DONE THINGS WITH MY LIFE
© 2000 PAWS, INC./Distributed by Universal Press Syndicate
BUT I DIDN'T
www.garfield.com
JIM DAVIS 10-9

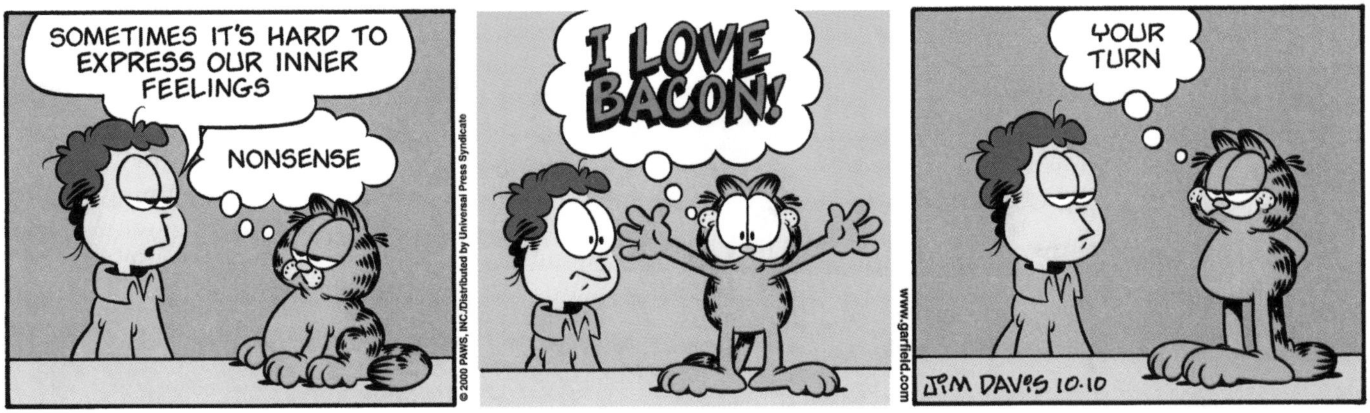
SOMETIMES IT'S HARD TO EXPRESS OUR INNER FEELINGS
NONSENSE
© 2000 PAWS, INC./Distributed by Universal Press Syndicate
I LOVE BACON!
www.garfield.com
YOUR TURN
JIM DAVIS 10.10

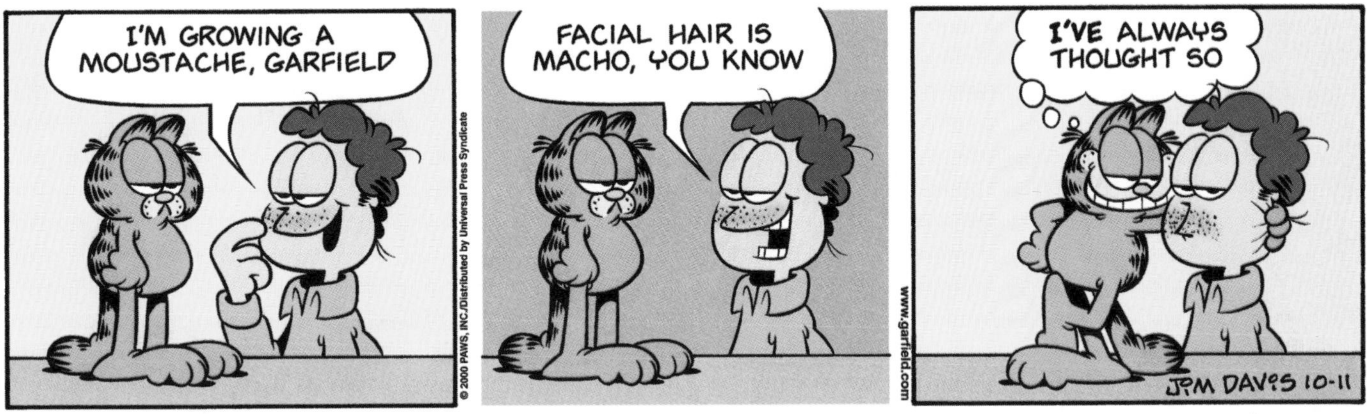
I'M GROWING A MOUSTACHE, GARFIELD
© 2000 PAWS, INC./Distributed by Universal Press Syndicate
FACIAL HAIR IS MACHO, YOU KNOW
www.garfield.com
I'VE ALWAYS THOUGHT SO
JIM DAVIS 10-11

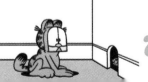

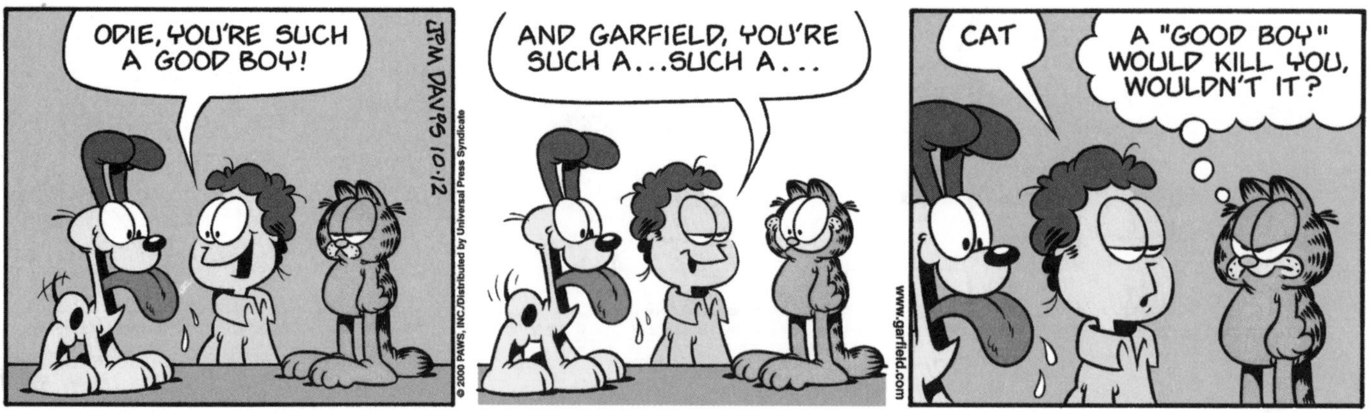
ODIE, YOU'RE SUCH A GOOD BOY!
JIM DAVIS 10-12
© 2000 PAWS, INC./Distributed by Universal Press Syndicate
AND GARFIELD, YOU'RE SUCH A...SUCH A...
www.garfield.com
CAT
A "GOOD BOY" WOULD KILL YOU, WOULDN'T IT?

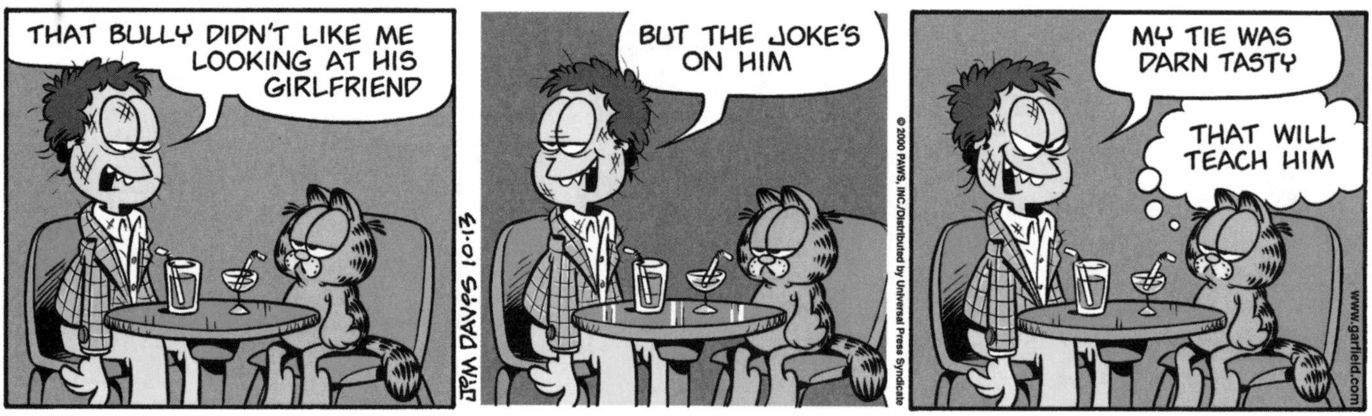
THAT BULLY DIDN'T LIKE ME LOOKING AT HIS GIRLFRIEND
JIM DAVIS 10-13
BUT THE JOKE'S ON HIM
© 2000 PAWS, INC./Distributed by Universal Press Syndicate
MY TIE WAS DARN TASTY
THAT WILL TEACH HIM
www.garfield.com

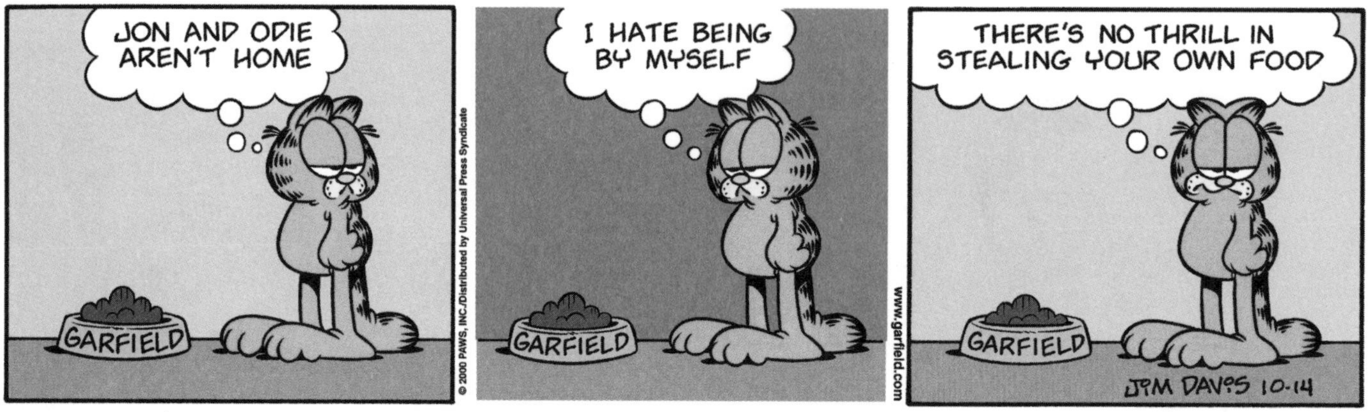
JON AND ODIE AREN'T HOME
GARFIELD
© 2000 PAWS, INC./Distributed by Universal Press Syndicate
I HATE BEING BY MYSELF
GARFIELD
www.garfield.com
THERE'S NO THRILL IN STEALING YOUR OWN FOOD
GARFIELD
JIM DAVIS 10-14

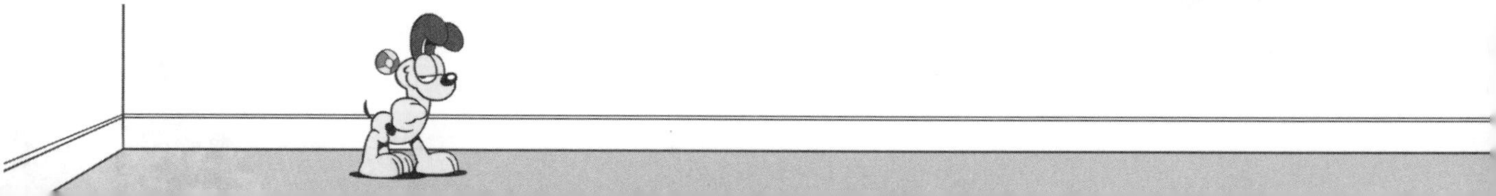

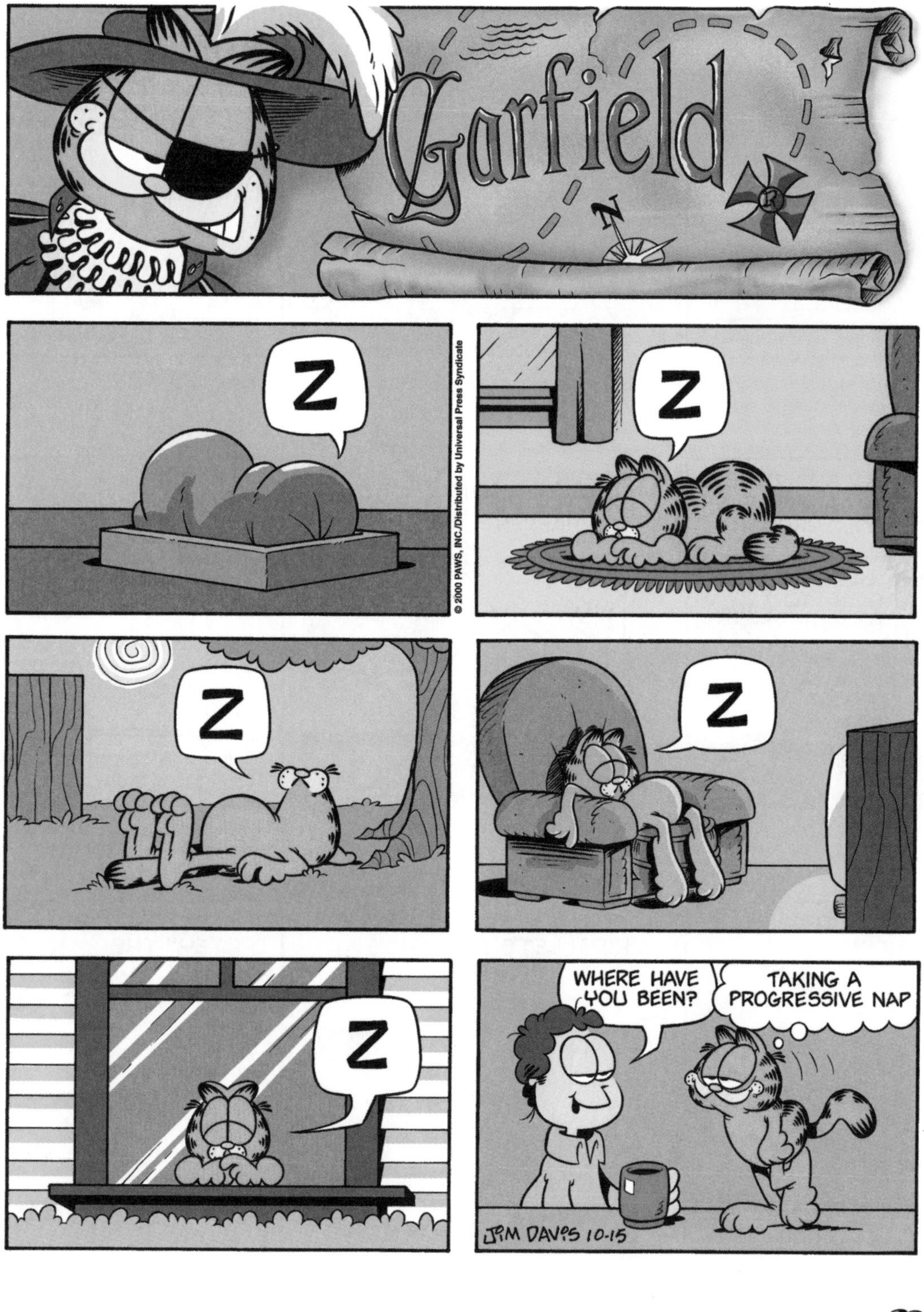
Garfield
© 2000 PAWS, INC./Distributed by Universal Press Syndicate
Z
Z
Z
Z
Z
WHERE HAVE YOU BEEN?
TAKING A PROGRESSIVE NAP
JIM DAVIS 10-15

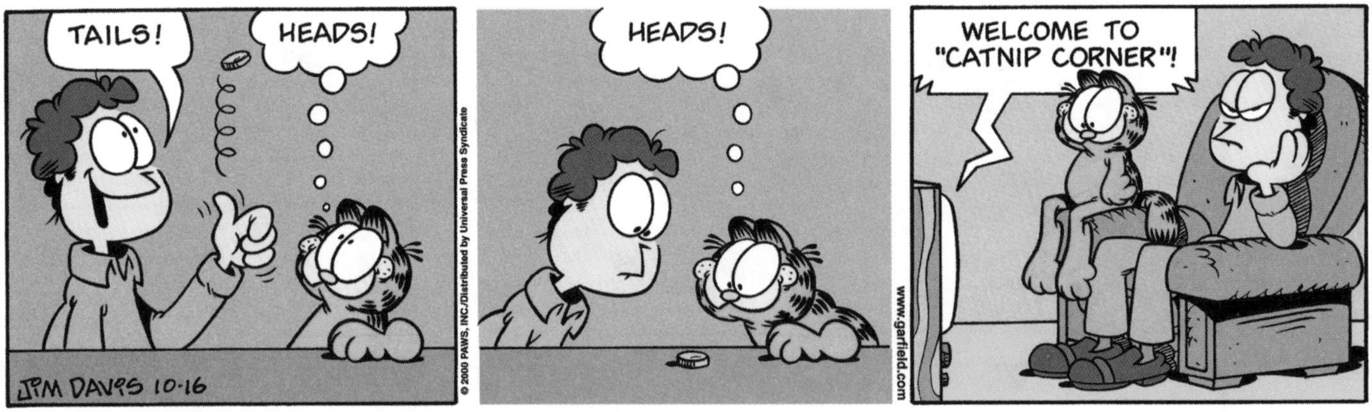
TAILS!
HEADS!
HEADS!
WELCOME TO "CATNIP CORNER"!
JIM DAVIS 10-16
© 2000 PAWS, INC./Distributed by Universal Press Syndicate
www.garfield.com

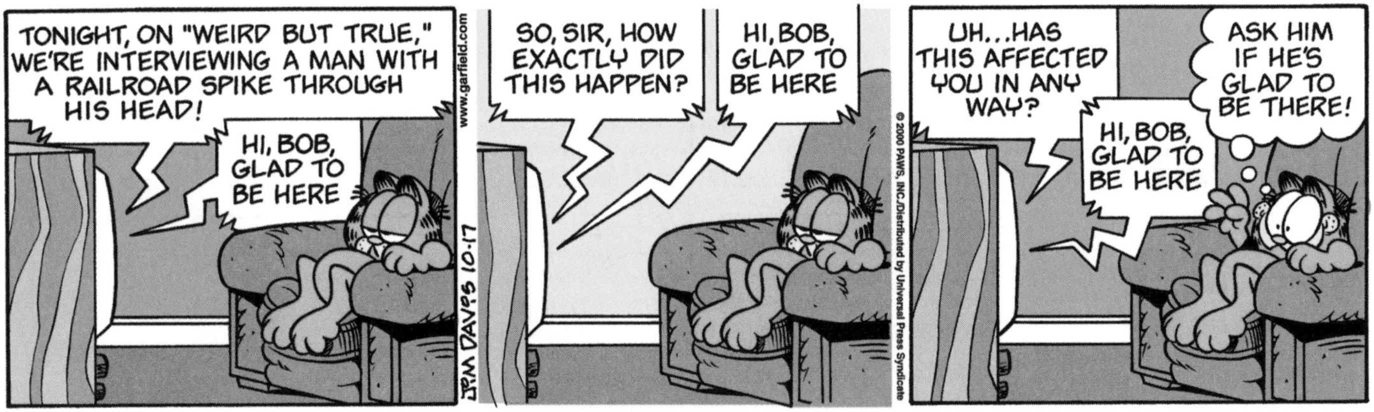
TONIGHT, ON "WEIRD BUT TRUE," WE'RE INTERVIEWING A MAN WITH A RAILROAD SPIKE THROUGH HIS HEAD!
HI, BOB, GLAD TO BE HERE
SO, SIR, HOW EXACTLY DID THIS HAPPEN?
HI, BOB, GLAD TO BE HERE
UH...HAS THIS AFFECTED YOU IN ANY WAY?
HI, BOB, GLAD TO BE HERE
ASK HIM IF HE'S GLAD TO BE THERE!
JIM DAVIS 10-17
www.garfield.com
© 2000 PAWS, INC./Distributed by Universal Press Syndicate

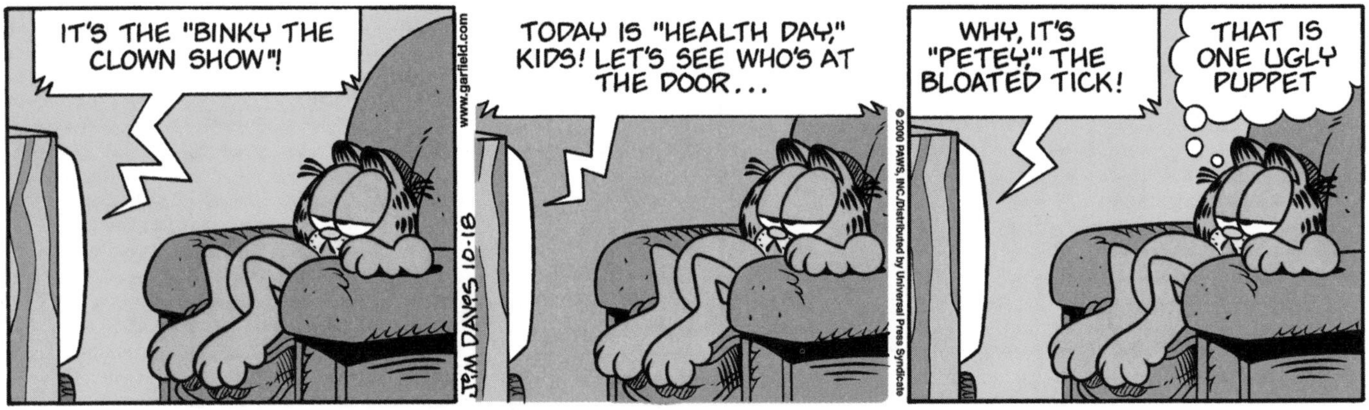
IT'S THE "BINKY THE CLOWN SHOW"!
TODAY IS "HEALTH DAY," KIDS! LET'S SEE WHO'S AT THE DOOR...
WHY, IT'S "PETEY," THE BLOATED TICK!
THAT IS ONE UGLY PUPPET
JIM DAVIS 10-18
www.garfield.com
© 2000 PAWS, INC./Distributed by Universal Press Syndicate

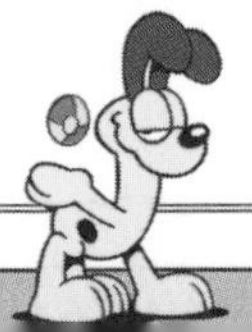

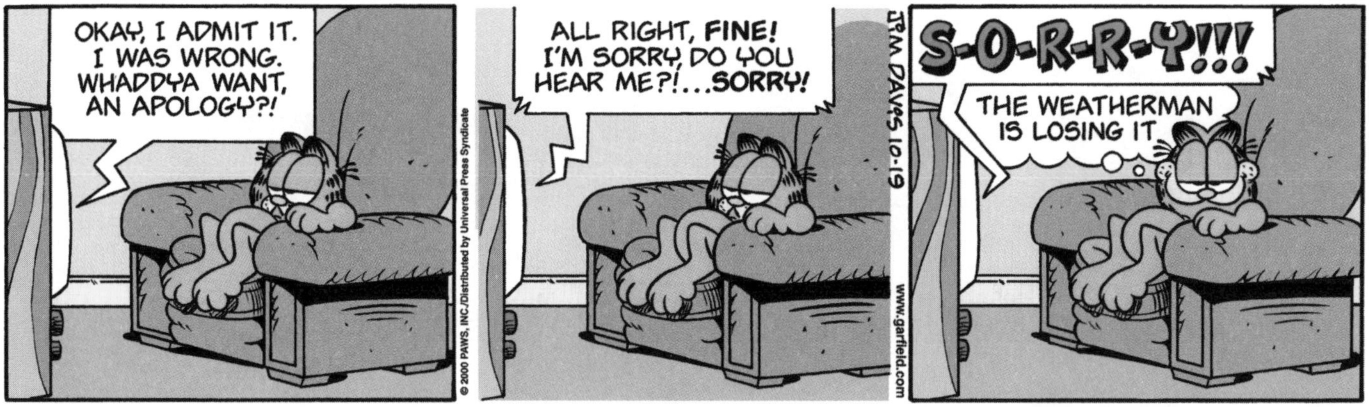
OKAY, I ADMIT IT. I WAS WRONG. WHADDYA WANT, AN APOLOGY?!
ALL RIGHT, FINE! I'M SORRY, DO YOU HEAR ME?!...SORRY!
S-O-R-R-Y!!!
THE WEATHERMAN IS LOSING IT
JIM DAVIS 10-19
© 2000 PAWS, INC./Distributed by Universal Press Syndicate
www.garfield.com

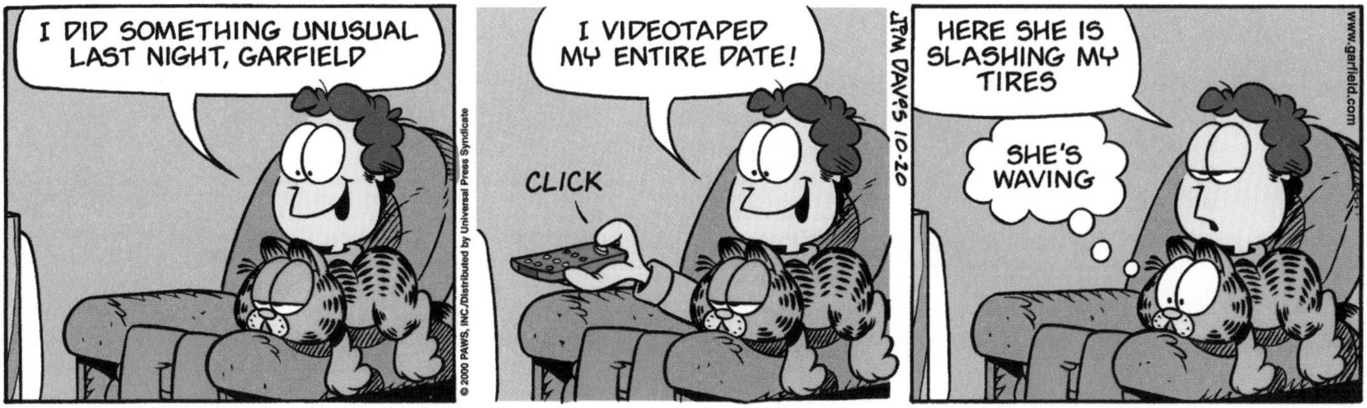
I DID SOMETHING UNUSUAL LAST NIGHT, GARFIELD
I VIDEOTAPED MY ENTIRE DATE!
CLICK
HERE SHE IS SLASHING MY TIRES
SHE'S WAVING
JIM DAVIS 10-20
© 2000 PAWS, INC./Distributed by Universal Press Syndicate
www.garfield.com

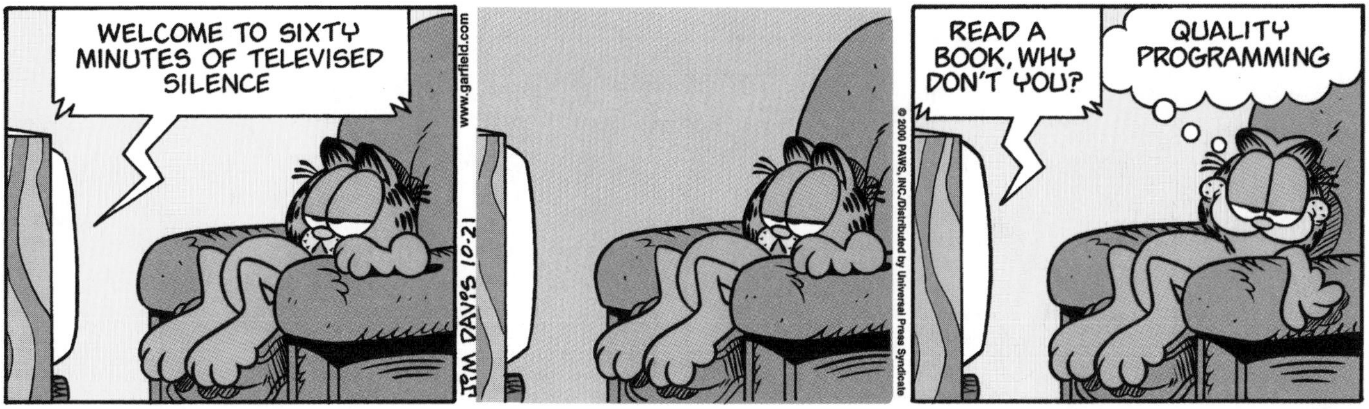
WELCOME TO SIXTY MINUTES OF TELEVISED SILENCE
READ A BOOK, WHY DON'T YOU?
QUALITY PROGRAMMING
JIM DAVIS 10-21
© 2000 PAWS, INC./Distributed by Universal Press Syndicate
www.garfield.com

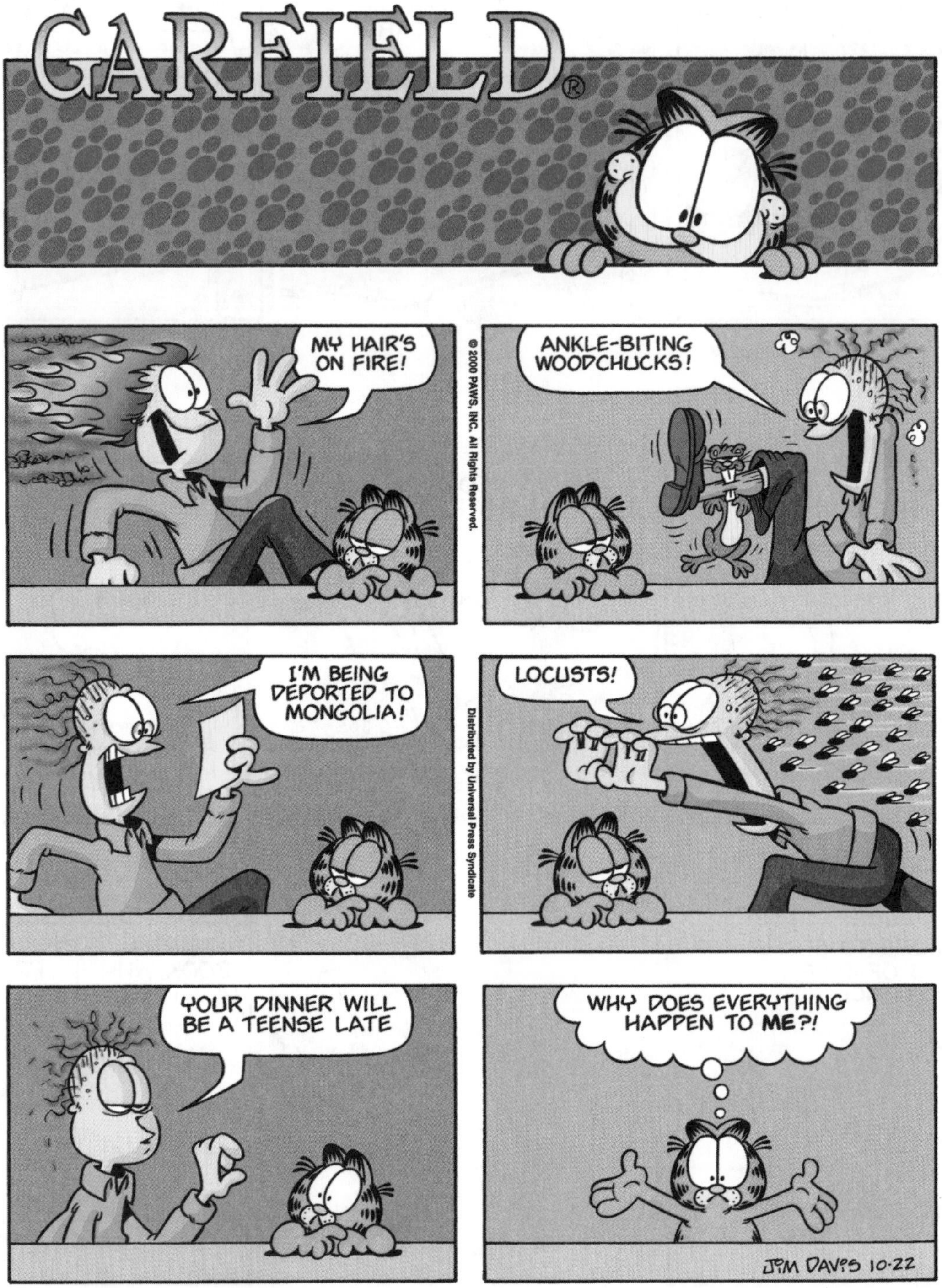
GARFIELD®
MY HAIR'S ON FIRE!
© 2000 PAWS, INC. All Rights Reserved.
ANKLE-BITING WOODCHUCKS!
I'M BEING DEPORTED TO MONGOLIA!
Distributed by Universal Press Syndicate
LOCUSTS!
YOUR DINNER WILL BE A TEENSE LATE
WHY DOES EVERYTHING HAPPEN TO ME?!
JIM DAVIS 10-22

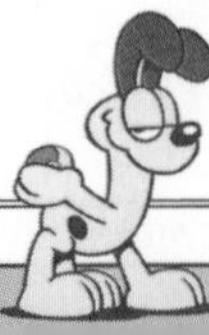

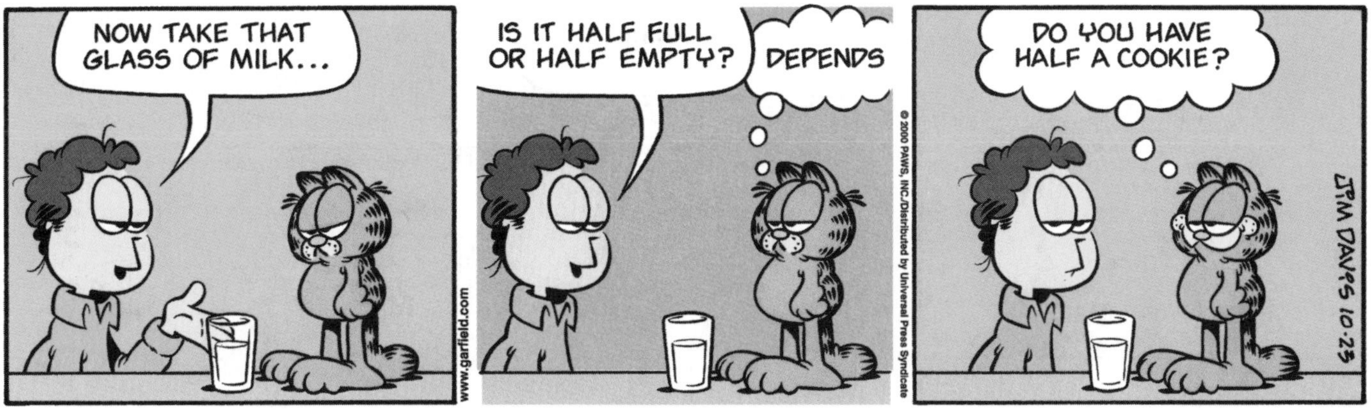
NOW TAKE THAT GLASS OF MILK...
IS IT HALF FULL OR HALF EMPTY?
DEPENDS
DO YOU HAVE HALF A COOKIE?
www.garfield.com
© 2000 PAWS, INC./Distributed by Universal Press Syndicate
JIM DAVIS 10-23

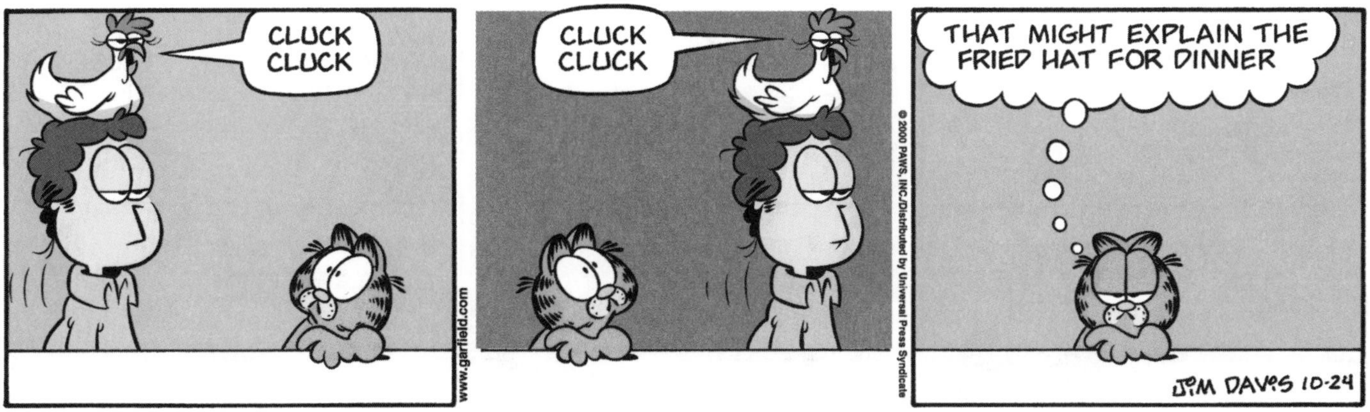
CLUCK CLUCK
CLUCK CLUCK
THAT MIGHT EXPLAIN THE FRIED HAT FOR DINNER
www.garfield.com
© 2000 PAWS, INC./Distributed by Universal Press Syndicate
JIM DAVIS 10-24

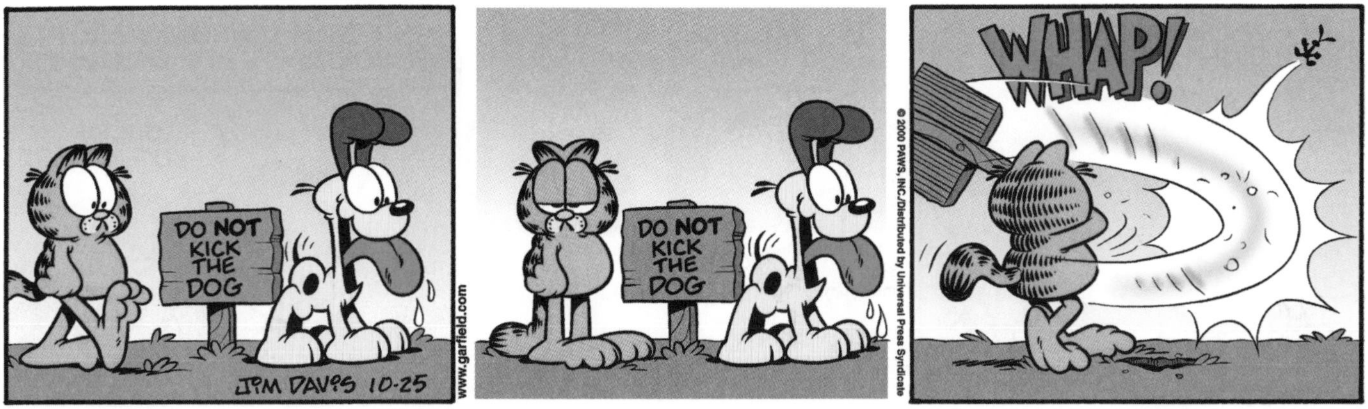
DO NOT KICK THE DOG
JIM DAVIS 10-25
www.garfield.com
DO NOT KICK THE DOG
© 2000 PAWS, INC./Distributed by Universal Press Syndicate
WHAP!

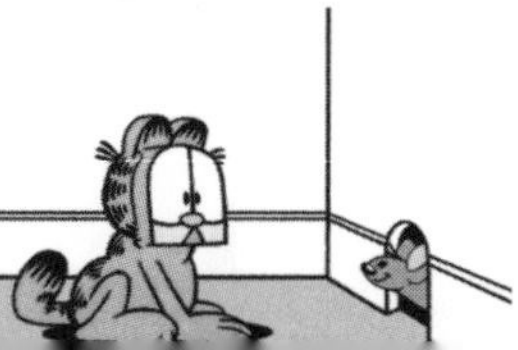

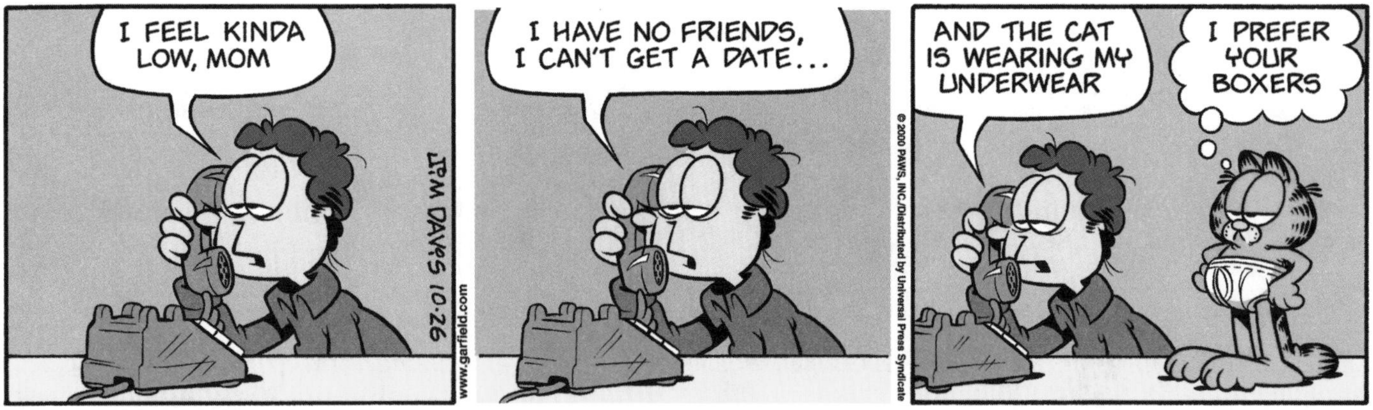
I FEEL KINDA LOW, MOM
JIM DAVIS 10-26
www.garfield.com
I HAVE NO FRIENDS, I CAN'T GET A DATE...
© 2000 PAWS, INC./Distributed by Universal Press Syndicate
AND THE CAT IS WEARING MY UNDERWEAR
I PREFER YOUR BOXERS

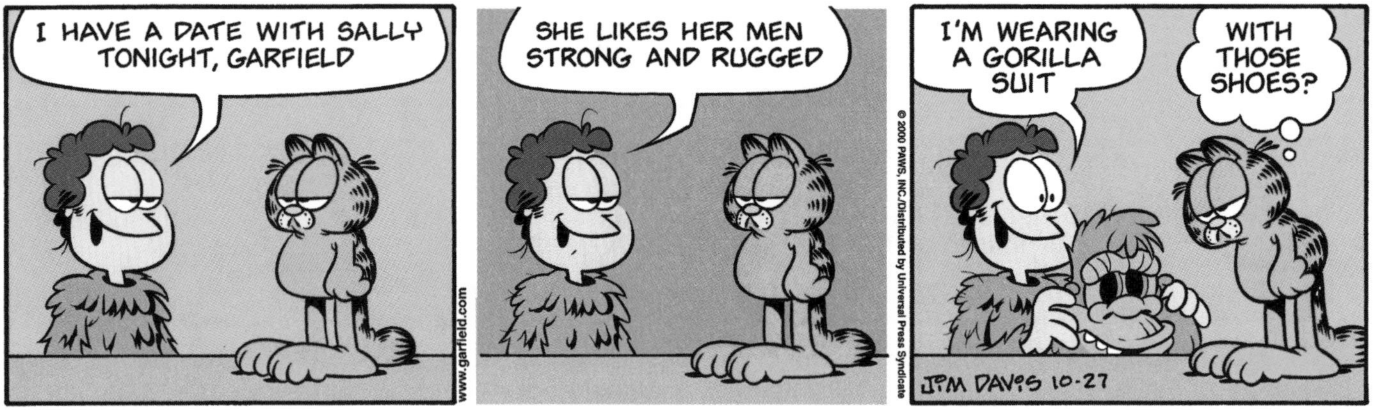
I HAVE A DATE WITH SALLY TONIGHT, GARFIELD
www.garfield.com
SHE LIKES HER MEN STRONG AND RUGGED
© 2000 PAWS, INC./Distributed by Universal Press Syndicate
I'M WEARING A GORILLA SUIT
WITH THOSE SHOES?
JIM DAVIS 10-27

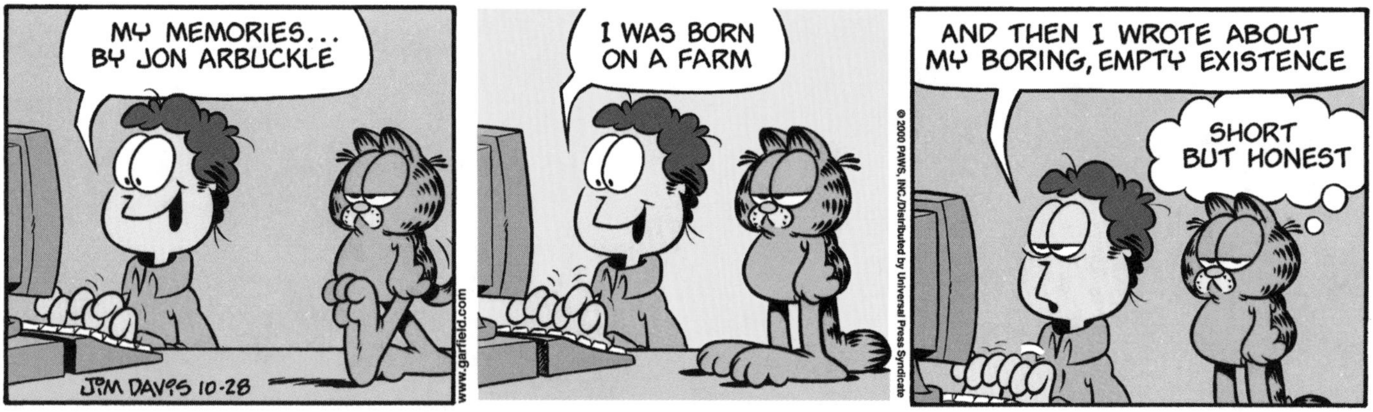
MY MEMORIES... BY JON ARBUCKLE
JIM DAVIS 10-28
www.garfield.com
I WAS BORN ON A FARM
© 2000 PAWS, INC./Distributed by Universal Press Syndicate
AND THEN I WROTE ABOUT MY BORING, EMPTY EXISTENCE
SHORT BUT HONEST

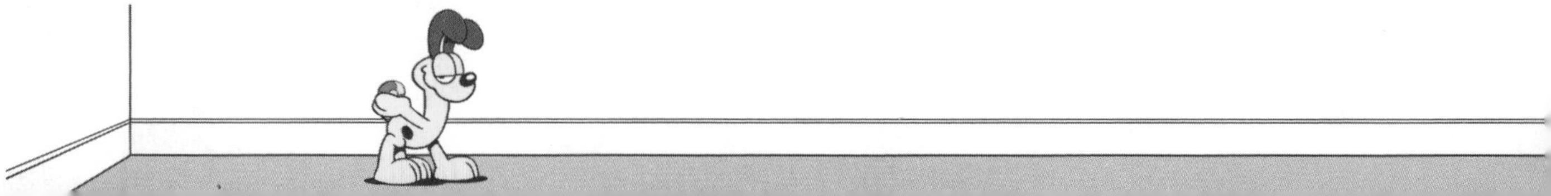

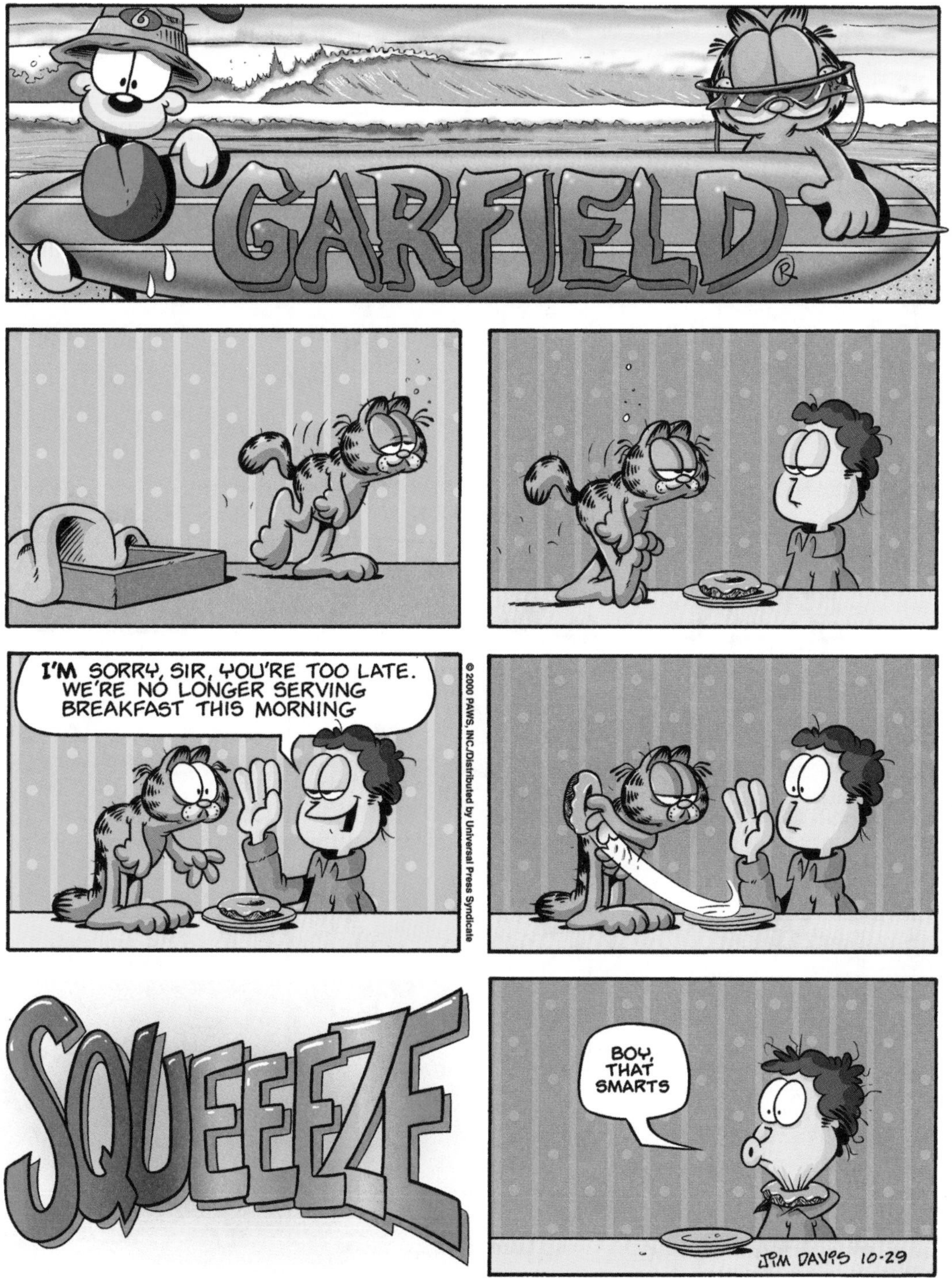
GARFIELD
I'M SORRY, SIR, YOU'RE TOO LATE. WE'RE NO LONGER SERVING BREAKFAST THIS MORNING
SQUEEEEZE
BOY, THAT SMARTS
JIM DAVIS 10-29
© 2000 PAWS, INC./Distributed by Universal Press Syndicate

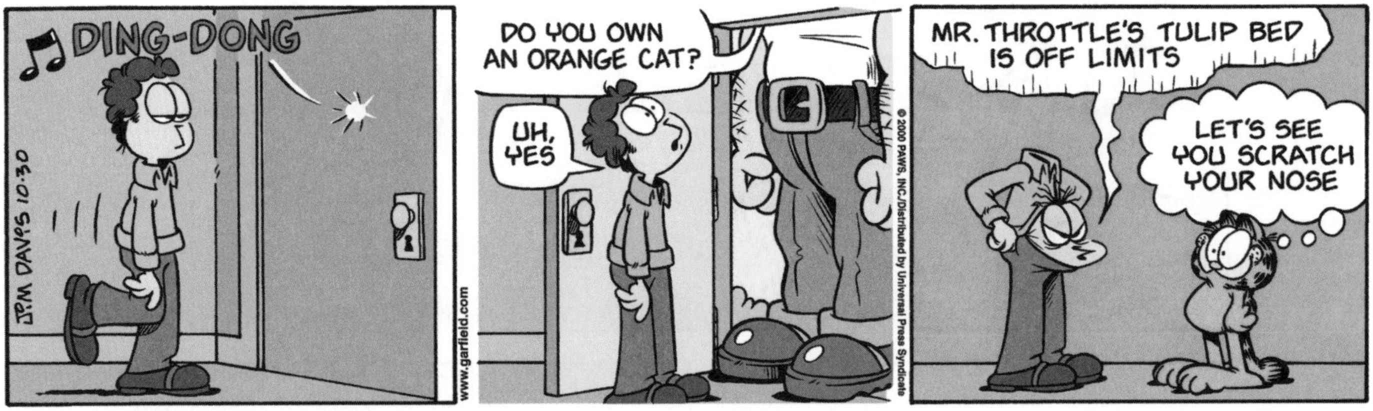
DING-DONG
JPM DAVPS 10-30
www.garfield.com
DO YOU OWN AN ORANGE CAT?
UH, YES
© 2000 PAWS, INC./Distributed by Universal Press Syndicate
MR. THROTTLE'S TULIP BED IS OFF LIMITS
LET'S SEE YOU SCRATCH YOUR NOSE

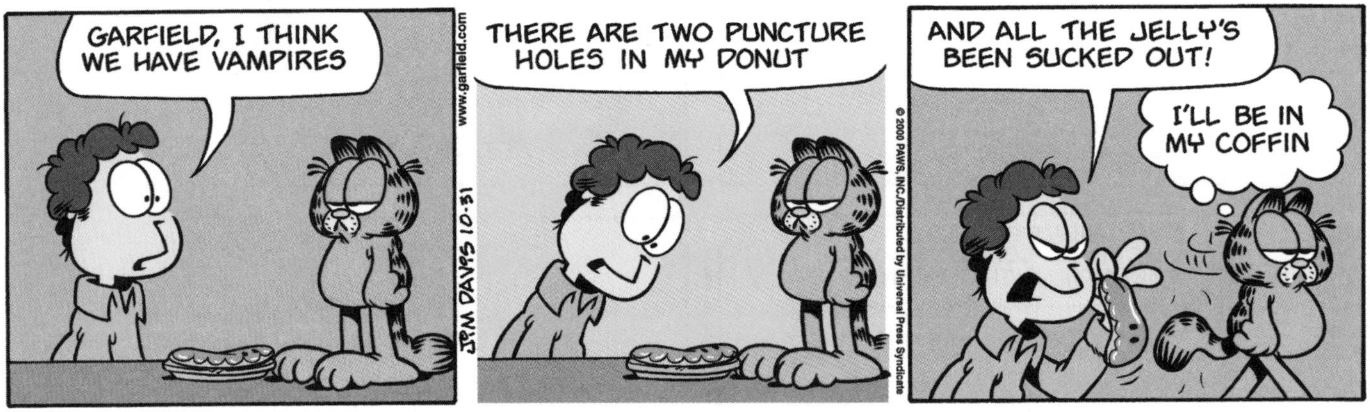
GARFIELD, I THINK WE HAVE VAMPIRES
www.garfield.com
JPM DAVPS 10-31
THERE ARE TWO PUNCTURE HOLES IN MY DONUT
© 2000 PAWS, INC./Distributed by Universal Press Syndicate
AND ALL THE JELLY'S BEEN SUCKED OUT!
I'LL BE IN MY COFFIN

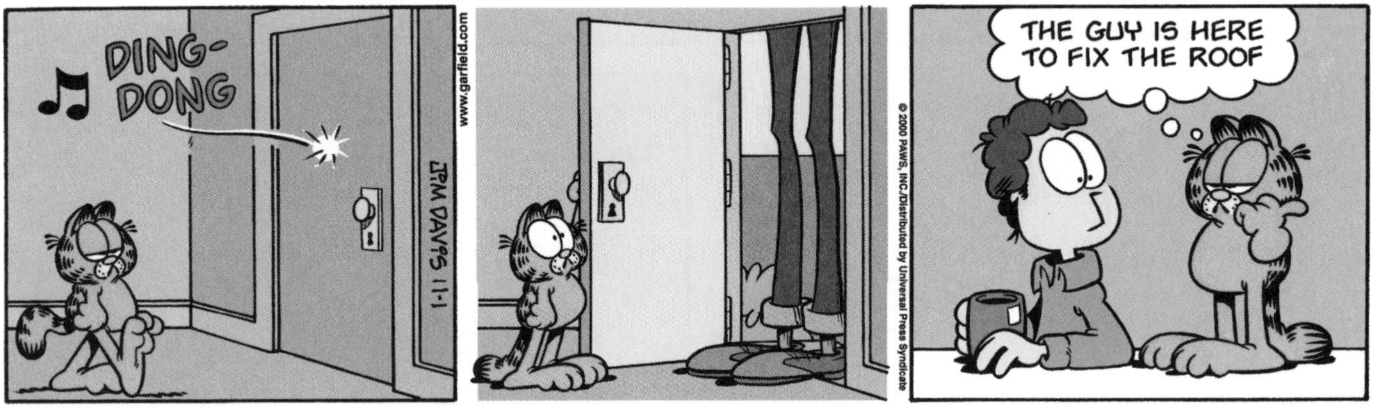
DING-DONG
JPM DAVPS 11-1
www.garfield.com
© 2000 PAWS, INC./Distributed by Universal Press Syndicate
THE GUY IS HERE TO FIX THE ROOF

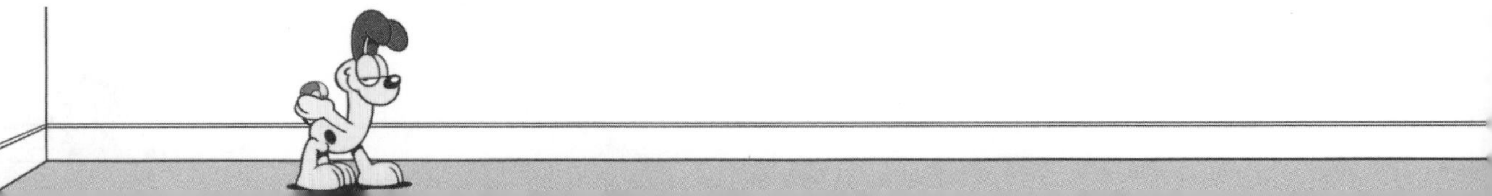

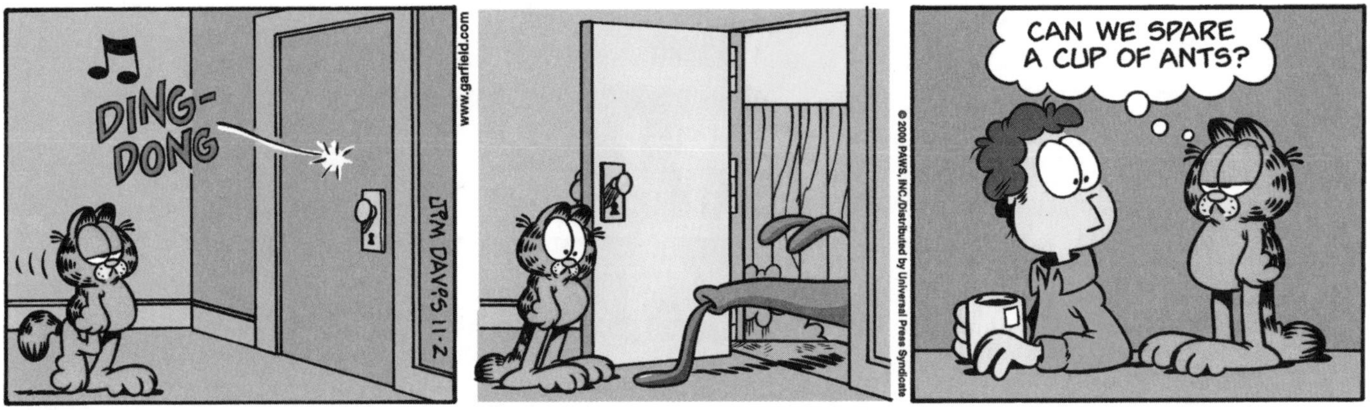
DING-DONG
www.garfield.com
JPM DAVPS 11-2
© 2000 PAWS, INC./Distributed by Universal Press Syndicate
CAN WE SPARE A CUP OF ANTS?

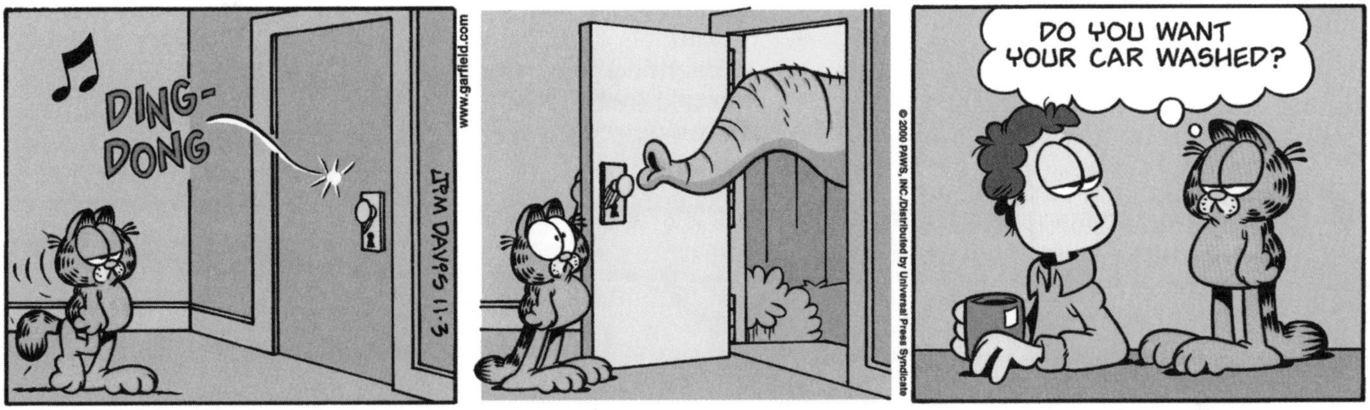
DING-DONG
www.garfield.com
JPM DAVPS 11-3
© 2000 PAWS, INC./Distributed by Universal Press Syndicate
DO YOU WANT YOUR CAR WASHED?

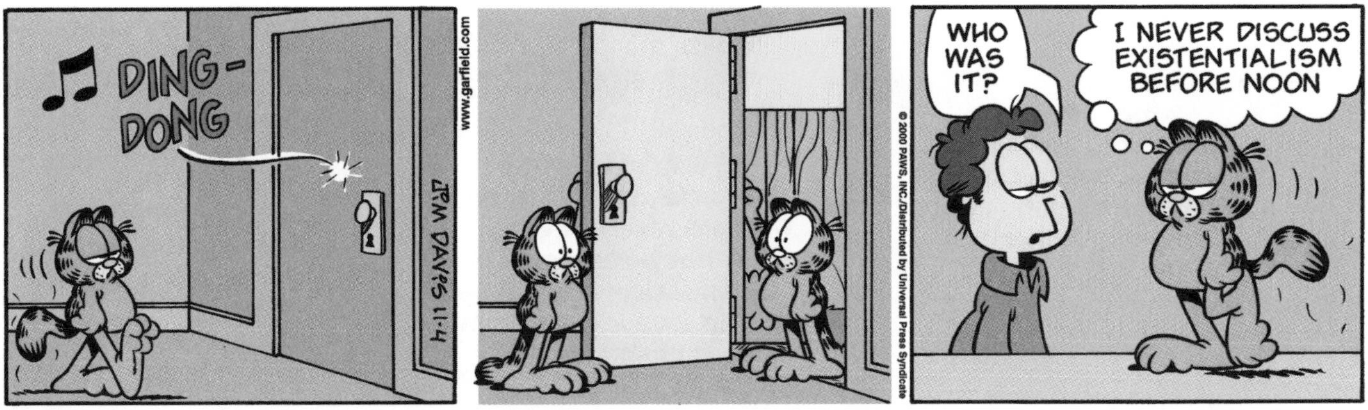
DING-DONG
www.garfield.com
JPM DAVPS 11-4
© 2000 PAWS, INC./Distributed by Universal Press Syndicate
WHO WAS IT?
I NEVER DISCUSS EXISTENTIALISM BEFORE NOON

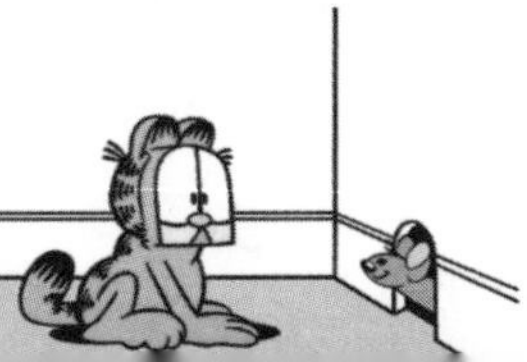

TAKE THE GARFIELD TRIVIA CHALLENGE!

Test your GQ (Garfield Quotient) with our brain-crunching quiz!

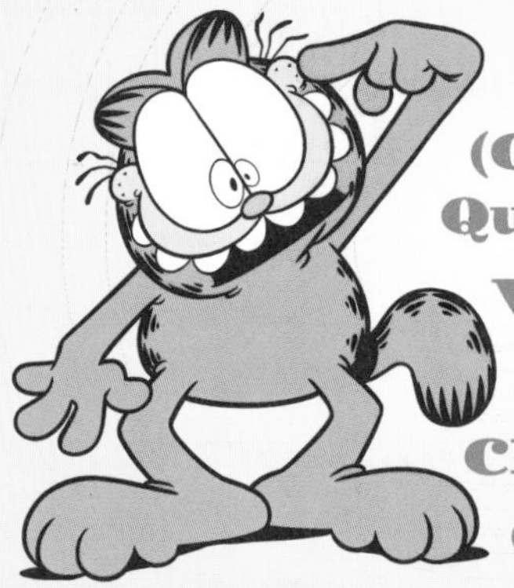

1 According to Garfield, there's nothing worse than a clever _____.
- A. Canine
- B. Arachnid
- C. Armadillo
- D. Insurance adjuster

2 What was the really, really hairy spider doing in Jon's bathroom?
- A. Waxing its legs
- B. Using Jon's comb
- C. Unwinding with a hot bath
- D. Using up all Jon's styling gel

3 In high school, Jon was voted Most Likely to ____.
- A. Become the Tri-County Polka King
- B. Date a kitchen appliance
- C. Become a figure skater
- D. Bring his mother to the prom

4 What did Garfield, Odie and Jon win in the TV special "Garfield Goes Hollywood"?
- A. A year's supply of jumbo paper clips
- B. A boat
- C. A "certified pre-owned" electric toothbrush
- D. An evening with Ed McMahon

5 In the Garfield Christmas TV special, what gift did Garfield give Grandma?
- A. A hairball shaped like a reindeer
- B. Old love letters from her husband
- C. Cash
- D. An autographed photo of Wilford Brimley

6 What did Garfield have tattooed on his chest?
- A. "Born to eat bacon"
- B. "My owner's a dork"
- C. "Caution: Wide Load"
- D. "USDA Choice"

7 What does Jon do on the first day of spring?
- A. Dress up as a bunny and hop around the living room
- B. Dress up as a flower and say, "Hello, Mister Springtime!"
- C. Dress up as one of Gladys Knight's Pips
- D. Dress up as a lawn sprinkler and spit on the backyard

8 When on the farm, what game do Jon and Doc Boy play?
- A. Hide the Heifer
- B. Touch the Udder
- C. Whack the Hoe
- D. Grease the Goose

ANSWERS:
1. B 2. B 3. B 4. B
5. B 6. B 7. B 8. B

THE CYBER CAT IS WHERE IT'S AT!

Check out the feisty feline on the Internet! Surf on over to
http://www.garfield.com
and get:

- Comics
- Fun & Games
- News
- Online shopping
- Official Fan Club
- Embarrassing photos of Jim Davis dressed as a giant possum (Well, maybe not!)

Want to get a cool catalog stuffed with great Garfield products?

Just write down the info, stuff it in an envelope and mail it back to us—or you can fill out the card on our Web site—www.garfield.com. We'll get a catalog out to you in two shakes of a cat's tail.

Get your daily dose of Garfield — absolutely FREE! Sign up now to get the comic strip e-mailed to you every day.
www.garfield.com/signup

LOVE ME, LOVE MY STUFF

Name _____

Address _____

City _____ State _____ Zip _____

Phone_____

Date of Birth _____ Sex _____

E-mail address _____

Please mail your information to:

**Garfield Stuff® Catalog
Dept 2BB38A
5804 Churchman By-Pass
Indianapolis, IN 46203-6109**

© PAWS

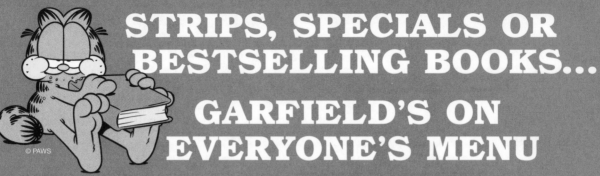

STRIPS, SPECIALS OR BESTSELLING BOOKS...

GARFIELD'S ON EVERYONE'S MENU

Don't miss even one episode in the Tubby Tabby's hilarious series!

GARFIELD AT LARGE **New larger, full-color format!** . . . .(#1) 0-345-44382-9
GARFIELD GAINS WEIGHT . . . .(#2) 0-345-32008-5
GARFIELD BIGGER THAN LIFE . . . . . .(#3) 0-345-32007-7
GARFIELD WEIGHS IN . . . .(#4) 0-345-32010-7
GARFIELD TAKES THE CAKE . . . .(#5) 0-345-32009-3
GARFIELD EATS HIS HEART OUT . . .(#6) 0-345-32018-2
GARFIELD SITS AROUND THE HOUSE (#7) 0-345-32011-5
GARFIELD TIPS THE SCALES . . . .(#8) 0-345-33580-5
GARFIELD LOSES HIS FEET . . . .(#9) 0-345-31805-6
GARFIELD MAKES IT BIG . . . .(#10) 0-345-31928-1
GARFIELD ROLLS ON . . . .(#11) 0-345-32634-1
GARFIELD OUT TO LUNCH . . . .(#12) 0-345-33118-4
GARFIELD FOOD FOR THOUGHT . . .(#13) 0-345-34129-5
GARFIELD SWALLOWS HIS PRIDE . .(#14) 0-345-34725-0
GARFIELD WORLDWIDE . . . .(#15) 0-345-35158-4
GARFIELD ROUNDS OUT . . . .(#16) 0-345-35388-9
GARFIELD CHEWS THE FAT . . . .(#17) 0-345-35956-9
GARFIELD GOES TO WAIST . . . .(#18) 0-345-36430-9
GARFIELD HANGS OUT . . . .(#19) 0-345-36835-5
GARFIELD TAKES UP SPACE . . . . . .(#20) 0-345-37029-5
GARFIELD SAYS A MOUTHFUL . . . .(#21) 0-345-37368-5
GARFIELD BY THE POUND . . . .(#22) 0-345-37579-3
GARFIELD KEEPS HIS CHINS UP . . .(#23) 0-345-37959-4
GARFIELD TAKES HIS LICKS . . . . . .(#24) 0-345-38170-X
GARFIELD HITS THE BIG TIME . . . . .(#25) 0-345-38332-X
GARFIELD PULLS HIS WEIGHT . . . .(#26) 0-345-38666-3
GARFIELD DISHES IT OUT . . . .(#27) 0-345-39287-6
GARFIELD LIFE IN THE FAT LANE . .(#28) 0-345-39776-2
GARFIELD TONS OF FUN . . . .(#29) 0-345-40386-X
GARFIELD BIGGER AND BETTER . .(#30) 0-345-40770-9
GARFIELD HAMS IT UP . . . .(#31) 0-345-41241-9
GARFIELD THINKS BIG . . . .(#32) 0-345-41671-6
GARFIELD THROWS HIS WEIGHT AROUND . . . .(#33) 0-345-42749-1
GARFIELD LIFE TO THE FULLEST . .(#34) 0-345-43239-8
GARFIELD FEEDS THE KITTY . . . . . .(#35) 0-345-43673-3
GARFIELD HOGS THE SPOTLIGHT . .(#36) 0-345-43922-8
GARFIELD BEEFS UP . . . .(#37) 0-345-44109-5
GARFIELD GETS COOKIN' . . . .(#38) 0-345-44582-1

GARFIELD AT HIS SUNDAY BEST!

GARFIELD TREASURY 0-345-32106-5
THE SECOND GARFIELD TREASURY 0-345-33276-8
THE THIRD GARFIELD TREASURY 0-345-32635-8
THE FOURTH GARFIELD TREASURY 0-345-34726-9
THE FIFTH GARFIELD TREASURY 0-345-36268-3
THE SIXTH GARFIELD TREASURY 0-345-37367-7
THE SEVENTH GARFIELD TREASURY . . . 0-345-38427-X
THE EIGHTH GARFIELD TREASURY 0-345-39778-9
THE NINTH GARFIELD TREASURY 0-345-41670-8
THE TENTH GARFIELD TREASURY 0-345-43674-1

AND DON'T MISS...

GARFIELD'S TWENTIETH ANNIVERSARY COLLECTION! 0-345-42126-4